Intolerant Interpretations

INTOLERANT INTERPRETATIONS

JOSH NEAL
AUTHOR OF AMERICAN EXTREMIST
& UNDERSTANDING CONSPIRACY THEORIES

ANTELOPE HILL PUBLISHING

Copyright © 2025 Josh Neal.

All rights reserved.

Second printing 2025

Cover art by Swifty.
Edited by CJ Miller.
Layout by Louis Condé.

Antelope Hill Publishing | antelopehillpublishing.com

Paperback ISBN-13: 979-8-89252-039-3
EPUB ISBN-13: 979-8-89252-040-9

CONTENTS

Proem 1

I. An Abbreviated Genealogy of Suspicion Culture 7

    Précis 7

    Postmodern Suspicion Culture of the Twentieth Century .. 11

    Hypermodern Suspicion Culture of the Twenty-First
        Century 67

    Legitimate and Illegitimate Suspicion 79

II. Contra Haidt: Rebutting the Moral Foundations Theory 91

    Are Liberals Really Less Morally Robust Than Conservatives?

    Mea Culpa 91

    A Righteous Find 93

    The Foundation of Haidt's Moral Foundations Theory 95

    Three to Six: Deficiency or (Over)Refinement? 99

    Conclusion 111

III. Conformity and Political Economy 113
   Answering the Question: How Did It Get This Bad?
      Corrosion of Conformity 113
      Hyperconformity and Its Consequences..........................119

IV. Kahneman, Ellul, and "Technocratic Psychology" 125
   Deconstructing the Nobel Prize-Winning Behavioral Economist's Celebrated Work, Thinking, Fast & Slow *With the Help of Philosopher Jacques Ellul and Psychologist Gerd Gigerenzer*
      Technocracy and Its Discontents......................................125
      Gigerenzer v. Kahneman 128
      Technique and "Technical Logic" 150
      Psychology of a Twenty-First-Century Technocrat 161

V. Paul Bloom's Racist Babies..169
   Disproving the Science of Racial Equalitarianism by Critiquing Paul Bloom's Lauded 2013 Publication Just Babies: The Origins of Good and Evil
      Ethnoscience as Information Warfare 169
      Just Racist Babies...173
      On the Origin of Good and Evil in Infancy.....................179

Addendum..217

Bibliography 225

PROEM

The following collection of essays ought to be understood as a continuation of the theses presented in my last book, *Understanding Conspiracy Theories*. Although they may also be understood in their own terms as a standalone work, the arguments contained within this book deepen the meaning and utility of the ideas I have already presented. In *UCT*, I sought to provide a basis for which my readers may arrive upon a genuine understanding of the present state of bewildering—and at times *overwhelming*—nervous paranoia, one which did not rely on psychologization (a technique which dominates contemporary discourse).

By and large, conspiratorialism is treated as a dysfunction of the mind. More importantly, it is studied as a dysfunction of *the individual mind*; in those instances where a broader view of the matter is permitted, the conversation takes on a distinctly partisan character. More precisely, we are only allowed to uncover the meaning of conspiratorialism from the view of equalitarian, consensist neoliberalism. I do not believe it is necessary to fully articulate the problems with this approach. As such, my intention for *UCT* was to provide a counterbalance—one which emphasized the epistemological tension between the two poles of American society: the folk and the regime.

I reoriented the idea of conspiratorialism as a rivalry between the consensist cult of expertise and the unsophisticated inductive reasoning of folk America. By no means do I intend any disrespect or denigration by describing folk logic as "unsophisticated." Rather, it is intended as a way of highlighting the extent to which the average American is deliberately misled as to the operational nature of his own country, his own civilization, and therefore left to his own devices (assuming he is even inclined to pursue an independent investigation into the ontic reality of his own circumstance).

Whereas *UCT* relied on a predominantly philosophical approach to excavating the true meaning of conspiratorialism, the essays collected in this work take a more empirical view of the matter. This is not to say that this book is narrower in scope; rather, each essay has its own character, and furthermore, approaches the problem of suspicion culture from a distinct point of view.

"An Abbreviated Genealogy of Suspicion Culture" examines the foundations of American paranoia, tracing its developments through the twentieth and twenty-first centuries before finally arriving upon a methodology for adjudicating the differences between legitimate and illegitimate conspiratorialism. This investigation, while limited (as the title suggests), nevertheless provides a solid basis for rejecting both the consensist view of conspiratorialism as well as the mutated strains of neo-populist conspiratorialism which have emerged since the early years of the Trumpist revolution in American conservatism. The essay begins with a brief summary of the concepts and arguments presented in *UCT* before moving directly into its own investigation.

"Contra Haidt" rebuffs the arguments presented in Jonathan Haidt's celebrated book *The Righteous Mind* by examining how the managerial revolution (as detailed by James Burnham) fundamentally altered the American electorate's consciousness, thereby producing the psychological strain of neoliberal progressivism which has led to our present moment of hyperpolarization. Haidt's thesis assumes a naive and atomizing individualism, leading him to unjustly portray left-liberal America as psychologically (and therefore *morally*) deficient. An avowed liberal himself, Haidt's book nevertheless presaged the cultural rightward shift which has culminated in three consecutive presidential cycles of Trumpism. To make my argument, I turn away from psychology and look towards the discipline of political science (aided by conservative luminaries such as Paul Gottfried and Sam Francis) for a more comprehensive explanation of the psychological differences between left-liberal and right-liberal America. While Haidt's intentions for *The Righteous Mind* were to fortify American liberalism by lending psychological credence to the conservative (or right-liberal) mindset, his publication had the unintended consequence of deepening rightist suspicion and resentment of "Liberal America" (while being utterly ignored by those to the left). This essay corrects his misunderstanding by providing a broader and less atomized view of human psychology.

"Conformity and Political Economy" utilizes the social theory of ecologically minded German psychologist Gerd Gigerenzer to explain how America ended up the way that it has. Politically punch-drunk and propagandized Americans struggle to understand how they woke up in a world where feminism, trans ideology, and anti-White propaganda melded into a single, awful, paradigm of injustice—ruling (and ruining) their every waking moment. We often hear about "the woke mind virus," and how well-meaning people have been "brainwashed" by race-Marxists and so on, but these explanations hardly scratch the surface of human social behavior and, moreover, tend to have the effect of inappropriately responsibilizing individual persons. In truth, we still fail to appreciate the unspoken and invisible rules of social organization which lead us to such disastrous conclusions. I believe that part of the solution to this problem lies in removing the individual ego, the individual mind, from the equation, and by looking at the broader group dynamics which do, in fact, dictate social conduct. This, of course, cuts against the grand American myth of individualism—a noble lie of the Platonic variety which, at this point, has done more harm than good. Our thoughts and habits are influenced far more by unconscious social forces than they are the rigorous and contemplative habits of the individual mind. If we can understand this, we can at least throw off the yoke of psychic guilt and undue responsibility which trap us within anti-social and atomic individualism.

"Kahneman, Ellul, and Technocratic Psychology" also makes use of Gerd Gigerenzer's work in conjunction with the thought of French sociologist Jacques Ellul to repudiate the heuristics and biases research program initiated by Israeli social scientist (and Israeli Defense Forces member) Daniel Kahneman. Kahneman's lifelong investigation into human decision-making has contributed greatly to the present-day climate of suspicion culture by undermining our understanding of (and confidence in) human cognition. His work (aided by long-time research partner Amos Tversky) has fortified the contemporary technocratic regime—which is synonymous with the cult of expertise—by "demonstrating" the alleged faultiness and unreliability of our native reasoning faculties. Kahneman's conclusions are now so ubiquitous that most Americans no longer believe in their own psychic sovereignty; arguably as influential as Freudian psychoanalysis (if not more so), it is now taken for granted that the human brain naturally militates *against* objective, factual, logical reasoning. The interest in artificial intelligence (and related technological developments) is partly informed by the belief—propagated by Kahneman and his ilk—that the deficiencies of human psychology are too intractable to resolve through social or political means, and as a result, we are freely giving away our independence, our agency, and ultimately, our very livelihoods to a psychopathic technocrat class whose ultimate aim appears to be the liquidation of mankind. Our technological society, as Ellul deemed it, has run amok. If we are to reassert our sovereignty we must first come to a more exacting and holistic understanding of the human mind. Gerd Gigerenzer's notion of a "human logic," once paired with Ellul's critique of technological society, helps us to achieve this.

"Paul Bloom's Racist Babies" applies a critical-psychological lens by which to understand the racially motivated reasoning of a certain class of social scientist. Here, I reintroduce the notion of an "ethnoscience" (albeit with a few key modifications) to demonstrate how it is that the scientific method may be utilized to advance partisan interests. Of the social scientists discussed in this book, Paul Bloom is certainly the least famous, but he is far from the least noteworthy. His 2013 publication *Just Babies* is truly an exemplar of logical and empirical deficiency, and as such, there is much to be learned from his work about how the modern-day academy truly operates. Furthermore, by critically analyzing his arguments, we stand to gain a far deeper understanding of what motivates the cult of equalitarianism. With a proper understanding, it is possible to reassert our psychic and political sovereignty.

Individually, each essay in this book tackles an aspect of suspicion culture. When taken as a whole, they reinforce an important point made in *UCT*: not only is biological race a real phenomenon, but political strife often emerges due to competition between the races. These two works emphasize the sociobiological element of political conflict, drawing upon the disciplines of psychology, sociology, political science, philosophy, and history to achieve this. While I do not consider myself a "race realist" in the way that the term is usually employed, I do believe in the ontic reality of group differences. I also believe that the White populations of the world are currently imperiled by a global tyranny, one hellbent on disempowering or even eliminating them.

In the age of so called "disinformation," where massive resources are deployed to disabuse the world's White populations of any sense of self-preservation, any sense of self-love, it has become more crucial than ever to achieve a proper understanding of the world and our place within it. The art of interpretation, then, is more important than ever before. As is appropriate for our age, let ours be *intolerant interpretations*.

I

AN ABBREVIATED GENEALOGY OF SUSPICION CULTURE

Précis

Let us take a moment to survey the terrain mapped out thus far, for the sake of comprehensiveness, before venturing deeper into unknown territory. At the outset we declared the problem of conspiratorial ideation to be a misdirection; the United States does not have an "information" problem (misinformation, disinformation, or otherwise); its problem is one of trustlessness. Many other arguments have been given to explain the collapse of a formerly high-trust Western world—be it a result of anomie or demography, decline in religiosity or increase in polarization; there are other explanations, all of them serviceable in one respect or another (though some are clearly better than others), but none seem to capture the problem we have called suspicion culture in its full dimensions. In short, we struggle with trust (e.g., trusting sources of information, trusting institutions, trusting our traditions, our communities, ourselves, others, et cetera) because our inherited wisdom is no longer in concert with our social ecology. But just why is that?

Assuming an imperial society rife with tribal conflict (which, as a description of contemporary multiracial America, is probably an understatement, sadly), the disciplines, institutions, and industries which govern human perception and action are not assumed to be owned, operated, or directed toward the betterment of native, folk interests. Instead, all available resources capable of giving form to our social ecology are directed towards the aim of the tribe(s) currently in possession of them. The managerial apparatus (including the universities, the press, and the culture industry), which emerged later in America's history and only in recent years appears to have passed its zenith, still works tirelessly to block the emergence of and organization around a native sovereignty. Owing to these efforts, we have arrived upon a permanent state of exception: the historical moment wherein the state alters its teleological course, slips into totalitarianism, and sacrifices internal cohesion for external expansion. This course correction, having been facilitated by the transition from folk sovereignty to alien sovereignty, culminates not only in the occlusion of folk sovereignty, but the ultimate alienation of the folk itself; its authentic way of living now effectively abolished, the marginalized folk is subjected to containment, what we have called neo-Reality (nR). nR replaces the normally, organically emerging social relations, filling the individual's phenomenal field with falsehoods and misdirection. Derealization, at least of the non-congenital and non-pathological kind, should be understood as occurring against this backdrop of a fraudulent world-image. When we think of the nR we may think of the Amerindian reservation life, Blacks living under Jim Crow (and more obviously, enduring the slave trade and plantation life), Southern Whites living under Reconstruction, the interwar Weimar period in Germany, communist occupations in the eastern hemisphere, capitalist colonization in the western hemisphere, et cetera. While the precise political contexts and relationships between the competing groups may differ from one example to the next, the common thread is as follows: a regime attempts to create both a narrativistic and social unity which provides itself with the legitimacy needed to govern. Old norms and traditions are appropriated, molded, and given new life—one amenable to the ascendant regime's aims. What is unique about our time is that this iteration of nR came to prominence under the veneer of civil, liberal democratic processes, perpetrated by the (supposedly) democratically elected elite against its constituency. This model was then duplicated in every other White nation of note. That this usurpation did not occur by the machinations of an outwardly and obviously recognizable enemy has frustrated

CHAPTER I   9

attempts to reverse this fate, and continues to do so.

Implanted directly into the core of folk consciousness, then, is a schizotic and joyless negation which drives the reproduction of suspicion culture, internally, from within both the individual and the collective consciousness. Reinforced from without (the aggregated powers of the Totalitarian Imperial State, hereafter abbreviated TIS) and from within (the internalization of freshly transvaluated axioms), suspicion (and, as will be elaborated more fully later, cynicism) becomes as ubiquitous and intangible as the air we breathe. Suspicion permeates, dictates, our every decision; respected men and women of their communities suspect their representatives, husbands suspect their wives, daughters suspect their mothers, students suspect their teachers, so on and so forth. Snap judgments (really, misjudgments) of character—based on nothing but the propagandizing "facts" of life in nR—now carry tragic, permanent, consequences (consequences which were never in need of accrual). Mass production of suspicion culture suppresses folk political organization, for a time at least, until it invariably resurfaces (as we are seeing now) in the form of estranged and deracinated mob politics (so-called "populism").

We also determined that the stereotype of the suspicion-addled individual fails to give us an accurate picture of contemporary, mass-produced (which is to say, mass-society—now a global society, as per McLuhan) suspicion culture. While it may have been possible to pigeonhole the suspicious American man (or woman) according to the prejudices and biases of bygone generations, this is no longer the case. Considering now that the archetypal demographic of the conspiracy theorist is no longer merely the pot-bellied and uneducated White American man, one might conclude that the conspiracy theorists of old were on to something all along! Democratization via the promulgation of advancing technologies (but also the spreading of indignities) has expanded suspicion culture beyond its initial boundaries; utilizing concepts developed by Marshall McLuhan, we examined how innovations in communication and information technologies over the last few decades have led to the uncontrollable brushfire of conspiratorial ideation presently confronting us. The Global Village that McLuhan predicted over sixty years ago has arrived, ushering in an era of psychopolitical control so total that its success surely must have surprised even the most optimistic among its architects. Twenty-first-century, hypermodern America now enjoys the luxury of mainlining suspicion directly into its very nervous system; every internet-connected man, woman, and child may participate in the now super-charged and "hotted up" Enlightenment tradition of doubt.[1]

Now that we have taken inventory of the positions as I have established them so far, we may resume our investigation. In this chapter I will speak more directly about the problem of suspicion, both as a political challenge (which we have already said a great deal about) but also as an epistemological one. Having already provided good reasons for affirming, or at least contextualizing, conspiratorial ideation (as broadly practiced, anyway), we must now offer some means for differentiating between legitimate causes for suspicion and illegitimate ones. In doing so we not only arrive upon a methodology for identifying relevant conspiracies but for competently prosecuting them, as well.[2] If we are ever to lift the culture of suspicion, we must turn a critical eye toward suspicion-merchants, and, importantly, towards suspicion as a commodity-form (making sure to give special attention to its distinctly libidinal features). Curiously, the pedagogical demand for "critical thinking," particularly now in the still fresh-faced youth of our new century, appears to be an incitement to doubt folk ways of living. Perhaps this was always the case; Peter Sloterdijk certainly seemed to think so. If to "think critically" is the same as to doubt, then we shall turn our critical eyes toward the obscurantist and mystifying powers of global

---

[1] In *Understanding Media*, Marshall McLuhan identified media as belonging to one of two categories: hot and cold. "Hot media" is high in information and requires little participation from its audience (e.g., the cinema), while "cold media" is the opposite: since it provides less sensory input, it therefore demands more participation from its audience (e.g., a telephone conversation). "Hot media" decentralize and break things apart, while "cold media," again, achieve the opposite.

[2] As will be detailed in this chapter, the invocation of conspiracy (within the context of a commoditized hypermodern suspicion culture, specifically) is a call to mystification. When everything in existence is itself already in doubt, and Man happily makes himself the executor of an Enlightenment will to demystify, the peculiar sight of a well-documented and well-lit conspiracy theory serves to direct attention away from actually-existing networks of influence, themselves eager to maintain their clandestine operation. That merchants encourage us to doubt a given practice, person, tribe, institution, or event should, itself, raise the alarm.

neoliberalism, fixing our gaze on those merchants of suspicion, and their underbosses. En route to the epistemological aspect of this investigation, we will discuss first the historical precedents (e.g., actors, institutions, and events) responsible for bringing about the present climate of hypermodern suspicion culture, for we cannot say anything useful about the matter without first understanding the uniquely American tradition of suspicion. We might better say something about the reasons to doubt by first interrogating those whose careers were predicated on the instigation of doubt.

Postmodern Suspicion Culture of the Twentieth Century

The United States was founded clandestinely, often pseudonymously, with its leadership fully conscious of existing geopolitical powers (and their rivalries). Its development, occurring within the context of a (relatively) freshly established global mercantile order, was fraught with uncertainty; not only were new threats and challenges constantly on the horizon, but the revanchist desires of old rivals frequently loomed large. Self-conscious of its place in the world (and, importantly, of its place in world-history), and soon to be pre-occupied with the political challenge of assimilating successive waves of "New World Europeans" (a demographic tsunami which would soon introduce peoples even more alien to the North American continent), we can acknowledge this much older and more historic (and thus also folkish) culture of suspicion on the North American continent.

Crises in Ireland and Germany drove immigration into America from an estimated 250,000 to 2.5 million in the years between 1820 and 1845 to nearly 3 million between the years of 1845 and 1852 alone.[3] Most packed into the cities, their presence a credible economic challenge as well as a potentially crippling ecological one. This very real demographic transformation of America led to the formation of one of its earliest third parties with the Anti-Masonic Party, a single-issue

---

[3] Boissoneault, "How the 19th-Century."

party that collapsed just a few years before the emergence of the Know-Nothing party;[4] hawkish on immigration but moderate on slavery, all the while walking a fine line between courting populists and progressives alike, the Know-Nothings were a nativist, pro-Protestant, and by some accounts pro-Jewish stop-gap party operating during the time between the decline of the Whigs and the ascent of the Republicans.[5] Though their stated aims and motivations differed, there could be no doubt that movements such as the Anti-Masonic Party and the Know-Nothing Party, among others of the time, were in touch with the demographic apocalypse looming forebodingly over folk America's future. On the subject of the Know-Nothing Party, it was founded by newspaper editor Lewis Charles Levin, a first-generation American and the first Jewish congressman in U.S. history, in the middle years of the nineteenth century, inaugurating, as it were, an early example of American suspicion culture. Founded on an opposition to immigration (though by some accounts Levin's motivations may have been specifically anti-Catholic and anti-papist),[6] the short-lived Know-Nothing Party (later, The American Party) set the tone for a distinctly conservative and "paranoid style" of American politics (Richard Hofstadter's coinage used to describe both the John Birch Society and Goldwaterism), one whose reverberations would be felt for the next hundred and seventy years.

Some have called into question the extent to which conspiratorialism was central to the suspicion-based parties of nineteenth-century America; the Anti-Masonic Party, for example, faced charges of ulterior motives, with the motivations propelling the party's outsized success ranging from a disgust for secretive, closed-door politics,[7] to fears about industrialization and its effects on American domestic life.[8] In fact, it was quite common for suspicion-based political movements of the time to expand their influence by appealing to populist issues, so perhaps this plurality of causes is explainable by assuming a practical,

---

[4] Little, "How America's First."
[5] Rabinowitz, "Nativism, Bigotry, and Anti-Semitism."
[6] Fitzgerald, "Philadelphia Nativists Riots."
[7] Cheathem, "Conspiracy theories abounded."
[8] Keller, "America's Three Regimes."

realpolitik attitude toward political organization and not the ideological style adopted by their hypermodern twenty-first-century progeny. The more successful of this progeny, like their forebearers, also attempted to straddle the line between, shall we say, righteous paranoia, and meat-and-potatoes populist politics. In many ways this represents a significant tension within the American Right: to successfully lead, representatives must maintain a credible big picture view of domestic and geopolitical intrigue, while simultaneously maintaining a foothold in day-to-day politics. The trend toward ever-increasing rigidity within rightist politics, however, has complicated successful attempts at such a maneuver.

It is the case now (perhaps it was then, too) that nativist and other suspicion-based political movements must answer the cynical charge of fomenting paranoia for the sake of self-aggrandizement. Whether conspiratorial ideation was central to the success of a given political organization or movement hardly poses a challenge to our analysis. We presume conflict in all things political, and furthermore the United States' history is defined by political conflict. To this very point: the decades leading up to the early years of the twentieth century were punctuated by episodes of shocking violence, often emerging due to foreign political intrigue. For instance: the labor and race riots of the 1870s and '80s, the transportation of anarchist movements into the United States which culminated in events such as the Haymarket affair, the rise of the Galleanists and their bombing campaigns (instigated by the activism of Italian anarchist Luigi Galleani), and the assassination of William McKinley at the hands of Leon Czolgosz, inspired by the Russian-Jewish anarchist Emma Goldman, who went to her grave defending the murder. That the disreputable may indeed cynically use the public's fear of foreign subversion for their own ends does little to obscure the historical fact of genuine political infiltration. But in the eyes of today's liberal consensus makers, the mainstream of twentieth (and twenty-first) century conservative, right-wing political movements is little more than a vulgar and parochial recapitulation of this paranoid and reactionary (and therefore illegitimate) nineteenth-century political strain, thrown in the same skeleton-filled closet which included the KKK, and later, the McCarthyites. Despite the credible threat posed by anarchists, socialists, and communists, America's paranoid tradition apparently lacks credibility in the mind of liberal elites. From our point of view, however, we can see that major disruptions of the conventional folk way of American life have historically preceded attempts at political organization, and with the deluge of "New World Europeans" giving way to an absolutely diluvial surge of Africans, Asians, Arabs, Hispanics, and post-Soviet Whites, such organization can only grow more (necessarily, justifiably) desperate.

It is important to note the presence of two distinct strains of suspicion that occasionally, uncomfortably mixed, though only the latter would win out rhetorically and strategically, proving to dominate the American Right without compromise. The first was an existential and domestically focused suspicion culture concerned with race relations, sex relations, labor relations and a variety of other causes that would eventually merge during the legal battle for civil rights (see Christopher Caldwell's *The Age of Entitlement*); the second was a primarily geopolitical and foreign-focused suspicion culture, preoccupied with the rising threat of international communism. Domestic concerns (e.g., internal subversion, proto-civil rights conflicts) plagued the country for the first half of the century (still, at the time, functioning in a more-or-less nationalistic mode of political identity), while the Soviet rivalry helped to formalize a new political identity for the United States, with the country moving unquestionably into an imperialist and faux-patriotic posture, and therefore, incapable of properly articulating—let alone confronting—internal challenges to stability in a morally upright manner. It is with the supposed end of the Cold War (really its submersion, as the present conflict between Russia and Ukraine has shown that beliefs, conflicts, and ideas do not die—they merely roll in and out like the tide) that American suspicion culture quickly turned farcical—more on that later.

The conspiracy theory, strictly speaking, serves one of two masters: truth, as in the disruption of the status quo, and power, as in the maintenance of the status quo. Both the conspiracy-theory-as-folk-history (or "the folk account of history") and the whistleblower-account-of-power (think Edward Snowden or Julian Assange) may fit into the first category, whereas the conspiracy-theory-as-psychological-operation and certain whistleblower accounts-of-power (the recent Facebook scandal which provided whistleblower Francis Haugen with her fifteen seconds of fame, for instance) belong to the second category.⁹ As we investigate the different forms of suspicion culture, we will more fully articulate the meaning behind these concepts, but suffice to say, the difference between truth and power, insofar as legitimacy is concerned, is also the difference between postmodern suspicion and hypermodern suspicion (or at least, *a* difference between the two).

Under hypermodernity, attempts at a folk account of history are transformed into cynical farces with scantly the power to expose the truth or implode would-be rivals, instead becoming subsumed into hegemonic psychopolitics. During the preceding century, however, the conspiracy theory was both alive and firmly tragic, as folk Americans lived through wave after unrelenting wave of violent transformations both architected and directed by the state, thereby making folkish suspicion an active force for resistance. Borrowing a term from Sloterdijk, postmodern suspicion culture manifested a "kynical" and authentic form of political organization, indicative of a truly revolutionary and anti-hegemonic spirit.¹⁰ It is with the progression into the hypermodern period of American history that this method of living lost its nerve and collapsed into cynical resignation. The conspiracy gave way to the conspiracy theory, toward a fatigued and neurotic discourse of already-uncovered-plots, half-baked imitations, reckless doubting, outright Machiavellianism, and toward, as well, an expansion of retrograde conspiratorial ideation into previously virginal psychic and social spaces.

The postmodern form of suspicion culture which I am here attributing to the twentieth century is that of the conspiracy itself: social, empirical, historical, but also a result of what has been termed "the collapse of metanarratives." For a certain kind of American, or even Westerner, the notion of a collapse of metanarratives is rather alluring, for it allows its believers to disassociate themselves from their actual tradition (liberalism), and to dismiss the fact of contemporary "woke," "postmodern," or "progressive" neoliberalism's legitimate heritage. It is a

---

[9] Diaz, "Facebook's New Whistleblower."
[10] Peter Sloterdijk, the German philosopher and cultural critic, places the ancient Greek tradition of "kynicism" in opposition to the contemporary practice of "cynicism," wherein the former was a legitimately subversive practice while the latter rendered a mere degeneration.

defense mechanism against the reality that liberalism's revolutionary ethos no longer requires their bodies, their values, their prejudices, and in fact was content to seek new ones with each successive generation. The chaos of today's world is not emergent; it was inherited. The view of postmodernism as militating against liberal norms rather than fulfilling them is a tragic but undeniably human shortcoming, one which remains with us to this very day. Having said this, it is critical to view this fulfillment as more of a hostile merger and not necessarily one of mutual beneficence. For both parties, however, it was a matter of necessity, of survival.

This error (or misunderstanding) is a characteristically folkish one; that is, the self-misunderstanding of Anglo-Saxon hegemony by its constituent members, and even itself. Blind to the dialectical movements occurring within its own canon, the innovating upon—or rather, the unfurling of—Enlightenment epistemology by its peripherally constituent elements was not something that the upper crust of Anglo-American power could fully take into view or accept as a fact of reality. As such, this self-misunderstanding was as critical to the emergence of twentieth-century suspicion culture as to its present incarnation. The so-called collapse of metanarratives was anything but. Postmodern suspicion culture was, in fact, the meeting between world-historical *ethnometanarratives:* the self-constituting mythological narratives of given ethnic groups. The previously assumed worldview (along with its justifications and explanations) suffered a repeated drubbing at the hands of rival ethno-metanarratives. This meeting took many forms, some collaborative, some antagonistic, still others ambiguous. In fact, the United States' relationship to communism at varying times constituted all the above (a complicating factor for suspicion-minded patriots). But it was the meeting of these ethno-metanarratives and the subsequent biopolitical and existential developments that followed in their wake which served to drive postmodern suspicion culture forward; postmodern suspicion culture manifested in the conspiracy itself, an authentic event which occurred against the backdrop of an utterly imperiled world civilization. The great tragedies of the preceding century were fundamentally grounded in the existential realities of identity. Inarguably, the domestic strife which transformed American life throughout the twentieth century was itself a conflict of and a confrontation between discrete identities. There was no collapse of metanarratives, only the submersion (or sublation) of the metanarratives of certain identity-groups into other ones. Even this notion of a "collapse" should strike us as insincere, as the binding mythological framework of American society did not suddenly, mysteriously, disintegrate but was instead sabotaged—or better yet, felled—by a more dedicated and sincere effort, a more *self-conscious* effort.

Because this meeting between ethno-metanarratives so strongly shaped America's domestic and foreign policy, and because it operated so clandestinely (often under the aegis of such nascent covert American institutions such as the OSS, the CIA, etc.), it conforms virtually completely to the textbook definition of the word *conspiracy*, but moreover, to the social reality of American political life. In the face of an ever-escalating intercontinental catastrophe, one which saw the West challenged by exoterically authoritarian regimes, liberal democracy very quickly descended into a mode of political organization that could only be described as governance-by-conspiracy. Liberal democracy, an esoteric form of authoritarian political organization, fortified itself on both the domestic and international fronts by rejecting the will of the people and asserting policies which would allow the state to militate against rival factions both at home and abroad. While our conventional historical understanding highlights the ideological dimensions of this conflict, they were at least (if not more so) motivated by primal and primary political realities, such as identity (a point to which we will return, repeat, and re-emphasize as much as is necessary). And so, the relevant identities (inclusive of their ethno-metanarratives) at play throughout the postmodern period of American suspicion culture (and by relevant, I mean hegemonic) would include the Anglophile powers of the United States and the more recently arrived ethnic Jews from Europe. The progression from kynical suspicion to cynical suspicion is very much a by-product of this meeting between historic Anglo-Saxon America and the ascendant European Jewish refugees, a meeting which saw certain intellectuals within this new Jewish-American cohort align themselves with hegemonic WASP liberalism against both international communism and the mounting domestic racial tensions caused by dissatisfied or otherwise yet-unassimilated ethnic Whites and the recently liberated Black population. Another way of describing these newer, ethnic

Whites (and the political turmoil caused by their presence): rivals. And not without reason, either, for the tidal wave of political chaos in the waning decades of the nineteenth century into the early decades of the twentieth manifesting in such forms as communism, anarchism, and socialism often arrived alongside these later generations of European immigrants.

Two mid-century writers are illustrative of this dynamic, and more to the point, their influence bears directly upon the question of contemporary suspicion culture: Richard Hofstadter and Karl Popper. Karl Popper holds a greater significance for us and our understanding of suspicion culture; after all, his work *The Open Society and its Enemies* more fully and audaciously extols the virtues of a liberal democratic state, even going so far as to offer ethical pronouncements against those individuals, groups, and ideologies which might threaten the open society. Not only did he write of the moral excellence of the open society, but in his essay "The Conspiracy Theory of Society" (a flimsy piece of writing which we shall turn our attention to momentarily), he places it outside of the reach of manipulative back-dealing. Popper's work lives on today in the efforts of men like Cass Sunstein and George Soros, career manipulators of the lowest moral fiber. Though not nearly as historically revered as Popper, Hofstadter's contribution to the discourse of conspiracy was nonetheless influential: because the memory of folk-historical movements (e.g., The John Birch Society) linger frightfully within liberal consciousness, Hofstadter's critique stays with us, too, and good for us that it has. Hofstadter's essay "The Paranoid Style in American Politics" expertly articulated the dismissiveness and absentee rigor of neoliberal consensist argumentation.

Through the work of Karl Popper and Richard Hofstadter we gain an insight into the sociobiological dimension of contemporary liberal democratic society and to the forces productive of American suspicion culture, offering us at last a way out of the game of philosophy (or ideology) which is so often played at our expense. It is the game of philosophy, and of ideas, which are so often deployed to protect the vulnerable, primal, plank of identity. To put it even more precisely: sophistic discursivity, in fact, is the preferred defense of the rivaling ethno-metanarrative. For if we were to raise identity to the level of a primary adjudicative object, rather than a peripheral (or even irrelevant) one, and demote the ideological or abstract discursive object, we might more easily get to the heart of the matter. I am not unaware of the pitfalls downstream of what I advocate for; we must not lose sight of the rational, for restoring dignity to the primal may incur a lustfulness (after all, it was denied this essential dignity for so long) which might thrust us into a similar, but inverted, controversy.

* * *

The legacy of liberalism is that of self-deception. Since its origin it has presumed that which was responsible for it, over time positing itself as its own cause. All these centuries later, it now self-assuredly attempts to impress upon us the irrelevance of firstness: the first and most primal things in life, those things which preceded civil society (and even all life as we know it). This is the central failure of liberalism, or perhaps a result of its over-succeeding, the something-for-nothingness which seeks to abscond from history with all its developments and contingencies while simultaneously declaring itself free of them. Without a doubt, this has aided in the creation and expansion of a global empire, but equally indisputably, it has hollowed out the spirit, leaving it ripe for exploitation.

This present battle of ethno-metanarratives, then, is a sort of joint effort in self-denial, paradoxically, for as much as the contest is a battle of wits and wills, ideals and aspirations, it is nonetheless a gentlemanly contest, predicated on just such an agreement: "We shall each suppress self-reflexivity in favor of delusion and egotism." The odd man out of this contest, then, is identity, and as such we find that on both sides of the confrontation is a kind of forgetfulness and a will to denial which comfortably meet each other in the middle. Unsurprisingly, they enjoin us to forget, too, not only so that the charade might continue unabated, but that we (in the shared spirit of democracy) might also forget ourselves. If we are right to place self-denial at the heart of liberalism, then it is also proper to view the political heresies of twentieth-century Europe as movements of rediscovery. They were not, as contemporary liberals like to think, necessarily bastions of sadism and depravity; rather, they were folk attempts at excavating an organic authority to defend themselves against the rising global tide of self-negation. To reason properly we must begin from a place of sure footing, hence the importance—nay, necessity—of identity for the proper adjudication of all matters, not the least of which includes the abolition of suspicion culture.

Through the writings of these two Jewish thinkers (Popper, an ethnic Jew from Austria-Hungary, and Hofstadter, an American Jew born to a German-Lutheran mother and Polish-Jewish father), we get an insight into the emergent post-war consensus which would carry the United States into its subsequent phase as an imperialistic and world-hegemonic force. The ethnic grafting of inbound Jewish migrants into the Anglo-Saxon upper class fortified the American state. However, it also relegated many ethnic American Whites to the status of second-class citizens. The integration of Jewish intelligentsia into the upper stratum of Anglo-Saxon America occurred during a time of great domestic strife, and the new Jewish elite shared an architectural role in responding to it. But this grafting was not due, necessarily, to ideological factors, or rather we ought to say that the ideological or abstract content was itself subject to an implied identitarian form. Both Popper and Hofstadter were Marxists in their youth, only to turn away from the cause later in life. For Hofstadter the breaking point was to be found in Stalinism. With Popper it was more personal and intimate. A 1919 failed coup attempt (which he was in attendance for) saw Popper grow disillusioned with communism, marking the beginning of a critical period for the young philosopher. While the immediate threat of national socialism impressed upon the man a deep concern with authoritarian regimes, communism would later occupy a similar place in his mind, thus becoming a target for criticism in his later writings. Within Anglophonic liberal democratic society, the two found respite from the persecutions of European living (for Hofstadter, and in fact many other conservative-leaning Jewish ex-communists, it was Stalin's purges of Jews while for Popper, it was the National Socialists' persecution of Jews), as well as prestige. Moreover, within Anglo-Saxon liberal democracy, ascendant Jewish intellectual elites like Hofstadter and Popper found a new avenue for the resumption of old rivalries. In representing history to their new neighbors (in the case of Hofstadter, American history while in the case of Popper, the history of the entire

Western political canon), a representation colored by their own consciously or unconsciously understood ethno-metanarratives, Hofstadter and Popper played crucial roles in validating the direction America and Western Europe would take following the calamity of the Second World War. But that is enough context for now; let us proceed with a direct engagement with their work.

Hofstadter's scholarly writings touched on a variety of issues close to the heart of upper crust liberal America (e.g., firearms, populism, anti-intellectualism), earning him quite the reputation as an academic historian, but one of his works was of the utmost importance—not only for its role in cultivating the neoliberal consensus, but for what it can tell us about suspicion culture. His essay, "The Paranoid Style in American Politics," while primarily a condemnation of then Republican presidential nominee Barry Goldwater and the ascendant John Birch Society (a successful though "fringe" conservative organization), was also a blanket dismissal of the concerns of millions of ordinary Americans. We will speak more directly to the bogeyman of paranoia that was (and remains to this day) the John Birch Society, but for now I will ask that the reader set aside that association for the time being. For the moment, at least, Hofstadter's words require our full attention.

In 1964, Hofstadter authored (or at the least, enshrined) the approach now common to regime polemics when he wrote of the "paranoid style" endemic to American politics. By tracing a straight line across the back of American history, Hofstadter presented a supposedly iron-clad case for the persistent continuity of a paranoid nucleus within its right flank. This tendency, Hofstadter enjoined us to believe, was present in causes as varied as anti-Masonry, anti-Catholicism, and most significantly, anti-communism. It was at work during the period of the abolitionist movement, returning with a vengeance in the form of the KKK and Jim Crow. The paranoid style of American politics was present, too, in the aftermath of the JFK assassination and all throughout the Goldwater debacle, Hofstadter assured us. If we take him at his word, right-wing talk radio, Buchanan-ite paleo-conservatism, the Tea Party, MAGA and QAnon, then, would necessarily be seen as following in this tradition.

"I am not speaking in a clinical sense, but borrowing a clinical term for other purposes," he tells us. "When I speak of the paranoid style, I use the term much as a historian of art might speak of the baroque or the mannerist style."[11]

It speaks poorly of the American establishment that such a nakedly and self-confessedly meritless analysis was heralded with thunderous applause. We will observe similar weaknesses in Popper's writings, as well. The function of this psychological language is not to foster understanding, but to characterize (and also to character-assassinate). Hofstadter's charge of paranoia carries an implicit condemnation of the American people for not understanding and accepting their own expendability, and furthermore, for failing to articulate a knowledge of their existential and political crisis in the manner befitting an erudite Ivy Leaguer. Liberal consensus-making, then, traffics in a narcissism of necessity; the empire has set a course, and that course is righteous. It is the people who are wrong. Of course, we are not merely speaking of liberal consensus, at least not in an unqualified sense. Here we observe a double narcissism—one that is politically constituted but also ethnically constituted as well. It is the intersection of needs between those of the declining Anglo-Saxon state and the ascendant Jewish diaspora which the reader should here take note of.

Hofstadter trafficked in a pseudo-perennialism, or political perennialism, by calling our attention to the repetition of certain tendencies and outcomes (e.g., paranoia, scapegoating, the combustibility of conspiracy movements, et cetera), as if drawing a circle around commonalities was identical to executing a diagnostically rigorous analysis. Similarly, Hofstadter applies a methodology of the superficial when he identifies certain relevant antecedental factors to the paranoid style (e.g., the ongoing displacement of Anglo-Saxon Protestants and German/Irish Catholics) but then pays them no further consideration. By painting a picture of faux comprehensiveness, Hofstadter put his stamp on the now standard practice of regime polemics (and apologia); through this static rendering of the ontic causes which drive human affect and action, consensists and apologists suggest a deeper and more definitive objectivity, or measured-ness, that does not extend to the analysis proper. Lip service, not thoroughness (a rather unsophisticated

---

[11] Hofstadter, *Paranoid Style*, 3–4.

method of persuasion that only succeeds because it is mandated to be as such), allows the liberal apparatchik to take tremendous and unconscionable license; by invoking such facts in passing, the author gains a certain plausibility or credibility in the eyes of his peers, one that allows all concerned parties to absent-mindedly neglect the fact that the author abuses this cachet for entirely self-serving reasons. The loose, dispassionate, and incomplete description of reality suffices for a meaningful and deliberate engagement with it, providing the cover for a deeper and more particular need for self-preservation. Buried deep within his essay are a handful of statements which fatally undermine the larger conceptual conceit at work (something we will observe again in Popper's work) and yet, somehow, they go unremarked upon. Hence, our investigatory work is made even more necessary.

In a passage now made remarkable by the very revelation of its facticity, Hofstadter uses the example of fluoridation in the water as a means for lambasting the paranoid conservative American:

> Again, it is common knowledge that the movement against the fluoridation of municipal water supplies has been catnip for cranks of all kinds, especially for those who have obsessive fear of poisoning. It is conceivable that at some time scientists may turn up conclusive evidence that this practice is, on balance, harmful; and such a discovery would prove the antifluoridationists quite right on the substance of their position. But it could hardly, at the same time, validate the contentions of those among who, in characteristic paranoid fashion, have charged that fluoridation was an attempt to advance socialism under the guise of public health or to rot out the brains of the community by introducing chemicals in the water supply in order to make people more vulnerable to socialist or communist schemes.[12]

Hofstadter offers us a very Lacanian line of reasoning here: yes, your wife may be having an affair but all the same it is pathological to suspect her of doing so! Or in this case: yes, your elected (or unelected)

---

[12] Ibid., 6.

officials may be contaminating the water supply for political reasons, but it is pathological to take notice of such a fact! Out of revulsion for folkish conservatism, Hofstadter condemns the irrationality of the common American who instinctively recognizes a bad deal yet fails to hit the mark with his or her conceptual analysis. That the American man and woman are deliberately lied to and manipulated—that critical information and motivations are withheld from them—is, in the final analysis, their own responsibility (and consequently, their own fault). At least, according to Richard Hofstadter and the liberal establishment of the time (and still today).

All of this begs the question: What is the meaning of paranoia, really? For Hofstadter, "[T]he 'paranoid style' is pejorative, and it is meant to be; the paranoid style has a greater affinity for bad causes than good." But in the very next sentence (and out the other side of his mouth) he reminds us that sometimes the paranoids get it right, and we shouldn't and can't outright dismiss an argument "because we think we hear in its presentation the characteristic paranoid accents."[13] Immediately following this, Hofstadter resumes his polemical writing, warning us of the dangers of what we are here calling the folk account of history, implicitly urging us to dismiss it. What are we, as readers, to make of such writing? A bit of ass-covering? Hofstadter's guilty conscience at work? Popper offers similar self-undermining statements, as we will see, and yet they have not seemed to penetrate the American liberal's mind in quite the same way as the more self-serving passages have. From the perspective of an enlightened, rational, and compassionate open liberal society, it would seemingly behoove us to not pejorativize "outsider" accounts of current events (or even historical ones, for that matter) and yet that is exactly what the liberal intelligentsia has done! It is this hardening of the liberal ego which contributed greatly to the later hypermodern manifestation of suspicion culture—a bitter pill for American liberals to swallow, no doubt.

Hofstadter uses equivocation to belittle the efforts of "paranoid" Americans when he highlights what in his mind (and the minds of self-deluding liberals, eager to have any reason—*even a non-reason*—for

---

[13] Ibid., 5.

dismissing competing accounts of history) is the smoking gun which delegitimizes, imploding from within, the "paranoid style."

This enemy seems to be on many counts a projection of the self: both the ideal and the unacceptable aspects of the self are attributed to him. A fundamental paradox of the paranoid style is the imitation of the enemy. The Ku Klux Klan imitated Catholicism to the point of donning priestly vestments, developing an elaborate ritual and an equally elaborate hierarchy. The John Birch Society emulates communist cells and quasi-secret operation through "front" groups, and preaches a ruthless prosecution of the ideological war along lines very similar to those it finds in the communist enemy. Spokesmen of the various Christian anti-communist "crusades" openly express their admiration for the dedication, discipline, and strategic ingenuity the communist cause calls forth.[14]

Using a quasi- (or proto-) Girardian logic, Hofstadter describes the "doubling" of counter-conspiratorial movements; by highlighting these similarities, it is supposed that any authentic difference between rival causes has been proven false, and that any reason for believing in one or the other (but for Hofstadter's purposes, exclusively the beliefs of "paranoid" Americans) can no longer be sustained.

We see in this passage that Hofstadter has demonstrated the absolute worst tendencies of psychologically-styled writing, as not only is nothing profound offered up in his analysis, but the fact of its banality is somehow taken up as proof of its salience. It is not that his analysis is incorrect; rather, it is that he has painted a picture of truth which withholds important contextualizing elements. It is not that he is correct, either, or that he has somehow successfully put us on our heels by the simple force of his logic; the correctness or incorrectness of Hofstadter's argument is immaterial because his writing serves a cynical power-function, and not a truth-function or knowledge-function. His artful psychologizing, no longer deployed merely for describing events,

---

[14] Ibid., 33.

now turns surgical—eviscerating the cause of folkish doubt with a mere stroke of the pen. Not only is this the best that post-war American hegemony has ever been able to conjure up in defense of itself, but the liberal mob's appetite for writing of at least this level of mediocrity has waned, and present-day torchbearers of liberal polemics are no longer capable of delivering even half as much as Hofstadter (or Popper, for that matter) did over half a century ago, which was already not very much at all. The fundaments of the paranoid style were declared, but Hofstadter never managed to convincingly demonstrate them. Then again, such works are intended to self-flatter and self-fortify the regime and humiliate the enemy. Here, successful persuasion is a distant—though welcome—outcome, but by no means a necessity.

Hofstadter offered up meaningless and distinction-less differences, seemingly intended only to distance the liberal consensus from folkish accounts of history syllabically, but not logically. This should be obvious when he says something like:

> [T]he distinguishing thing about the paranoid style is not that its exponents see conspiracies or plots here and there in history, but that they regard a "vast" or "gigantic" conspiracy as the motive force in historical events. History is a conspiracy, set in motion by demonic forces of almost transcendent power, and what is felt to be needed to defeat it is not the usual methods of political give-and-take, but an all-out crusade.[15]

For the paranoid style to be operational in some way, Hofstadter must privilege conspiratorial ideation by granting it a centrality within the mind of the paranoid American, rather than viewing it as a natural consequence of living through chaotic and disordered times. Paranoia is granted a psychical firstness that is not only unjustifiable, but is in fact demonstrated (in passing, as we have noted) to be the by-product of world-historical social circumstances rather than individual (or even group) consciousness. But it is not obvious why Hofstadter provides this distinction, nor is it obvious how he sees it as justifiable, as

---

[15] Ibid., 29.

representative of reality; furthermore, it is not obvious why this "fact" is necessarily objectionable even if we were to accept it as true of the paranoid style in the first place.

The only purpose seemingly served by Hofstadter's characterization is the need to reduce the power of folk accounts of history, and to reduce the power of producing (or attempting to produce, even *wanting* to attempt to produce) alternative accounts of novel events. Hofstadter achieves this by attributing an unsophisticatedness, a lack of rigor, and a superstitious childishness to Americans captured by the paranoid style. Is he correct? Perhaps, but not for any of the reasons provided. What would the further meaning of this be if he were correct, from the point of view of administrative justice? It is unclear. What is clear, however, is that Hofstadter pioneered the liberal style of hand-waving away non-hegemonic attempts to articulate or otherwise participate in the discourse of the day; even when the paranoids are right, they are wrong because their justifications, their account of the motive for politically covert actions, did not accord with reality. That reality, of course, is the reality-image as constructed by the regime (and yet it is the "paranoid" American and his folkish methodologies which require the combined weight and power of the managerial class, liberal academia, the culture industry, and the judicial apparatuses to keep in line).

Even if it were the case that a "paranoid style" had swept across America, or more to the point, that American conservatism was somehow at its core paranoid, and that all of mainstream (and underground) right-wing political activity was also operating under the sway of this paranoid style, what would that mean, and why would it be a problem for us in the way Hofstadter (and the generations of liberal polemicists and apologists following in his wake) has deemed it? What would it mean to be paranoid during a time of radical upheaval, such as the racial strife which culminated in the Civil Rights Act? Or during a period of high-profile assassinations of public figures, such as the ones that ended the Kennedy dynasty? Or during a time of economic uncertainty and massive restructuring of the economic sector, as was the case with the events leading up to the New Deal? What would it mean to be paranoid at a time when the entire moral infrastructure of your society was being redesigned without consideration or care for your or your progeny's inclusion? Would paranoia be a fit response? Would this deferral to (pseudo) psychiatric conceptualization even be the proper term for it?

By artfully appropriating the language of psychopathology, Richard Hofstadter told us what it meant to be paranoid during these times. It not only meant you were wrong to be concerned, or that you were crazy for doubting the regime, but that you would be lampooned for it, marginalized for it, and, ultimately, left behind. To be paranoid means to be worthy of dehumanization. As such, whether we speak of the paranoid style, or of American pseudo-conservatism (another of Hofstadter's back-handed concepts), we must speak of them within the context of liberal democracy's existential need for fortifying rhetoric. And if we are speaking of the post-war period in American history, we can only speak of and understand paranoia within a framework of dueling ethno-metanarratives. Affects are never isolated and individual phenomenon; rather, they arise from a time and a locale. More importantly, affects inform the shape and color of our ethno-metanarratives, i.e., they tell us what is important and what is worthy of neglecting. Our ethno-metanarratives drive affect, too; the one cannot be disentangled from the other, and as such, we should guard ourselves against the privileging of logos over pathos when adjudicating competing ethno-metanarratives. To read Hofstadter's rebuttal of the folk account of history strictly in terms of its consistency, coherency, and accordance with the facts without considering the person behind the argument is to disarm oneself before the battle has even begun. This, too, is the fruit of self-deceptive liberalism.

Before turning our attention to the work of Karl Popper, it is worth our while to say a few things about the John Birch Society and the role it played in the history of American conservatism, for Richard Hofstadter was not the only one who bristled at their success. Though the two (Hofstadter and Birch) are now inextricably linked, the story of the John Birch Society is a great deal further-reaching. The John Birch Society was a rather atypically competent conservative outfit; though ultimately unequipped to meaningfully spearhead a folk-conservative countermovement, it still managed to strike fear into the liberal establishment. A testament to their success, the John Birch Society was even targeted by the Anti-Defamation League in an operation that saw the ADL align itself with "the White House, sometimes the Department of Justice, depending on the issue, the NAACP, Americans for

Democratic Action, labor unions, the union-backed Group Research Inc. in tracking and marginalizing the 'far-right.'"[16]

To this day, despite what amounts to a devastating and near-total psychic victory over folk-conservative America by imperial (neo)liberalism, the name John Birch Society cannot strike a pair of liberal ears without triggering horror or disgust, if not both. Ludicrous as it may seem, deep within the most paranoid and psychotic corners of liberal America lies the belief that, in fact, it is the John Birch Society which dominates American political culture! This is, of course, a contortion which, as extreme as it is, nonetheless bears a relevant truth. Within the theatre of American politics, the John Birch Society has—to great effect—shaped rightist rhetoric and strategy; this much is undoubtedly true. But within the realm of American politics, "Bircherism," or shall we call it "Neo-Bircherism," is but one more liberal trapdoor, forever forestalling an authentically folk-conservative revolution. The fatal conceit of Bircherist (and subsequently of Neo-Bircherist) political strategy was its inability, or unwillingness, to step outside of its own ethno-metanarratives. Bircherist commitment to patriotism, but even more so, its strategic commitment to over-privileging ideology when interpreting political matters, ultimately doomed folk-conservatism, even if—at least at the level of the Spectacle[17]—it appeared to be gaining steam. While Neo-Bircherist sentiments and stratagems are functional within the contemporary rhetorical economy, they are not meaningfully active at the level of policy. The liberal panic, being motivated by a certain ethnic partisanship, betrayed a very Popperian (as we shall soon see) intolerance toward the interests and concerns of other ethnic sovereignties. While the influence of Bircherism was never a quantitative threat (some estimates placing peak membership at 100,000), the mere presence of an organized folk interest has often proven justification enough for persecution by liberal hegemony.

We must take note that the failure of Bircherist conservatism

---

[16] Elia-Shalev, "How an ADL spy."
[17] In Guy Debord's book The Society of the Spectacle, Debord details the condition by which authentic, organic social life has been supplanted by its representation: the spectacle. "Being" descends into having, before sliding into its final stage: appearing. Social life is then dictated, or mediated, by imagery.

mirrors the broader failing of the Anglophone New World project: a failure of self-misunderstanding. Embedded within this failure of self-misunderstanding, complicating this challenge while illuminating it all the same, is self-forgetting. Liberalism's role in this self-forgetting is that of an ideological euthanizing agent, which, in tandem with the world-historical success of the Old-World Anglo empire, created the conditions for a fluidity of self-concept molded by pragmatism. That which was self-evident (the foundational principles of identity, for instance) was forgotten, while that which was expedient (spook concepts like "individualism" or "propositionalism," for example) was elevated. The self-forgetting of the Atlantic-Anglo powers led, tragically, to a misunderstanding of themselves as existential beings and, furthermore, to a misunderstanding of the events transpiring within their territories; no meaningful progress has been made on this front and consequently, political conservatism has languished ever since. The true legacy of the John Birch Society is that of a "hotted up" and tumultuous nation-state (e.g., "the culture war"), but an ice-cold and stable political subculture (e.g., "the Deep State"). On this point there is still more to say, but for the time being let us turn our attention to the contemporary re-fixation by liberal hegemony, or what may otherwise be known as "Birch fever." While some readers may consider this exercise repetitive or tedious, I would counter by suggesting that we can better understand this phenomenon of ethno-metanarrative and the conflict between the self-concepts of differing people-groups by indulging the propagandists of liberal hegemony.

Before proceeding any further, I should make it known that I have taken most of my understanding of the John Birch Society ("JBS" henceforth, for brevity's sake) from D.J. Mulloy, who penned a commendably objective (and concise) history of the JBS titled *The World of the John Birch Society: Conspiracy, Conservatism, and the Cold War* in 2014.

Writing for *The New Republic*, Chris Lehmann makes similar observations about the kynical-to-cynical influence of Bircherist thought, though he draws entirely different conclusions from our own. Published in late 2021, Lehmann says of the JBS:

For Trilling and the other apostles of America's postwar liberal consensus, Welch and the Birchers were a terminally backward-looking movement, ill equipped for the complex challenges of sober governance and distrustful of anything resembling modernity and progress. In this analysis, the reactionary right of the 1950s and beyond was profoundly maladaptive, steeped in cultural resentments, status anxieties, ethnic and religious bigotries, and grandiose conspiracy-mongering. The reactionary right sought to restore a world order that was, in essence, everything that the modern world was not: proudly Christian and Americanist over against a doubt-ridden regime of science-bred skepticism; morally Manichean in opposition to a new age of statecraft that embraced agonizing complexity; culturally confrontational and traditionalist in an era of upheaval in the universities, the press, and the country's civic life writ large.[18]

Remarkably, the JBS were temperamentally (and ideologically) about as radical as the Tea Party of the 2010s, adhering very closely to a conventional and classical conception of liberal political philosophy and social theory. Demographically speaking, they were very similar as well: the JBS membership was largely comprised of well-to-do, upstanding, and conformist Americans, themselves possessed by at least a moderate sense of civic duty. Made up in large part by working professionals and business owners (beneficiaries of American free enterprise, in other words), we might best describe them as bourgeois in the Schmittian sense of the word: concerned but otherwise preoccupied. We might even apply Sam Francis' term here, "the post-bourgeois proletariat," which better captures the sense of the average card-carrying JBS member as belonging to the class of prototypical "forgotten Americans" (thereby providing a defense against the charge of "backwardness"). Despite smears to the contrary, these people were not extremists—a charge which ought to shock the senses considering how anarchistic left-wing political violence dominated the country during the 1960s and '70s (periods of peak JBS influence, by most accounts). Neither

---

[18] Lehmann, "We All Live."

were they necessarily parochial and backwards; rather, they were simply ordinary American citizens. Writers like Richard Hofstadter worked hard to concoct the image of a retrograde and irrationally prejudiced, anxiety-wracked convention of back-country nobodies, in stark contrast to the ontic reality of the circumstance. That the civil rights fiasco was clearly on the minds of many JBS members made the work of people like Richard Hofstadter much easier, and as the result of a great deal of propagandistic effort, this image has since tragically cemented itself within popular consciousness.

> Yet on the far side of the midcentury liberal consensus, it's clear that figures like Welch were much closer to the emerging ideological mainstream than any Cold War liberal could have imagined. In his new biography of Welch, *A Conspiratorial Life*, Edward H. Miller makes a provocative and persuasive case that Welch was a vanguard figure rather than a retrograde one. The Birch society was the first major group on the right to pioneer modern culture warfare, with committees opposing the Equal Rights Amendment, abortion, high taxation, and sex education. And once Ronald Reagan—who drew heavily on Bircher ideas, though without any formal affiliation with the group—ascended to the presidency in 1981, Welch's organization became known "for its espousal of any issues that the Reagan revolution . . . cared about."[19]

Robert Welch, Jr. was the founder of the JBS, an entrepreneur himself, and—insofar as his political activism was concerned—something of a pugilist as well. Highly publicized controversies with President Eisenhower and William Buckley, Jr. of the National Review cast the JBS in an outsider light, giving them an edginess and territoriality that mainstream conservatives of the day sought to distance themselves from while at the same time still seeking ways to exploit. This places Welch and the JBS within that comfortable "inner revolution" or "identity crisis" tradition of American conservatism; this tradition, or dialectic

---

[19] Ibid.

between a conventionally liberal understanding of "conservatism," and that of the radical folkish expression, works to animate the electorate without seriously threatening liberal hegemony. For as long as I have observed, and probably longer still, the internal political culture of conservatism has been dominated by this tradition (with the JBS merely operating as the instantiation of a seemingly factual metapolitical reality). If Welch was a vanguardist, it was certainly not of any kind of conservative ideology. But in his organization and sheer zeal, surely, we can agree with Lehmann's assessment.

In the decades since, a series of national political leaders have embraced and modified the hard-core Bircher gospel to the point where it has become the stock-in-trade messaging of the Republican Party. Welch, who died in 1985, would doubtless relish the rise of a nakedly conspiracy-obsessed, twenty-first-century right, intoning its grievances against a "deep state" and bruiting the notion of corrupt power elites' complete treasonous control of the electoral system. Yesterday's maladaptive crank has become today's defender of the true and pure rightwing creed; whereas Robert Welch toiled in the mocked and marginal fringe of the "paranoid style," today scores of prominent GOP leaders—from Josh Hawley and Tucker Carlson to J.D. Vance and Marjorie Taylor Greene—proudly wave the Bircher standard of ultrapatriotic elite-baiting and victimhood.[20]

By the time of the JBS, America had already gone through several rounds of communism-induced hysteria, and perhaps, if we can permit of some conjecture, Welch's framing of the issues of political sovereignty and internal subversion represented the failed final gasp of American anti-communism. That his own messaging became wilder, more speculative, and, comically enough, less dependent on actually existing communism, left subsequent generations of patriotic conservatives with little room for maneuvering. Because the space for intellectual analysis had already been compromised (negated, as we have said, by the self-forgetting, self-misunderstanding, and subsequent overcompensation by way of liberalism-as-ethno-metanarrative), Welch's intellectual progeny could only trade in bluster and bombast (consider, for

---

[20] Ibid.

example, Alex Jones and *InfoWars*). The hypermodern form of suspicion culture as represented by Marjorie Taylor Greene, for instance, demonstrates the ideological impotency of patriotic anti-communism while at the same time still suggesting (to rival partisans like Chris Lehmann or Richard Hofstadter, for instance) the virility of folk-conservativism and of its own ethnically partisan suspicion culture. Civil rights—an issue that animated JBS members but was not as front-and-center rhetorically speaking—frustrates hypermodern suspicion-merchants in much the same way. Trapped between the metapolitical tendency of conservatism to make explicit concessions to progressivism (moving rhetorically and even ideologically from "there are only two genders" to acceptance and even employment of prominent trans celebrities like Blair White and Caitlyn Jenner) and the often-unspoken desire of its constituency to turn the tides of history more aggressively, the movement simultaneously signals impotency while also obscuring a latent potentiality. What Lehmann would have us believe was necessarily true of the JBS can only really be said of its illegitimate political children.

Lehmann, himself a partisan engaging in the battle of ethno-metanarratives, easily and correctly sees the tradition of outsider folk conservatism at work but cannot avoid pathologizing it rather than directly engaging it, just like his intellectual and ethnic ancestor, Richard Hofstadter. It is only "paranoid" because within the open society of liberal democracy there is no "reason" for the particular or the primary—in fact such barbaric vestiges are threats to us all and to the Good itself (though in his analysis, open society luminary Karl Popper would not trouble himself with notions of "the Good"). Pathologization, then, is the first step on the path to "liquidation"—but we will speak more comprehensively to Popper's strategy for defending the open society momentarily. What Robert Welch and other patriotic conservatives call "communism" we can merely call another ethno-metanarrative, and to the extent that America had already internalized "communism" (said differently, its political structure had already ingested outsider ethno-metanarratives, diluting its capacity for rational action and thereby diminishing its own sovereignty), it had also immunized itself against the type of analysis Welch and the JBS put forth.

Ultimately the legacy of the JBS is of organization and outreach, not ideology or analysis. Liberal hegemony feared it because while politically inconsequential (that is to say: no conspiracy was ever uncovered and no tribunal was ever convened), the JBS demonstrated the capacity for folk-conservatism to materialize and operate outside of the conventional political machinery. Welch and the JBS understood the American political scene in a structural and functional but ultimately impersonal way—a failing which hampered the potential success of the JBS at the same time as it stunted the intellectual development of radical folk-conservatism itself. It is this failure which, if anything, led to the "collapse" of the JBS. According to Welch and the JBS, internal subversion was the result of a discrete and external other, and therefore as an incursion not representative of the agency or accountability of America itself, but of some other hostile and irrational will. This invasion, in the view of the JBS, occurred along the plain of ideology and economy, not tribal identity, and so the JBS's failure to articulate anything about the invaders themselves was the necessary result of this conceptual blind spot. Welch's later speculations about a conspiracy beyond communism are indicative of this fact; something else was going on, but what it was no one could say. Neo-Bircherism continues this charade, only more farcically, as the conflict between ethno-metanarratives has only grown more explicit in the years since Welch's death. Consider these facts in the light of our contemporary situation: the rightist establishment within the United States speaks loudly of infiltration by the Chinese Communist Party but says nothing about Israeli spy Jonathan Pollard; this returns us to our earlier point about the way in which, in America's contemporary imperial phase (and just prior to it), the conflict between ethno-metanarratives found ways of harmonizing with one another, at the least, aspects of the one found a place within aspects of the other. The Anglo-American elite needed a new lease on life every bit as much as the incoming Jewish migrants did; it is conceivable that this mutual need, to say nothing of the long-standing and historical Anglo-Jewish alliance of the Old World, worked out a rationale suitable to the curious political behavior of Jewish-Americans. It is also conceivable that Welch's vision was stunted by his patriotism, class status, or any other of several possible causes presently unknown to us. What is known to us now, beyond a shadow of a doubt, is that the rightist tradition of resignation in the face of domestic revolution and overcompensation in the face of foreign turbulence was very much solidified by the JBS, continuing well into the present era. That liberal hegemony invokes the JBS despite its complete lack of cultural relevance and aspirational power signifies the historical importance of the JBS and its role in formalizing not only dissenting folk-conservatism, but the identity of liberal hegemony itself.

Liberal consensists worked tirelessly to discredit Welch and his ideas, but proving an idea wrong does not stop people from lining up behind it. As Steven Monacelli observed in a report written for *The Texas Observer*, some people are still lining up behind Bircherism.[21] Citing Alex Jones and Donald Trump as exemplars of culturally resurgent Neo-Bircherism, Monacelli offers us the boots-on-the-ground proof:

> Now that central Bircher tenets have effectively become embedded into the fabric of the conservative movement, explicit interest in the John Birch Society appears to be growing. In 2017, an article by Austin freelance journalist John Savage noted growing membership in the group across Texas. Local chapters in Dallas, Houston, and Central Texas have been active in recent years. Now, Fort Worth, where Birch himself attended seminary, boasts its own chapter.[22]

If you aren't terrified yet, then just buckle up. Monacelli continues:

> Today, North Texas continues to be an epicenter of Bircherism and the variety of far-right movements that have digested its ideas—some of which have more violent or extreme tendencies. Consider that North Texas is also home to a significant number of participants in the January 6 insurrection, and has been a site and center of activity for extremist groups like the Proud Boys, Oath Keepers, Patriot Front, and far-right militias like This Is Texas Freedom Force (TITFF).[23]

---

[21] Monacelli, "John Birch Society."
[22] Ibid.
[23] Ibid.

CHAPTER I 37

The battle of ethno-metanarratives, itself an abstraction of the battle between folk-sovereignties, does not easily permit slain foes their eternal rest. The open society is, itself, sustained by the vilification of folk-sovereignty and, as we are currently witnessing, whether it takes the form of a defeated and neutered political opponent (former President Donald Trump) or a long-since felled international rival (such as Soviet Russia), as that pearl of Hollywood wisdom goes, "no one is ever really gone." Even the JBS, a relic of twentieth-century suspicion culture whose founder, having been dead for nearly a half-century (and furthermore, whose image does not posthumously inspire seditious feeling), must be reanimated in defense of the open society. A quick Google search will unveil page after page of liberal handwringing over a "resurgence" of Bircherism going back well over a decade, and while new editorials are published seemingly every year, the much-prophesized nuclear holocaust of Bircherist insanity is not on the horizon.

* * *

Let us now turn our attention to Karl Popper, beginning with his essay, "The Conspiracy Theory of Society." Popper, who like Hofstadter was a liberal maximalist influenced by the social theorizing of Adorno, Horkheimer, and the other Frankfurt School thinkers, offers us similarly flimsy reasoning as to why the "paranoids" are so wrong about liberal democracy. His reasoning, as was the case with Richard Hofstadter, follows the same paralogical formula: arguments are declared but never substantiated. We will see, however, that an important way in which Popper differs in his analysis from Hofstadter is his forthrightness in admitting his distaste for the manners and methods of the so-called "closed society" (thereby providing us an avenue for attack against his argumentation by way of his own standards for analysis). Hofstadter never let slip his personal distaste for the subject matter—certainly not in the transparent way Karl Popper did. But to elaborate further would be getting ahead of ourselves: let us focus on the arguments as presented in this brief essay.

Popper criticized what he termed the "conspiracy theory of society," which is the view that powerful people or groups, godlike in their efficacy, are responsible for purposely bringing about all the ills of society. This view cannot be right, Popper argued, because "nothing ever comes off exactly as intended." Of the "conspiracy theory of society," Popper says the following:

> I shall call this theory, the "conspiracy theory of society." The theory, which is more primitive than most forms of theism, is akin to Homer's theory of society. Homer conceived the power of the gods in such a way that whatever happened on the plain before Troy was only a reflection of the various conspiracies on Olympus. The conspiracy theory of society is just a version of this theism, of a belief in gods whose whims and wills rule everything. It comes from abandoning God and then asking: "Who is in his place?" His place is that filled by various powerful men and groups—sinister pressure groups, who are blamed for having planned the great depression and all the evils from which we suffer.[24]

Here Popper trades in anti-teleological thinking, enjoining us to attribute some heretofore unknown privilege to governance by liberal democracy. "Things happen, even bad things, for no reason at all. Nobody uses the power of the state methodically, purposively, especially not to harm or marginalize opponents. Not in a liberal democracy!" (Except when they do, as Popper advises over the course of his work.) Popper wishes us to believe that there are neither plans nor leaders within the open society. We are aware that there is no God in a liberal democracy, but are there not men? Anti-teleologism, then, is the antidote to conspiratorial ideation—or rather, it is the antidote to the folk account of history. The folk account of history, marginalized and often left to languish in unconscious solitude, operates by inductive reasoning almost out of necessity. Patterns emerge through experience which ultimately lead to the production of some conclusion. That conclusion may be inaccurate or incomplete, but the wrongness of this method is due in equal parts to the folly of the reasoner himself (or herself), as well as to

---

[24] Popper, "Conspiracy Theory of Society," 13.

the leadership and management of the open society itself. Nevertheless, it is the folk historians who, through their process of covert induction, reverse engineer the intentions and identities of the powerful agents operating within (and upon) liberal democracy. When they fail it is largely because the open society necessarily obfuscates itself and the reality it produces to militate against and contain its most problematic constituents. According to Karl Popper this is not only a necessity for the preservation of the open society, but is also a good in and of itself.

This framing also serves to reinforce Popper's juxtaposition between the rationalism of the open society and the irrationalism of the closed society: the closed society is superstitious and paranoid, unable to understand the complexities of the open society that is liberal democracy. The closed society is Manichean, while the open society is Enlightened. The closed society is preoccupied with elevating a sophistic and subjectivist notion of "the Good" to the detriment of all, while the open society organizes to root out an objective Evil (the liberal maxim to "reduce suffering") for the betterment of all. Though if we learn to read between the lines, we see that Popperian liberal democracy is every bit as paranoid, sophistic, and Manichean as the closed society, if not more so.

Popper continues his diatribe in the subsequent paragraph, saying:

> The conspiracy theory of society is very widespread, and has very little truth in it. Only when conspiracy theoreticians come into power does it become something like a theory which accounts for things which actually happen (a case of what I have called the Oedipus effect). For example, when Hitler came into power, believing in the conspiracy myth of the learned elders of Zion, he tried to outdo their conspiracy with his own counter-conspiracy. But the interesting thing is that such a conspiracy never—or hardly ever—turns out in the way that it is intended.[25]

That "a conspiracy never—or hardly ever—turns out in the way that it is intended" does nothing to invalidate the folk account of history; rather, the statement operates as a thought-terminating cliché. Invoking

---

[25] Ibid.

this phrase is an admonition against further interrogation into the nature of suspicion culture and its constituent elements. How many events or happenings occur "according to plan," whether they were covertly designed or not? Defense of the open society, and of liberal democracy, mostly takes the form of paralogisms: just as Hofstadter did, Popper is merely working to deflate attempts at a folk account of history through his authority as a representative of the open society.

In *The Open Society and Its Enemies*, Popper takes this even further when he says:

> Conspiracies occur, it must be admitted. But the striking fact which, in spite of their occurrence, disproves the conspiracy theory is that few of these conspiracies are ultimately successful. Conspirators rarely consummate their conspiracy.[26]

Popper reinforces one non sequitur with another. How does this statement elucidate the ones which preceded it? As with Hofstadter in his own writing, Popper boldly declares the truth of reality but apparently never feels the need to substantiate his claims. Rather than affirm some truth of reality, or clarify problematic social dynamics, both statements instead leave us with an unending production of questions—questions that the suddenly incurious Karl Popper, it would seem, considers unworthy of even posing, such as:

1) What are these conspiracies that never turned out as intended/were never consummated? Why did they turn out as they did?
2) What conspiracies did turn out as intended/were consummated? Why was this so?
3) What does it mean for something to "not turn out as intended?" Who are these intending conspirators?
4) Why are all conspiracy theories generalized as such, rather than being adjudicated on a case-by-case basis?
5) Why is "conspiracy" a legitimate category but "conspiracy theory" is not?

---

[26] Popper, *Open Society*, 307.

If we were to pose these questions and pursue them honestly, we might very well undermine the core conceit of the open society. As a result, liberal democracy itself may crumble. The other outcome, of course, is that we might simply come to doubt Mr. Popper's reasons for exalting the open society. We might begin to look at the apologetics of individuals like Richard Hofstadter and Karl Popper not as labors of objective intellectual discernment, but rather as the sleight of hand of motivated partisans. We may not invalidate the concept of an open society, or of liberal cosmopolitanism writ large, but we might come to an uncomfortable conclusion regarding the sociobiological aspects of post-war liberal hegemony. Yet again, unfortunately, we have gotten too far ahead of our place in the argument. Let us stay the course just a little longer.

Popper continues:

> This remark can be taken as a clue to what is the true task of a social theory. Hitler, I said, made a conspiracy that failed. Why did it fail? Not just because other people conspired against Hitler. It failed, simply, because it is one of the striking things about social life that nothing ever comes off exactly as intended. Things always turn out a little bit differently.[27]

Or in other words, national socialism was felled by unpredictability. Popper's argument does not even rise to the level of speciousness. We are encouraged to believe that Hitler didn't fail because of strategic incompetence, or by being overwhelmed by the forces of his opponents, or because massacring the weak is wrong. Rather, he failed because he incorrectly perceived social life. Which (or even, whose) "social life"? It is unclear. It also, to be frank, does not matter. For Popper, national socialism as a political paradigm and as an iteration of the closed society failed because it could not produce good social theory, whatever that means. Popper's semi-tautology here is worse than embarrassing: it is an insult. Surely the architects of liberal democracy did not achieve their success by virtue of somehow anticipating all possible future developments. Truly, is liberal democracy a successful political institution

---

[27] Popper, "Conspiracy Theory of Society," 13.

on account of having a successful social theory? The arrogance of the social theorist knows no bounds.

Just beneath this layer of articulation, however, is the following converse assumption: had Hitler correctly perceived the social life—that is, were his social theory more accurate—then his conspiracy would have succeeded. It would seem then that what Popper truly means here is that victory is validating. Liberal democracy survived while national socialism did not, which from the point of view of the social theorist implies that the open society "got it right" and, consequently, was able to conjure a victory. The open society is not "more moral" than the closed society just as liberal democracy is not "more virtuous" than national socialism. It is simply more ontically true. One conspiracy wins out over another and is thereby made just. This veiled presumption of might-makes-right appears to be the true meaning behind Popper's anti-cognitive non sequiturs, which should trouble readers familiar with Popper's theorizing, as he flatly rejects might-makes-right elsewhere in the text. The sudden poverty of rigor in his logic and paucity in his language provokes the instinct to doubt; we presume, due to his status as an academic and a social theorist, that the whole of Popper's analysis is guided by a commitment to painstaking objectivity, but at the pivotal moment he falls short. That he spends much of his time coining terms to characterize his opponents (e.g., "historicism"), and—especially in the penultimate chapter of his book on the open society—agonizing over the meanings and contradictions inherent to his usage of commonly understood concepts (e.g., "rationalism") employed in service of his polemic speaks to the trap of partisan ethno-metanarratives Popper finds himself mired within. In attacking the historicist collectivism of the closed society, Popper commits nearly identical trespasses as those he accuses others—Plato for instance, one of his key intellectual antagonists—of committing.

Rather than continue his sustained, rationalist polemic against the closed society and against totalitarianism, Mr. Popper turns away, offering instead a pithily obfuscating dismissal. Throughout his text *The Open Society and Its Enemies*, Popper is rather forthcoming about his personal feelings on the matter, taking special care to inform the reader when he was breaking the fourth wall of philosophy by admitting to his own partiality. Here, however, he sloppily blends the partial and the impartial, suggesting a deeper ambivalence about—and in fact, an a priori indebtedness to—the open society on grounds that cannot be adjudicated rationally and dispassionately. Which is to say, they can only be adjudicated on terms that would invalidate (or at least fatally recontextualize) his open society apologia. Assuming the correctness of my analysis, we may dismiss Popper's claim that the open society represents the overcoming of tribalism, much less the rejection of collectivism. For is a society not a collective, and is adherence to liberal political norms not to identify with a tribe? So-called collectivist societies like the ones described in Plato's *Republic* are based, Popper tells us, on prohibitions against the pursuit of an individual's unmoored personal freedoms, but would liberal democracy tolerate an individual who behaved antithetically toward its norms? We know for a fact that it does not. But once more we find that we are ahead of the analysis. Let us continue.

We employ thought-terminating clichés and non sequiturs (e.g., "it is what it is," "that's just the way it goes," "things always turn out a little bit differently," et cetera) to assuage our nerves and to compel others toward some action, usually our preferred action, or at least, the actions of another introjected through us. When Popper says that conspiracies fail because "social life turns out a bit differently," or that "conspirators never consummate their conspiracies," he is issuing an injunction against investigating the matter any further. He issues the injunction to himself as well, in effect conforming to the dominant ethno-metanarratives of his own community, and so internally the cliché operates in equal measures as a disciplinary technique as well as a therapeutic one. (We can assume this dual directedness for reasons I shall soon provide.) Externally, however, the imperative serves a strict disciplinary function.

To better understand this disciplinary function, we must now—finally being able to give it our full consideration—turn our attention to Popper's notion of the open society. In doing so we will make explicit his motivations for championing the open society, for they bear directly upon our investigation into ethno-metanarratives and their role in the formation of suspicion culture. I have selected some dozen or so excerpts from his text, *The Open Society and Its Enemies* which I feel are illustrative of the conflict between ethno-metanarratives, of how this conflict foments a society-wide epidemic of suspicion, and perhaps most importantly of all, of the ultimately sociobiological underpinnings of contemporary hypermodern neoliberalism.

    Born to an upper-class family of Lutheran Jews, Karl Popper would later flee his home in Vienna to escape persecution at the hands of Hitler's national socialist regime. Raised in an exceptionally literate and inquisitive household, Popper's academic inclinations were informed by his firsthand experience with authoritarian (or in his terms, totalitarian) regimes, first as a teenager during an early and nearly fatal flirtation with Marxism, and then later as an adult seeking refuge from the Third Reich. These experiences drove him to adopt a dichotomous view of European political history: the closed society versus the open society. His reading of the Western canon (taking the specific form of a polemic against Plato, Hegel, and to a lesser extent Marx), colored by his own personal experience of political terror (and, permitting a small bit of probable conjecture, an inherited ethno-metanarrative of fear and terror) led him to project the violence and perceived irrationality of the twentieth century's fascist and communist revolutions directly into the foundational texts of European political and social theorizing. Through this lens, Plato became indistinguishable from (as well as an indelible prelude to) the forms of political violence which threatened to expel all liberal democracies from the face of the world during the middle of the last century. In dissecting Plato's *Republic*, Popper saw both a proto-Hitlerian eugenics program and a proto-communist move against private property. The blood-and-soil myth which animated European folkish authoritarian movements was presaged, so Mr. Popper argued, by Plato's support of the "noble lie." He saw Marx's theory of class struggle in Plato's *Republic* as well. In Hegel he saw an obvious and direct predecessor to the authoritarian regimes of the subsequent century, but more importantly he reviled Hegel for being, in his view, a sycophant more concerned with career trajectory than truth. (One could easily imagine a twenty-first-century incarnation of Karl Popper cursing Hegel for being a "mediocre White man.") In Hegel's writing Popper saw the essentially mystical justification for the irrationalist "isms" of the closed society (e.g., nationalism, nativism, et cetera) which, he argues, are as old as European political theory itself. I am not concerned by Popper's indictment of Marx, and I am to an even lesser extent interested in his view of Hegel. For our purposes it suffices to review Mr. Popper's remarks against Plato if we are to validate our counter argument.

Popper, a friend to the Freud family and one time student of Alfred Adler, donned his psychoanalyst hat when describing Plato as a reactionary of the Heraclitan kind and a man petrified by change, utterly fixated on arresting it.[28] Popper contextualizes Plato's thought further by highlighting the tumultuousness of the time in which he lived, emasculating the great philosopher's theoretical body by reducing it, effectively, to the level of a coping mechanism. According to Mr. Popper, Plato looked everywhere and yet saw only chaos; as such, he marshalled his tremendous intellect to forever halt the tides of history. Change, which is uncritically held up in Popper's analysis as "good," appears to be the main foe of the closed society. Attentive readers will recognize this similar style of psychologistic argumentation from our discussion of Hofstadter's essay; would it invalidate Popper's theorizing to point out that his persecution at the hands of the ascendant German regime provoked him to recoil at the mere discussion of ethno-political sovereignty found in Plato's *Republic*? Or that, because the authorities of his day made an enemy of him and his heritage, that Mr. Popper wasn't in fact motivated to return the favor to the very notion of authority itself? Perhaps it might. At least, it would certainly provide as illuminating a context as Mr. Popper believed doing so would in the case of Plato and his "totalitarian" philosophy. It might further injure Popper's credibility to note that he was complicit in the very same scholastic sins which he condemned Plato for committing, namely the preoccupation with essentials, the fixation on origins, and his psychologistic approach to social theorizing. Karl Popper was no less interested in identifying the nature or essential character of things when it came to the question of how one could identify the closed society, or

---

[28] Psychoanalysis demonstrates itself to truly be an exemplary ideology of the harmonized ethno-metanarrative. Freud, like Marx, stood apart from the Enlightenment of the British Isles and yet was deeply indebted to it, contributing his own puzzle piece to the dialectic between the Isle-Anglo and Continental-Jewish expressions of rationalist Enlightenment theorizing. Hence its warm acceptance among the Atlantic powers (the United States and Great Britain). While Karl Popper considered psychoanalysis to be "on the side of irrationalism" (and thus opposed to the open society), he nevertheless armed himself with a psychoanalytic approach to aid in his deconstruction of Plato's thought.

historicism (the main villain in Popper's reading of history). Similarly, his experience as a refugee pushed him into much the same predicament as Plato found himself in, namely one of trying to find out just where things all went wrong. Very early in Popper's analysis we find little that differentiates him, in practice, from his historicist enemies other than his disapproval for their interests in identifying and preserving a primary political sovereignty.

Plato's *Republic* is the most significant text for analysis in the man's corpus, not only because of its intensive focus on social engineering and investigation into political sovereignty, but because of the way in which Plato slanders Socrates, the man Mr. Popper believes to be the archetypal hero of the open society. On the one hand, we have Socrates, the individualistic freedom lover devoted only to truth; on the other hand, we have Plato, the collectivistic censorious tyrant, concerned only with power. Not only was Plato a traitor against the open society, but he was (in Popper's view) a traitor against his own master, Socrates. But we are less concerned with adjudicating this supposed rivalry; rather, what interests us is the way in which this rivalry is used to establish a specific dichotomy. This framing of individualism and collectivism has proven to be one of the most harmful rhetorical devices ever constructed in political history, for no sooner does one invoke one or the other concept than does he find himself victimized by the very same invocation. Aided by this rhetorical movement we come to see the through line of a vulgar solipsism coursing throughout Popper's thought: the tribalism he spends so much time resisting may be much closer to his own heart than his theory suggests.

> I believe that Plato's political program, far from being morally superior to totalitarianism, is fundamentally identical with it. I believe that the objections against this view are based upon an ancient and deep rooted prejudice in favor of idealizing Plato.[29]

Plato labored mightily in producing an accurate understanding of Man's fundamentals, building from the ground up a worldview which

---

[29] Popper, *Open Society*, 84.

would provide the justification for a particular kind of regime—specifically, a regime capable of providing the conditions for authentic and eternal flourishing. (Popper insists that Plato seeks to arrest change when it would be more accurate to say Plato sought an end to degeneration—a point which Mr. Popper concedes in his writing. What, then, would be the motivation for impugning Plato's mission given the facts of the matter, I wonder?) At the heart of this understanding are concerns over what constitutes "the Good" and "the Just," so that a state could emerge which possessed a concrete and jointly understood civilizational ethos capable of delivering both. For Popper, all of this is unnecessary, and furthermore, participation in a program such as this portends disaster. It is sufficient that life exists at all, with the only questions of importance being just how we will go about executing and preserving a liberal moral framework. Several times throughout the text Popper mocks the so-called historicist's preoccupation with the epistemology of authority, showing a clear preference for an ethics of authority (for example, Mr. Popper directs us against asking "Who shall the rulers be?" suggesting instead "How shall we rule, as equalitarians?") over an ontology of authority. Why, exactly, are liberal values necessarily superior? Popper tells us it has to do with the importance of equality, and of the necessity for exalting the freedom of the individual above all else. And why, exactly, are these to be the organizing principles of Western society? This is never sufficiently explained, though it may have to do with Popper's a priori dependence on liberal norms.

See, Mr. Popper lauds the sociological theorizing of Plato's *Republic*, recognizing in it a deep understanding of human psychology and social behavior. It is precisely this understanding which Popper recognizes and rejects, a priori dismissing the juridical conclusions Plato derives from it, for this wisdom when enacted necessarily precludes the open society (at least, that is what he claims). Understanding man as he did, Plato understood as well the multiplicity of predative influences upon him and of the dangers they bring to bear upon man's pursuit of an authentic living. If we disabuse ourselves of the intense scrutiny which Popper brings to this investigation, then we might see Plato's "utopian social engineering" (Popper's term for the teleologically-informed style of social organization, juxtaposed against his own "piecemeal social engineering," which is not dissimilar from the contemporary "nudging" style of social engineering originated by Cass Sunstein) as a sincere attempt at protecting Man against the sociobiologically motivated attempts to rob him of his joy—a joy which fundamentally informs the whole of society (an observation which Mr. Popper himself offers up to us, as well). The "deep rooted prejudice in favor of Plato" is neither different from nor more extreme than the respect and regard a young man holds for his grandfather and grandmother; Plato is not simply part of the European political tradition—he is part of its foundation, and as such he holds a special place in the extended European canon. The very characterization of this reverence as "prejudice" highlights the hostile and beguiling affect guiding Mr. Popper's critique. Liberal values are necessarily superior to those of the closed society, for they are the necessary precursor to the inclusion of groups who would seek to influence the systems and institutions of a liberal society. And for those of you who are familiar with the text, you will likely not fail to recall the necessity Mr. Popper places on the control of a society's institutions.

Consider the dilemma we are here investigating under less grandiose conditions: a man and a woman fall in love and marry for seventy long and happy years. During that time, they may grow to know each other well, perhaps even too well. Consequently, they may learn to forget aspects of themselves, each other, or even their own history so that they may keep their love alive. It is their decision to do so, delusion or not. If a delusion it is, then it is their delusion (and they are right to pursue it). Of course, it may only appear delusory from the outside, which is precisely the position Popper operates from throughout his critique. The fluidity or stability, or better said, the intelligibility (or lack thereof) of a community's self-concept is its alone and is not subject to the interrogations and investigations of disinterested passersby. Liberalism's self-forgetting renders itself vulnerable to precisely this kind of external motivated reasoning. It may be that no self-concept maintains its coherence once being rendered self-less; all that we may do in the face of such a fact is affirm the dignity of the self (and its native social ecology) and discourage the kinds of motivated deconstruction which passes itself off as reason. While I am not defending irrationalism per se, I am extolling the beauty and necessity of the irrational core of human experience, the "irrationality" of love, belonging, and joy, all of which crumble under too watchful a gaze.

And now back to Mr. Popper himself:

> What did Plato mean by "justice"? I assert that in the republic he used the term "just" as a synonym for "that which is in the interest of the best state." And what is in the interest of this best state? To arrest all change, by the maintenance of a rigid class division and class rule. If I am right in this interpretation, then we should have to say that Plato's demand for justice leaves his political program at the level of totalitarianism; and we should have to conclude that we must guard against the danger of being impressed by mere words.[30]

Karl Popper's admonition that we not be "impressed by mere words" is a curious one, for it is only by "mere words" that Plato's theory may be reduced to a desire to arrest change. Popper's sociobiological commitments to liberalism require him to excavate the personal prejudices which inform the "true meaning" behind Plato's words. For Popper, "change" is an unalloyed good, though this apparent fact is, yet again, never demonstrated as such; it is left to us as readers, then, to answer the question: how could any rational person ever oppose "change"? In considering Popper's argument, the mind does wander to the possibility of a totalitarian liberalism, however. For if a state were to exist somewhere, one which decides to organize itself in the manner Plato describes, the mere fact of its thriving should not pose an existential threat to the liberal project—and yet it somehow does. If the success of such a state drove liberal democracies to militate against it (in the case of the United States: Iraq, Syria, Iran, Libya, and so on), are we left with any other way in which we might describe liberalism but as a totalitarian ideology? Can we truly valorize Popper's commitment to freedom if, upon reviewing his argument, we find that he was only ever committed to the liberal paradigm of freedom? Increasingly we see that Mr. Popper is not committed to freedom, or any other virtue for that matter, on its own terms; rather he is committed to a certain kind of freedom arising from within a unique social ecology. It would seem then that the great

---

[30] Ibid., 86.

lover of Socrates resembles more closely the sophists who opposed him than the great master himself.

With each page of *The Open Society and Its Enemies* we find that the sociobiological interpretation wins out over the game of philosophy. Consider the following excerpt, for instance:

> But was Plato, perhaps, right? Does "justice" perhaps mean what he says? I do not intend to discuss such a question. If anyone should hold that "justice" means the unchallenged rule of one class, then I should simply reply that I am all for injustice.[31]

The legacy of Karl Popper's open society is exactly that which he was dedicated to forestalling: the unquestioned rule of the many by the few. The very title of his book would itself serve as the inspiration for and namesake of the most disreputable institution of liberal tyranny known to most of the Earth (that institution, of course, being the Open Society Foundation, founded by George Soros, who was not only influenced by Karl Popper but in fact studied directly beneath him). In today's world liberalism is synonymous with unaccountability, a fact which is not owed to any misapplication of Popperian theory, either. Real liberalism has been tried—and quite successfully in fact! Now that we find ourselves fully ensconced within the international age, the whole Earth itself is an open society lying in wait (which is exactly how liberal oligarchs like George Soros conduct themselves). The preservation of the open society no longer finds itself in a commitment to abstract moral principles, but rather, it is grounded in a particularistic and sociobiological posture of self-preservation. This is why someone like George Soros can use his massive store of wealth and extended network of influence to affect the desired juridical outcomes in regimes on the far side of the planet. Can we plausibly call this equality? Or should we call it self-defense? Consider the following statement made by Isadore Zack (the man who led the ADL's infiltration of the JBS) which brings to the surface the very prejudice we are now suggesting, "[It] was only in a democracy that the Jewish community has been allowed to flourish

---

[31] Ibid., 87.

and so, if you want to defend Jewish Americans, you also have to defend democracy."[32]

Did Karl Popper (or Richard Hofstadter, or any other liberal consensist, for that matter) value the liberalism of the open society for purely rational reasons, or did he also labor under ethno-metanarratives of his own? When we consider that many of the Jewish refugees from Central and Eastern Europe (notably the ones who would later form the new American intelligentsia) were influenced by Frankfurt School theorists and their allies, it only grows more difficult to ignore the role ethno-metanarratives played in the formation of the post-war neoliberal consensus. Frankfurt theorists like Herbert Marcuse and Theodore Adorno sought to transform society—specifically European society—by moving it away from its historically tribal social structure, beginning with an attack on its monogamous and sexually-restrained familial unit. While the Critical School was not a strictly Jewish affair, the Frankfurt School was, and its adherents drew from their own experiences of persecution at the hands of authoritarian European regimes to develop their social theories (as did Karl Popper). Frankfurt and critical thinkers agreed with Popper that tribalism was the cause of "totalitarianism," though they attributed it to the presence of an authoritarian personality style which arose from intact family structures led by strong men. The solution, as they saw it, was the dissolution of the family itself. As a result, freedom became the ultimate moral value in the war against European ethno-political sovereignty, also known as the closed society, finding its strongest supporting arguments in works such as Erich Fromm's *Escape from Freedom* and, as we are all familiar with, Karl Popper's *The Open Society and Its Enemies*. While Mr. Popper did not take up the whole of the Critical-Frankfurt school's theoretical foundations, he nonetheless carried forth the tradition of defending democracy and freedom against European tyranny.

Despite the differences between their individual accounts, this generation of Jewish intellectuals found a new home within American universities and government to carry out their latest ethno-metanarrative: "Never again." Never again would the Jewish people suffer the indignity

---

[32] Asaf, "How an ADL spy."

of judgment at the hands of European political sovereignties. The disciplinary function behind Popper's use of thought-terminating clichés begins to come into focus considering the (brief) historical context provided here: why should we not think through the consequences of our competing ethno-metanarratives? Because the survival of the Jewish people demands it. We observe the therapeutic function of the specifically Jewish ethno-metanarrative of "Never Again" (and the clichés conjured up in defense of them), for it not only operates to extract compliance from other people-groups, but it extracts compliance from within the Jewish ethnos. Thought-terminating clichés ameliorate mental suffering, bind the community, and coerce obedience from the constituent members of the tribe, regardless of their truth-value or knowledge-function. They are part of the "condition-of-delusion" which all people-groups ostensibly depend on for their existence. Given these facts (supplementing, as it were, our critical reading of Popper's own writings) it is difficult to review Mr. Popper's argumentation and not see this prejudice at play in his text.

In an interview for *The Times of Israel* (the same interview we have already cited earlier in this investigation), Matthew Dallek, the author of a recent book on the JBS, further exposes the prejudice inherent to Jewish ethno-metanarratives:

> There certainly were other threats at the time, but the Birch Society was seen by liberal critics, including the ADL, as a very secretive group that promoted conspiracy theories about communists who often became conflated with Jews.[33]

Once more I ask: was Karl Popper's condemnation of Platonism as "closed society totalitarianism" strictly an intellectual and philosophical conclusion? Or Hofstadter's claim of a paranoid American style, for that matter? Was it, perhaps, the result of a transference—a projection of his own personal nightmare-experience? Or, perhaps even more radically, are the two propositions not in fact one and the same motivation, contained within a single experience of life? For if it is in fact the latter,

---

[33] Ibid.

we see that the identitarianism which Mr. Popper (and other advocates of his open society) decries truly reigns supreme over liberal abstraction. Liberalism's social theory does not appear to be strong enough to override the firstness of identity if its champions cannot overcome their own personal prejudices enough to fortify their advocacy. Should our own analysis hold true, then we must conclude that the post-war neoliberal consensus was the result of a harmonization between Anglo-American self-forgetting and Jewish over-remembering of the self.

Let us commit ourselves to the greatest of liberal sins: proper contextualization of The Most Uniquely Evil Event in all Human History. The Third Reich arose out of the existential conflict Germany faced at the hands of both the Weimar regime and the just-over-the-horizon threat of bolshevist communism, both of which were vehicles for the deliverance of Jewish ethno-political sovereignty.[34] The closed society of German national socialism appears, in this view, to be motivated not by an exclusive and irrationally pathological hatred of an out-group, but by the very real clash of civilizations, namely the meeting between opposing ethno-metanarratives. That Karl Popper retreats into faceless, history-less abstractions like "collectivism" and "historicism" in the face of these facts betrays his total capitulation to the dominant ethno-metanarratives of his own people. Submission to one's own prevailing ethno-metanarratives manifests psychologically as solipsism and chauvinism, and perhaps even, paradoxically, in the abolition of agency (individual and collective alike). Because the function of the ethno-metanarrative is to provide fortifying ego defenses (at least, that is one of its functions), the truth of one's actions never (or rarely ever) rise to the level of articulation. Consequently, the collective is banished, psychologically speaking, into the realm of the shadow, thereby obfuscating the ability to properly adjudicate their own actions. (It is ironic that Mr. Popper should have lionized Socrates, exalting him as the patron saint of the open society, without ever internalizing the most well-known of Socratic dictums—to know thyself.) While Popper's defense of the open society does not appear outwardly chauvinistic, the superficial preoccupation with liberal identity-signifiers like "the social

---

[34] Frantzman, "Was the Russian Revolution Jewish?"

scientist" allow the primal voice to speak, disinterred as it were, and express its own private bigotries in a manner palatable to the liberal point of view. Bound to the power of the unconscious ethno-metanarrative, liberal ideology loses its claims to reason and objectivity, becoming instead a battering ram used to break apart rival ethno-political sovereignties.

> The Republic is probably the most elaborate monograph on justice ever written. It examines a variety of views about justice, and it does this in a way, which leads us to believe that Plato omitted none of the more important theories known to him. In fact, Plato clearly implies that because of his vain attempts to track it down among the current views, a new search for justice is necessary. Yet in his survey and discussion of the current theories, the view that justice is equality before the law (isonomy) is never mentioned. This omission can be explained only in two ways. Either he overlooked the equalitarian theory, or he purposely avoided it.... I do not see how Plato's method of impressing upon his readers the belief that all important theories have been examined can be reconciled with the standards of intellectual honesty; though we must add that his failure is undoubtedly due to his complete devotion to a cause in whose goodness he firmly believed.[35]

In his *Republic*, Plato is quite transparent about his opposition to equality. Consider his "Myth of the Metals" which deals rather explicitly with the inherent inequalities built into human society. Why then would it be rational to expect Plato to include a theory of justice which he considers axiomatically illegitimate? Karl Popper observes Plato's belief in an axiomatic inequality of man, and furthermore, suspends his predilection for doubt to acknowledge the good faith position which Plato took. To my eye it appears that Mr. Popper merely seeks to weaken the power of Plato's argument through relentless critique, even if his own critique is, itself, impotent and irrational. Where is the dishonesty in

---

[35] Popper, *Open Society*, 90.

excluding that which one is axiomatically, categorically, opposed to? Well, the problem is in the fact of Plato's exclusivity, for our sociobiological view holds that Popper's critique is not about philosophical rigor, or the philosophic pursuit of truth and knowledge, but rather about securing one's place within a favorable social ecology. Popper's preference for equalitarianism is informed not by intellectual rigor, but by group survival strategies formulated over centuries upon centuries of human development. And what exactly does our dear liberal apologist intend when he invokes the concept "equalitarianism"? Thankfully Mr. Popper provides his definition of equalitarianism, which I shall share with you here: "Equalitarianism proper is the demand that the citizens of the state should be treated impartially. It is the demand that birth, family, connection, or wealth, does not influence those who administer the law to the citizens."[36] From the point of view of Plato's holistic, organic, view of the state there can be no true juridical impartiality. We may aspire to (and even succeed in) upholding a rational and objective system of justice, but the eye cannot be impartial to the kidney any more than a mother can be impartial towards her infant daughter. To be clear, in making this argument I am not encouraging or condoning sycophantism, nepotism, or despotism. But in keeping with the theme of liberal self-forgetfulness, we must be careful to distinguish between good faith critiques of injustice and sociobiological strategies of inclusion. The state is the political apotheosis of a people; it contains them, nourishes them, and when necessary, disciplines them. But the state is not separable from the people themselves, and the demand that all primary markers of firstness be cast out in favor of a blind commitment to impartiality strikes us as a plea to lower the legal standing of the indigenous population. Here, the abstract commitment to liberal moral values masks once more the command to forget oneself and abandon his style of life. We should not forget either that the demand to uphold equalitarianism is motivated by an a priori rejection of the native population's authentic manner of being.

If any reader should doubt the pernicious influence of open society equalitarianism, one need only look at contemporary society and note

---

[36] Ibid., 91.

how the commitment to equality has not only devastated whole industries and spheres of everyday life (e.g., athletic competition, education, military recruitment, et cetera), but has even rendered conceptual understanding and simple communication virtually impossible. Karl Popper's legacy of equalitarianism can be seen in the present-day inability to define manhood or womanhood, for instance, out of the irrational fear that such definitions lead inexorably to genocide. We also see how this legacy of equalitarianism, or equality before the law, has manifested itself as its opposite. Equality before the law has come to mean the privileging of the open society's subject(s) over the folk population. With each passing generation, cultural developments produce new subjects who are celebrated as "true representatives of the American way of life," who by the very fact of their exaltation are intended to cast aside the actually existing representatives of American life: the folk. And this manifestation, it must be said again, has not arisen out of incoherence or misapplication, but from the very legacy of the open society itself. It would appear that the true meaning, or ethos, of the open society is an indefinite militating against the closed society—specifically its biological type(s). The pursuit of "freedom" and "individuality" in the face of the law is thus to pursue a further extending of biological types into the open society, fortifying it against the alleged parochialism of the closed society. Because defense of the open society is an existential challenge, equalitarianism can only have the meaning of an attack on entrenched habits and modes of being, and those beings themselves who thrive under the reign of "parochialism."

Thanks to the following excerpt we see more nakedly how Popper's argument for the open society is predicated on a deliberate misunderstanding of Platonic thought—a misunderstanding that careens dangerously into outright hostility:

> The sole purpose of [Plato's] argument is to impress upon the reader that "justice," in the ordinary sense of the word, requires us to keep our own station, since we should always keep what belongs to us. That is to say, Plato wishes his readers to draw the inference: "It is just to keep and to practice what is one's own. My place (or my business) is my own. Thus it is just for me to keep to my place (or to practice my business)." This is about as

sound as the argument: "It is just to keep and to practice what is one's own. This plan of stealing your money is my own. Thus it is just for me to keep to my plan, and to put it into practice, i.e. to steal your money." It is clear that the inference which Plato wishes us to draw is nothing but a crude juggle with the meaning of the term "one's own.". . . But in such a principle Plato himself does not believe; for it would clearly make a transition to communism impossible."[37]

Karl Popper betrays his commitment to a social scientist's impartiality in two critical ways: first by repeatedly impugning Plato's motivation and secondly by reading into history his own autobiographical experiences. Throughout his analysis, Mr. Popper concedes the good faith position which Plato takes, but because he is hostile to Plato's program, Popper works to convince his audience of the sinister double-meaning lurking behind each passage of the *Republic*. We are asked to accept that Plato, who was doggedly committed to a kind of "class collaboration," was in fact a secret despot who sought to plunder the lower classes. Moreover, Popper twists Plato's conception of "justice," lending to it a suspiciousness that would not be possible from a direct reading of Plato himself. As for the final statement excerpted above, we need not agree with Plato's program (in fact, there remains to this day a great debate over how much of his own program Plato truly accepted) to see that his treatment of the Guardian class was a far cry from the communism of twentieth-century Europe. But to fulfill the ethno-metanarrative of "never again" demands we construct a *new* understanding of the history of Western social and political theory—one that is compatible with the partisan sociobiological strategy of the West's new intelligentsia.

But Popper continues his libelous analysis of Plato's political theorizing:

> We see here that Plato recognizes only one ultimate standard: the interest of the state. Everything that furthers it is good and virtuous and just; everything that threatens it is bad and wicked

---

[37] Ibid., 93–94.

and unjust. Actions that serve it are moral; actions that endanger it, immoral. In other words, Plato's moral code is strictly utilitarian; it is a code of collectivist or political utilitarianism. The criterion of morality is the interest of the state. Morality is nothing but political hygiene. . . .

Totalitarianism is not simply amoral. It is the morality of the closed society, of the group, or of the tribe; it is not individual selfishness, but it is collective selfishness.[38]

Plato's standard for statecraft is predicated on the strict axiomatic definitions he provides for the relevant criteria (e.g., "the good" and "the just"). The state, then, is merely the executor of a social will teleologically informed by the theory of Forms/Ideals. We can accept or reject the theoretical underpinnings of Plato's model of statecraft, but we cannot dismiss them as utilitarian—at least, not without disposing of the commonly accepted definition for the word. Operating from within the Platonic framework of holism (as Popper sees it), the state and the people are one; that which is "good" permeates the whole of the social organism, reflecting the "goodness" of the realm of Forms/Ideals. To accept Popper's critique, we would need to discard the entire framework Plato presents to us as justification for his model of Man and politics. Mr. Popper fails to provide sufficient reason for doing so. Rather, we are simply expected to read into Plato's own descriptions a sinister dimension which is not apparent.

In fact, Mr. Popper provides us with an excellent reason for dismissing his own critique: the supposed virtue of the open society is nothing more than a sociobiological projection of the necessary criteria for securing the inclusion of the Jewish peoples into Western societies. Is this not manifestly "political utilitarianism"? Is it not "collective selfishness" to denigrate other people-groups' right to self-definition? Is it not "totalitarian" (if not outright genocidal) to demand the abolition of all folk tribal ways in favor of a global open society?

If one seeks to persuade another of the superiority of his position, he must answer the following question: "Why should I care?" Why

---

[38] Ibid., 102–103.

should proponents of "the closed society" care if their authentic way of living is incompatible with the needs of the stranger living half-way across the planet? Popper gives us no reason for condemning the closed society on our own terms, thereby failing to give his rhetoric any true persuasive power. Ultimately, we are expected to concede to the authority of a liberal academic, whose own arguments, being rooted firmly in solipsism, veer fearfully into narcissistic chauvinism.

The following excerpts focus on Popper's critique of sovereignty, to which we can re-introduce our concept of the atrocity of power, presented in the first chapter of *UCT*. On the question of sovereignty, Mr. Popper shares the following:

> It is my conviction that by expressing the problem of politics in the form "Who should rule?" or "Whose will should be supreme?", etc., Plato created a lasting confusion in political philosophy.... It is clear that once the question "Who should rule?" is asked, it is hard to avoid some such reply as "the best" or "the wisest" or "the born ruler" or "he who masters the art of ruling."
> ... But this leads to a new approach to the problem of politics, for it forces us to replace the question: "Who should rule?" by the new question: How can we so organize political institutions that bad or incompetent rulers can be prevented from doing too much damage?
>
> Those who believe that the older question is fundamental, tacitly assume that political power is essentially unchecked. They assume that someone has the power—either an individual or a collective body, such as a class. And they assume that he who has the power can, very nearly, do what he wills, and especially that he can strengthen his power, and thereby approximate it further to an unlimited or unchecked power. They assume that political power is, essentially, sovereign. If this assumption is made, then, indeed, the question "Who is to be the sovereign?" is the only important question left.
>
> I shall call this assumption the theory of (unchecked) sovereignty, using this expression not for any particular one of the various theories of sovereignty, proffered more especially by such writers as Bodin, Rousseau, or Hegel, but for the more general

assumption that political power is practically unchecked, or for the demand that it ought to be so; together, with the implication that the main question left is to get this power into the best hands. This theory of sovereignty is tacitly assumed in Plato's approach, and has played its role ever since.

I am inclined to think that rulers have rarely been above the average, either morally or intellectually, and often below it. And I think that it is reasonable to adopt, in politics, the principle of preparing for the worst, as well as we can, though we should, of course, at the same time try to obtain the best. [39]

I introduced the concept of the AoP (atrocity of power) in the first chapter of *UCT*, and now we may at last apply it on more concrete grounds. But before doing so I must admit that I am somewhat sympathetic to Popper's skepticism of the ruling class. The routine failure of leadership, whether we speak of its vanity, incompetency, or any of the other commonly observed negative characteristics of today's leadership, is almost enough to drive good hearted men and women of all backgrounds into the arms of anarchism. This, however, is why I have introduced the concept of the AoP: to highlight Man's natural struggle to fulfill the role of authorship, but as well, his duty to do so despite himself. Ultimately, I am afraid, Mr. Popper's skepticism is akin to the skepticism of the non-believer, or outsider. This is demonstrated by his refusal to entertain investigations into the epistemology of authority. For advocates of the open society, the only reliable metric of authority is in how dutifully it protects the liberal norms of the open society, which is to say, Popper does not seek *good* leaders, rather, he seeks *his* leaders (those who would self-forget and turn away from their own customs and tribal relations in favor of those of the open society, as well as those whose identitarianism is obscured by paramoralizing and universalistic rhetoric). When seen from this sociobiological view, does the defense of the open society not appear to be a utilitarian one? Hence our charge that the Popperian polemic against the closed society is a projection of the open society's reflexive hostility toward all styles of

---

[39] Ibid., 114–116.

life outside its own purview. After all, the only question Mr. Popper is interested in, and considers to be worth investigation, is the question of how authority can work for the open society. No attention is paid to what authority is (ontology) or how we can know authority (epistemology), only a realism which recognizes existing institutional power structures and seeks to win them to the side of the open society (utility, or para-ethics). The question of what makes an authority just can only be answered by a consciousness in touch with the ontic reality of the AoP; rather than dismiss the inquiry as faulty or problematic, we must confront it with the utmost grim commitment. Failure to do so can only ensure that some other style of sovereignty fills the vacancy.

Popper is also correct to point out the cognitive errors we often make in understanding authority; sovereignty often finds itself in similar circumstances to the rest of us, namely those circumstances of negotiation, compromise, and defeat. Sadly, that one is a ruler does not mean that he or she will rule, unquestioned, as they see fit. By this I mean to say that the problem is not (as Popper sees it) of an unchecked will; rather, the true problem is of a will that is not truly strong enough to rule properly. Plato's theory of political power and social organization answers the problem raised by Popper insofar as it anticipates the ways in which sovereignty can deteriorate over time. Far from proposing an unchecked sovereignty, however, Plato painstakingly details the factors and forces which impinge upon sovereignty, in effect lessening or diminishing it (as opposed to Popper's assumption of a "liberated" sovereignty). But this, too, is part of the AoP. We as temporal beings lack the grace necessary to move the masses of man permanently toward the ultimate Good. It is a lifelong struggle to keep ourselves on that path. In this respect, sovereign rulers are hardly different from the rest of us. Popper sees in this fact the necessary justifications for abandoning teleologically informed authority in favor of a technocratic one. Thus, he offers his piecemeal engineering instead, opting to incrementally nudge the population away from pain and suffering, and wherever possible towards "the Good." What is "the Good"? Well, while Mr. Popper dismisses its existence, he nevertheless possesses a meta-ethical structure, one bound up within liberal norms like "equality." We will say more on this in the following paragraphs so I will not belabor the point further.

To return to the AoP, I would like to reiterate the factual status of the concept, lest readers interpret it as another form of power apologia. We observe in our own lives the reticence to discipline, to discern, and to demarcate (the three Ds of authority, perhaps?) and the consequences accrued for failing to do so. For most of us, our stomachs cramp and knees weaken at the hour of decision, that moment of choosing where we are confronted with the truth of our moral agency. Only a few of us are equipped with the strength to act despite our cowardice (most of us require the proverbial moral education; more importantly, we require the fortification to act reliably), and a subset of that group are clinical psychopaths. Action, then, is itself obfuscated by the actors who commit to it and the social fog of cowardice which consequently materializes, thereby only furthering the reach and scope of the AoP. I think readers will begin to understand why interrogating the epistemology and ontology of authority is critical, for the ontic reality of human action does not permit us to accept institutional authority at face value. Certainly not the institutional authorities of the open society. In our own time, we see how the unfettered and unquestioned field of human action which constructs and preserves institutional authority fuels, and ends up elevating, the production of suspicion culture.

Suspicion culture does not arise solely out of the competing sociobiologies of tribalism, but out of the immanence of human failure and weakness. We doubt, in part, because action is difficult and consequential, often fatally so. Superstitions propagate because we do not always understand the parameters shaping our action, nor the structure of the ecologies we find ourselves within, especially the ones we construct for ourselves. Our condition-of-delusion, or propensity for self-delusion, is tightly bound up within this socio-ecological blindness, typically finding itself only punctured by visionaries (e.g., the shaman, the artist, the avatar, et cetera) whom we rely upon to bring the truth of existence safely into our lives. (The other rupture arises from calamity, with no guarantee that we will survive it, let alone excavate some meaning or truth from it.) For these reasons, it is often easier for analytically minded outsiders to map the structure of a foreign social ecology, therefore justifying our need for a capable and robust civilizational immune system. Given our demonstration of the open society as a predatory social ecology, and how competing ethno-metanarratives operational within the open society can only, by their very nature, make circumstances worse, none should then contest the necessity for and privileging of man's "right" to the condition-of-delusion. Part of the success of an act is that it goes, at least for a time, uninterrogated. When I speak of this antagonism toward our condition-of-delusion, I am speaking to the desire we all share in to unmask, to draw back the curtain, to doubt. Human life cannot thrive if it is permanently subjected to a doubting gaze; eventually we must declare the investigation complete. All these phenomena are canopied within the AoP, for the powers of creation and of vision are, themselves, atrocious.

The question of Mr. Popper's anti-teleologism has come up several times throughout our investigation, and to that point we turn our attention once more. Let us look to his discussion of "utopian" and "piecemeal" engineering for a better understanding of its meaning and consequence:

> Before proceeding to criticize utopian engineering in detail, I wish to outline another approach to social engineering, namely, that of piecemeal engineering. It is an approach which I think to be methodologically sound. The politician who adopts this method may or may not have a blueprint of society before his mind, he may or may not hope that mankind will one day realize an ideal state, and achieve happiness and perfection on earth. But he will be aware that perfection, if at all attainable, is far distant, and that every generation of men, and therefore also the living, have a claim; perhaps not so much a claim to be made happy, for there are no institutional means of making a man happy, but a claim not to be made unhappy, where it can be avoided. They have a claim to be given all possible help, if they suffer. The piecemeal engineer will, accordingly, adopt the method of searching for, and fighting against, the greatest and most urgent evils of society, rather than searching for, and fighting for its greatest ultimate good."[40]

---

[40] Ibid., 148.

Popper's "piecemeal engineering" (the ideological precursor to Sunstein's notion of "the nudge") neatly combines his anti-holism with his antagonism toward teleological thinking into a style of governmentality which preserves the open society by subdividing and atomizing society itself. If society itself is not a unified whole, with its various domains of social life helplessly, hopelessly, spilling over into one another, then it is a series of self-contained spheres which bear no relation to one another. For instance, a state with plummeting fertility rates, a housing shortage, and a catastrophic immigration policy, is a state with three separate and unrelated challenges which all operate within their own spheres, irrespective of the others, and each with its own targeted goals and objectives (which might, in fact, conflict with one another were we to view the scene in terms of what Popper calls the "biological theory of the state"). Bearing this in mind, we might then describe Popper's view as anti-integralist, for it seeks to blind itself to the multitudinous relations which inform a society's domains of being (anti-integralism as the autism of political and social theorizing). If there were in fact no relations, no interstitial tissue connecting the various domains of social life, and no good reason for believing such, then we might find ourselves able to accept Popper's proposed method of governmentality. However, Mr. Popper commits a similar error as he accused Plato of, only in reverse: piecemeal engineering is only possible—preferable even—from the standpoint of an irrational commitment to individuality; if Plato's so-called "collectivism" compelled him to deny the reality of the individual's need to pursue freedom, then Popper's "individualism" compels him to deny the embeddedness and interrelatedness of the various sub-domains of sociality, thereby subjecting the individual to an unceasing wave of totalitarian interventions, each nebulously aimed at reducing "unhappiness" and rebuking "evil." Here, Popper's commitment to anti-teleologism shows itself to be rather detrimental to the goal of proper statecraft, for if there is no "plan" then to what end are the micro-adjustments of piecemeal engineering intended? How are we to know when to "nudge" and when to relax this habit of chronic state intervention? Of course, if the point of such interventions is to perpetually militate against the closed society and its types, then we have, in fact, a genuine civilizational telos! Once more we see the accusations hurled by Popper against the closed society are at least as true of the open society; if the open society orients itself around a continual battle against evil, is liberal democracy not also Manichean in nature? Mr. Popper's open society suffers a parochialism of its own; while we tend to associate liberalism, democracy, and cosmopolitanism with open-mindedness and curiosity, the open society of post-war neoliberal democracy—beset as it is by partisan ethno-metanarratives—exhibits a trauma-bound narrowmindedness (e.g., "Never Again") which undermines its own supposed virtues.

The open society of twenty-first-century neoliberalism lacks what we might term "an affirmative morality"; in both theory and in practice, the open society fails to honor its commitments (e.g., commitments to pluralism, free discourse, and equal participation), and so when it makes an overture to some rival other, a Big Other even, it always does so with threats and never by extending the proverbial olive branch. "Affirmative morality" is not synonymous with tolerance per se—certainly not the tolerance we know today. It does not denote obsequiousness or self-flagellation. Rather, affirmative moralities are those which approach other(s) with a non-coercive, non-exploitative desire or aim. Affirmative morality presupposes the dignity of the other, and as such, permits the possibility of a genuine mutual encounter or exchange. In short, it is of the order of pure generativity or genuine productivity. Something real emerges from it. Hence why Mr. Popper rejects a teleological notion of statecraft, and of the Good (castigating the former as irrational and the latter as impossible), for the reconfiguration of liberal norms was never intended to occur on rational and philosophical (or even scientific) grounds, but on irrational and sociobiological ones. The open society of contemporary neoliberalism is a group survival strategy, not a political or sociological experiment.

Before we turn our attention away from Popper's work, let us consider these final few quotations:

> In what follows, the magical or tribal or collectivist society will also be called the closed society, and the society in which individuals are confronted with personal decisions, the open society.
>
> A closed society at its best can be justly compared to an organism. The so-called organic or biological theory of the state can be applied to it to a considerable extent. A closed society

resembles a herd or a tribe in being a semi-organic unit whose members are held together by semi-biological ties—kinship, living together, sharing common efforts, common dangers, common joys and common distress. It is still a concrete group of concrete individuals, related to one another not merely by such abstract, social relationships as division of labor and exchange of commodities, but by concrete physical relationships such as touch, smell, and sight. And although such a society may be based on slavery, the presence of slaves need not create a fundamentally different problem from that of domesticated animals. Thus those aspects are lacking which make it impossible to apply the organic theory successfully to an open society.

As a consequence of its loss of organic character, an open society may become, by degrees, what I should like to term an "abstract society." It may, to a considerable extent, lose the character of a concrete or real group of men, or of a system of such real groups.[41]

What "personal decisions" can be made by individuals who have been denatured by ideology? Who are these new people, anyway, and from whence do they derive their personhood? Mr. Popper seems to believe that the trade-off between the firstness of identity and the "freedom" of individuality ultimately vindicates his project. (Recent data, sadly for proponents of the open society, invalidates this presumption.)[42] To his credit, Mr. Popper is willing to acknowledge that not only does the open society militate against the closed one, but that its final victory is secured by erasing the folk ways of organically constituted peoplegroups. From the sociobiological point of view, postwar neoliberal democracy functions as genocide by way of ideology.

---

[41] Ibid., 165–166.
[42] Clifton, "Global Rise of Unhappiness."

CHAPTER I 67

Hypermodern Suspicion Culture of the Twenty-First Century

Contrasted with the postmodern form of twentieth-century suspicion is our contemporary, irrationalist mode of doubt which I am calling "hypermodern suspicion culture." Whereas postmodern suspicion culture was, as we have already said, social, empirical, historical, and occurring against the sociobiological backdrop of a fortuitous but ultimately hostile merging of ethno-metanarratives, hypermodern suspicion culture ought to be understood as parasocial, solipsistic, technological (often invoking a "pre," or lost, or unconscious history), and emerging out of the near total subsumption of all ethno-metanarratives to a singular hegemonic self-concept, the self-understanding inherent to the neoliberal open society. Under the reign of hypermodernity, suspicion most regularly takes the form of a commodity, purged of all dignity, thereby resigning itself to the status of a farce. Hypermodern suspicion culture's farcical nature is not exclusively a byproduct of commodification, however; instead, it more directly results from two discrete but related events: 1) dismissal of the folk account of history; and 2) by the replacement of communal folk ways of relating with the virtual sociality birthed by revolutions of information and communication technology. By disrupting (and in many cases suspending) originary processes of consensus-making (e.g., the family, the community, and so on), the open society affected a regression in man, thrusting him into a panicked and primordial psychological state given to hysteria and misjudgment, the secondary effect of which was the intensification of taboos. We should also note that the move from postmodern suspicion to hypermodern suspicion is synonymous with a movement from the preoccupation with events, to a preoccupation with conjectures and discourses. Said differently, it is the movement from "the conspiracy" to "the conspiracy theory," consistent with the abstracting and obfuscating tendencies of the open society neoliberalism. It may be said that the discursive abstraction of reality facilitates the avoidance of violating newly imposed taboos (e.g., racism, anti-Semitism, homophobia, et cetera).

To elaborate further on the farcical nature of hypermodern suspicion, we ought to say something first about the tragedy of postmodern suspicion. The word "tragedy" should not conjure imagery of the suffering endured by the various societies of the twentieth century, prodigious as it may have been. Rather, it is used here to encapsulate the momentousness of the political challenge which confronted Americans, pointing specifically to its (at the time) not-yet-decided nature. Hope and the feeling of optimism for the future were not yet extinguished; there was a sense in which things could still be done to avert disaster, and that there were still men and women willing to do something—anything—to overcome defeat. It was, in a word, patriotic. Twentieth-century suspicion culture may be described as tragic in the sense, as well, that the choices made and actions undertaken needn't have unfolded as they did—that there was no great invisible hand driving man's action, but rather the decisions of postmodern man were part of a genuine striving toward and wrestling against fate. We can look back upon recent history and plausibly declare, "It could have all been different." This, for us, is the meaning of tragedy.

No such feeling exists within our contemporary hypermodern suspicion culture, only the feeling of resignation, for patriotism has been replaced by solipsism. Man's psychic regression is synonymous with (or a consequence of) his defeat and subsumption into the new paradigm of ethno-metanarratives, manifesting itself as hysteria and acting out, juvenility being the natural state of conquered peoples.

We may illustrate the farce that is contemporary suspicion culture by contrasting it with a well-known hero of postmodern suspicion culture: Maury Terry. For readers who may be unfamiliar with the name, Maury Terry was a journalist who devoted his life to uncovering the secret behind the "Son of Sam" killings. His hypothesis still lingers in the air, having been neither satisfactorily proven nor disproven—not that we will be taking a side on the matter. It is a hypothesis he built slowly, hesitantly, and in isolation over the span of many years, namely that David Berkowitz was but one actor out of many, operating under the direction of an entity known as "The Children" (a group with connections to the Process Church, Charles Manson's "family," and the Church of Scientology). Just prior to his interest in the Berkowitz/Son of Sam killings, Terry had been covering the race riots which occurred in the wake of MLK, Jr.'s assassination. Having seen with his own eyes the violence and chaos which savaged the streets of America in the aftermath of Dr. King's death, Terry was shocked to find his accounting of events dismissed in favor of a more flattering depiction. This, by his own admission, lit the spark which would later erupt into an all-consuming flame during the years in which the Son of Sam killings took place (1975–1977).

Law enforcement showed no interest in Terry's folk account, just as they showed no interest in investigating the suspiciously loose threads pulled by Berkowitz's arrest (e.g., the lack of conformity between eyewitness sketches, Berkowitz's own evolving testimony). Eager to put the "Son of Sam" murders behind them and reassure the public of a return to normalcy, it was thus left for Terry to pull those threads and see where they led. Terry's skepticism was provoked by the disharmony between Berkowitz's appearance and the eyewitness sketches of the murderer, as well as the cryptic messages Berkowitz left to the public in the wake of each murder, leading Terry to eventually suspect the involvement of Berkowitz's neighbors, John and Michael Carr. (Their father, Sam Carr, had already been implicated as the owner of the dog "responsible" for inciting David Berkowitz to kill). Adamant that Berkowitz—in league with the Carr brothers—was part of a Satanic cult, Terry's investigation was hampered by the brothers' deaths in the years shortly following Berkowitz's arrest. Both deaths were shrouded in mystery: Michael Carr died as the result of an alcohol-induced car accident (he was not known to drink, as he apparently had a genetic aversion to alcohol), while his brother John was believed to have died of a self-inflicted gunshot to the face (John's body was found with the number "666" marked on his hand).

One such thread, the murder of Arlis Perry (which was only solved in 2018), proved significant in that the details of the murder seemingly supported aspects of Terry's folk explanation. Arlis Perry was a North Dakota native who had moved to California with her husband of two months, Bruce Perry. It was in California, Stanford University specifically, where she would be brutally and ritualistically murdered. Arlis was only nineteen years old at the time of her death, victimized repeatedly inside the Stanford Memorial Church. The investigation into Perry's murder had gone cold until Berkowitz sent a copy of *The Anatomy of Witchcraft* to Lt. Terry Gardner, a deputy sheriff from Ward County, North Dakota bearing a note which read, "Arlis Perry, hunted, stalked and slain. Followed to California." And, "Stanford Univ." Berkowitz would soon prove less than helpful, claiming that if he said anything else about the Perry murder, "they are going to think I am a snitch" and "they'll kill my father." Many of Berkowitz's disclosures matched this formula—insinuation, followed by a retreat. David Berkowitz clearly wanted to invite others into his world but feared the consequences. Fortunately, the limited assistance he did manage to offer was rather significant: with the aid of a DNA sample, Stephen Crawford (the man Maury Terry had suspected of murdering Arlis Perry), was proven to be the killer. Tragically for Terry's investigation, Crawford took his own life before law enforcement, attempting to enter his apartment, could arrest him. Inside his apartment, however, was the jacket to Maury Terry's book *The Ultimate Evil* and a two-year-old suicide note written sometime after being interviewed by the sheriff's detective.[43] While Arlis Perry was not directly linked to the "Son of Sam" killings, there were too many synchronicities surrounding the details of her death. One such detail relates to the alleged suicide of John Carr.

It was in North Dakota at the Minot Air Force Base where John Carr succumbed to a fatal gunshot, reportedly a suicide, though local law enforcement had their doubts. Those doubts were informed by a most curious event: only a few short months before expiring, John was admitted to a local hospital where he claimed (rather incoherently, according to Mike Knoop, the patrol officer for the Minot Police Department), that he had been thrown from a car and had been drinking blood and urine from a chalice. Minot, North Dakota was apparently a hot bed of Satanic activity according to Glenn Gietzen (then sheriff's deputy), who was the officer on scene at the time of Carr's death. Gietzen had seen this activity for himself firsthand, responding to reports of stolen religious items from Catholic churches in Minot as well as breaking up Satanic gatherings where participants "gathered around tables set up in a cross formation, passing around chalices containing human urine" after mutilating and sacrificing over a half-dozen dog carcasses.[44] Gietzen and Knoop were not alone in their belief that Carr was involved in cult activities: Lieutenant Terry Gardner, a deputy

---

[43] Louie, "Suspect in 1974 Stanford."
[44] Huebner, "North Dakota Link."

sheriff who was also part of the investigation into John Carr's death, was quoted as saying, "There is no doubt in my mind, based on interviews I conducted and information I have obtained, that John Carr and Berkowitz knew each other well."[45]

While Maury Terry would eventually become something of a media spectacle himself, the bulk of his investigation occurred alone in the shadows, away from the seductive pull of commodification and media titillation. His investigation into the Berkowitz killings is an interesting example of the folk account of history colliding with the "official" narrative provided by law enforcement and the juridical establishment. Berkowitz's capture was won by concerned citizens, just as the conspiracy behind his actions was only uncovered by citizen journalist Maury Terry (assisted by others), themselves operating outside of hegemonic law. (The Berkowitz murders were also a forerunner to the so-called "Satanic Panic" of the 1980s, another historical example of the conflict between the folk account and the hegemonic liberal interpretation of history.) While the truth of the Son of Sam killings is in no danger of being revealed to us anytime soon, we are not here to discuss the merits of such investigations, but rather to view them in their proper historical lens and contrast them with similar investigations occurring today. Unglamorous, slavish, and painstaking: this was the nature of the postmodern conspiracy.

Let us consider the story of Maury Terry in contrast to a contemporary hero of hypermodern suspicion culture: Alex Jones, the filmmaker and one-man-phenom responsible for making *InfoWars* a household name.

While Terry's legacy verges on the bombastic, his dedication to swimming against the current—not just the current of apathy established by law enforcement and the legal structure more broadly, but also the current of liberal anomie which had dispossessed Americans of their religious consciousness—lends a tremendous authenticity to his work. His investigative work was not complicated by grand ideological commitments or fortuitous connections to the intelligence community; as was characteristic of his time, Maury Terry was obsessive—a true

---

[45] Tron, "How the 'Son of Sam.'"

man of conviction. Alex Jones is an obsessive, too, as well as a man of conviction (who, in the wake of the Sandy Hook trial is now, also, a convicted man) and his early documentary work adheres more closely to the postmodern style of suspicion. As American as any man God ever made (at least, the persona of Alex Jones is as such), Jones brought the ethno-metanarrative of the rugged frontiersman with him into battle against the discourse of "The New World Order." Before *The Alex Jones Show* regressed into a multi-million-dollar cult of personality, it was every bit the vehicle for bootstrapped folk-account Americana. Whether it was in revealing the secret dealings and misdeeds occurring in his own backyard of Texas, or showing secretly recorded footage of the (then relatively unknown) Bohemian Grove gatherings, or perhaps most disturbing of all, releasing training documents and footage of law enforcement seminars exposing the turn-of-the-century Patriot Act era pivot towards targeting law-abiding Americans, the early years of Jones's journalistic career were as commendable and dignified as any folk-historian of the previous century.

In truth, the downfall of *The Alex Jones Show* was not wrought by tyrannical censorship and partisan lawfare; rather, it was the result of Jones's own slide into hypermodern suspicion. Over time (specifically in the years following then-President Obama's first term), the *InfoWars* operation grew steadily less factual and less discerning, evidenced by the shift in guest appearances, having gone from booking former heads of state, investigative reporters, and credentialed subject-matter experts to anonymous "insiders" with top secret security clearances and bottom shelf rhetorical skills. Owing to Alex Jones' unique bond with his audience, guests like, for example, ex-State Department, board-certified psychiatrist, and psychological operations expert Steve Pieczenik could appear on the show and make dubious or otherwise ill-supported claims (e.g., that Sandy Hook was a false flag operation, that the alleged 2020 election fraud was permitted by the Trump administration as part of a sting operation, et cetera) that would slip past the defenses of the audience because of the parasocial relationship cultivated by Jones himself. An even better example would be Donald Trump's own appearance on *The Alex Jones Show*, which helped fortify the persona of Trump as a secret patriot; telling the audience of Alex Jones (and Alex Jones himself, no less) that they would be "very proud of him" and the work he would do as President of the United States. This secured the future Commander-in-Chief's street cred with the schizo-paranoiacs, the radicals, and the conservatives alike. It didn't just validate Trump; it validated Jones as well, leading many major media outlets to anoint him as the leading voice of radical conservatism.

While it was not obvious at the time, by aligning himself with the Trump team, Jones had hoisted himself by his own petard. Long after it stopped being plausible to believe that Mr. Trump was in control of his own administration and agenda, personalities like Alex Jones continued to hold water for the failing administration. It was not simply a poor choice of bedfellows which instigated Jones' decline; his degenerating credibility occurred in tandem with his increasing overreliance on technology and his own descent into solipsism. Alex's "information war" was also a technological one: moving from public access television to the world wide web; a tailor-made app bringing *Prison Planet* content censorship-free direct and to the audience; emergency broadcasts conducted by smart phone; zealot that he was, the urgency in getting his message to as many people as possible was not followed by an urgency to refine and review the message itself. As his program became more technically impressive, more professional, the substance of the message itself degraded badly. The duration of each broadcast began to expand, as did the number of advertisements, thus causing a contraction of actual content. The number of broadcasts per day increased while the clarity of the message steadily decreased. Jones' own message increasingly became incoherent, incapable of even being communicated over the course of a single four-hour broadcast. Mr. Jones' exasperation with the circumstances of his business grew increasingly apparent as he would regularly break down and cry or regress into hysterics while on air (performative or otherwise). *InfoWars* and the persona of Alex Jones, though a devout Christian his whole life, increasingly took on Messianic overtones as his program and career lapsed more fully into commodification and sycophancy.

Like Robert Welch, Jr. of the JBS before him, Jones's list of antagonists and opponents grew more ephemeral and euphemistic over time, too. In the late 1990s into the early 2010s, the list of villains included individuals like Janet Napolitano and Donald Rumsfeld, institutions like the Department of Homeland Security, policy initiatives like the

Patriot Act, to name a few. But in the years following his breakthrough into mainstream success, his narrative took a Manichean turn, one in which the side of Evil was populated by "globalists," "goblins," and "interdimensional vampires"; in other words, no one in particular, no one that could be traced, much less challenged. What started out as an earnest investigation into the declining political state of American life became an exercise in tedious and incomprehensible esoterica that only Jones could decipher but never satisfyingly articulate. None of this is to imply that Jones was the driving force behind hypermodern suspicion culture; rather, he was merely one of its clearest expressions. In truth, the whole of North America was swept up by the same technologically induced solipsism, resulting in dangerous mass movements organizing around the dueling conspiracy theories of "QAnon" and "Russiagate." We have already spoken about the meaning and significance of these two events in the first chapter of *UCT*, so let us close out this juxtaposition between the postmodern and the hypermodern, between Terry and Jones, before moving at last to the question of legitimate suspicion.

Whereas Terry (and other folk-historians of the postmodern period) was the medium, the vehicle for delivering the folk-account of history (the message of which was simply the sum of his investigative labor), Jones is both medium and message. Rather, the message is Alex Jones. Under hypermodernity, there is no longer any pretense toward "raising consciousness" or "speaking truth to power," just as there is no longer, in fact, a conspiracy to expose (much less to theorize over). That we are now caught amid an over-proliferation of theory speaks to this fact. Reality no longer demands the same kind of interpretation or ideological framing as it once did. In most instances, ontic reality is characterized by bare fact and pure expression. Therefore, the regress to theorizing serves a crucial ego function, namely that of self-delusion, rather than an express truth function (that of revelation). This is the farce of hypermodern suspicion culture—that there is, in fact, no longer a conspiracy—or, said more exactingly, that "the conspiracy" has simply become the normative mode of political action and conduct. We live in Byung Chul Han's transparency society, after all: the Council on Foreign Relations publishes a podcast, available for download on your phone or computer; presidential whistleblowers and election manipulators publish the truth of their machinations in the most widely circulated magazines and endure no scrutiny; sporting competitions and other cultural events are preceded by bizarre and perversely esoteric dances or demonstrations, seemingly designed to instigate folk-suspicion. For the doubt-stricken American man and woman, daily life is an exercise in confirmation bias. Theorizing has ceased to be a primarily folk endeavor and is now the domain of hegemony (with the general thrust of the investigation taking the form of, "Why aren't the people accepting of our tyranny?"). In the face of the transparency society, folk theorizing loses its analytic and social power, though it has yet to lose its appeal.

Whereas it was once necessary to explain or interpret how the President of the United States was felled by a single shot despite the bullet's perplexing trajectory, it is now necessary to account for why men in dresses don't attract attention from heterosexual males. And if the difference between the two seems slight, while it is the case that both accounts primarily serve an ego-function (a defense of the hegemonic ego), we locate the fact of this distinction in the underlying affect and context which distinguishes between the two. The one is constituted by conquest and erotism, and the other, by enforcement and anti-erotism. Under a state of exception (e.g., the assassination of a sitting president), hegemonic theorizing "plugs the hole" of suspicion by providing a conclusive and authoritative account of the event so that the regime may return to the business of politics. Hegemonic theory operates quite differently during the permanent state of exception (PSoE), however. Under the PSoE, the "business of politics" is found in applying unrelenting pressure against the folk population, thus necessitating an accompanying investigative discourse throughout.

Hegemony itself validates our claim about the remission of folk theorizing, if only in its own convoluted and half-accurate way. Consider the following excerpt taken from a recent interview in *The Economist* featuring Nancy L. Rosenblum and Russell Muirhead (both political scientists from Harvard who co-authored the book *A Lot of People Are Saying: The New Conspiracism and the Assault on Democracy*):

> The Economist (TE): Though conspiracy theories have always existed, they note that today something is different and dangerous: "Conspiracy without the theory."

Nancy Rosenblum & Russell Muirhead (NR & RM): "Its proponents dispense with evidence and explanation. Their charges take the form of bare assertion," they explain in an interview. "It is a powerful force, with the capacity to animate popular fury, to delegitimize political opposition, and to hijack government institutions."

TE: Conspiracies have always been a part of life and politics. Is it more of a thing now, and if so, why?

NR & RM: "Conspiracy theory has always been part of political life. So long as those who exercise power are secretive and self-serving—and so long as democratic citizens value vigilance and even a degree of mistrust—it always will be. Some theories are far-fetched, but sometimes the dots and patterns that support a conspiracy theory prove the charge.

NR & RM: What we're seeing today is something different: conspiracy without the theory. Its proponents dispense with evidence and explanation. Their charges take the form of bare assertion: "The election is rigged!" Yet the accusation does not point to any evidence of fraud. Or take Pizzagate, the claim that Hillary Clinton is running a child sex-trafficking ring in a pizzeria in Washington, DC. It doesn't connect to a single observable thing in the world—it's sheer fabulation. And in America, this new conspiracism now comes directly from the president, who employs his office to impose his compromised sense of reality on the nation.[46]

From the point of view of the hegemonic ego, the folk account of history is irrational and baseless. Whereas we see the absence of theorizing as resulting from an experience of life within the transparency society, the hegemonic ego sees it as a pitiful expression of solipsistic prejudice and parochialism. Once more, we see suspicion culture boil down to a confrontation between the open society and the closed society (evinced by the authors' repeated concerns over the damage done to liberal institutions and experts by the folk account of history).

---

[46] N.C., "Conspiracy theories are dangerous."

CHAPTER I   77

This "new conspiracism" is comparable with our concept of "hypermodern suspicion culture" insofar as they both recognize a discrete and contingent break in the relations between folk-sovereignty and hegemony. But the hegemonic ego, hyperinflated and decadent as it is, cannot truly understand the problems posed by folk-sovereignty and the folk-account of history, much less understand these folk entities themselves. Even in our present statistically driven psychopolitical era, where every institution and every domain of life labors ever more intensely to penetrate the consciousness of the individual and extract every morsel of information about him or her possible, the state cannot get inside the folk and understand them as they are (instead of understanding them as they need to be understood in the minds of a sociobiological rival). After all, they are "the open society"; the open society is the result effected by mutating liberal political philosophy into an ideology of extremist partisan intolerance, one whose entire cause for being is predicated upon rooting out heretics (the existing folk-sovereignty).

That Rosenblum and Muirhead understand the importance, not only of vigilance (necessary for full extirpation of folk-sovereignty) but of institutions (necessary for establishing and enforcing liberal hegemony), places them comfortably within the tradition of the open society. Not only are they part of that tradition, but their own intellectual contributions also advance it. Hypermodern liberalism therefore represents the complete and total victory of Popperian social theorizing; this fact is demonstrated anytime we look at the political landscape of North America, that titanic apotheosis of exclusionary cosmopolitanism and oligarchic tyranny.

Rosenblum and Muirhead's "new conspiracism" proves itself inferior to our concept(s), however, by virtue of its overcommitment to the values, strategies, and discourses of the open society, the foremost of which is the open society's tendency toward negative morality. The strictly negative morality of the open society forecloses the possibility of understanding, leaving the social field open to colonization by accusation and bad faith interpretation. We say negative here to denote the open society's axiomatic invalidation (or negation) of alternative folk claims to sovereignty, authority, and history. Contrast this with our own process: we arrive at concepts like hypermodern suspicion or the folk-account of history by practicing affirmative morality, or the a priori non-negation of sociobiological competitors and their ethno-metanarratives, thereby granting us privileged access to the necessary psychological states which transform the possibility of understanding into a reality of understanding. Simply stated, we do not suspend or deny the dignity of another, were doing so to stymie a mutual understanding and recognition or even the very possibility of understanding for ourselves.

One should, in fact, always speak of affirmation and negation rather than of inclusion and exclusion, for the rhetoric of the open society often amounts to little else but self-preserving and thought-terminating clichés (inclusivity results in defenestration; exclusivity is demonized while practiced in secret). Our own framing does not negate or reject other folk-claims to sovereignty or folk-accounts of history, but it also does not make of them a fetish, thereby inappropriately privileging them over our own. We can preserve the dignity of competing sociobiological groups without subjecting them to derisive and incoherent neoliberal concepts.

This negational tendency is, itself, an expression or manifestation of the paranoiac wing of the open society, whose membership is comprised of the most partisan (and erratic) agents active within hypermodern neoliberal hegemony. Owing to this extreme and pathological posture, we will never see a "final success of the open society," for its own origins and constitution are too dysfunctional to persist with the kind of longevity observed in certain "closed societies." Consider that the dual problems of "misinformation" and "disinformation" are really the challenges posed to hegemony by a technologically enabled pluralism of resentful ethno-metanarratives, all unleashed simultaneously. These are resentments, mind you, that were stoked by the institutions of the open society to aid in the dispossession of folk-sovereignty (the causes of said resentments which were also, as part of the program of dispossession, attributed to folk-sovereignty). Concocting resentful ethno-metanarratives and then disseminating them through the power of liberal institutions creates the phenomenon of mass solipsism we see operating across hypermodern America, a process greatly aided by the proliferation of screens and the predominance of the culture industry. The overwhelming majority of Americans, now being technologically ensconced within their own minds, use their rational faculties almost exclusively in service of some ego-function, whether in advancement or defense of their own particularized sphere of suspicion. So, while on the one hand, hypermodern suspicion culture can be understood as the ascendance and dominance of a single ethno-metanarrative against all others, it must also be understood as a space of precarity and combustibility, barely containing rival ethno-metanarratives (a circumstance unlike any previously observed in human history, not even earlier empires-in-decline).

That the various domains of life each, in their own way, fortify the open society—that the individual man and woman can willingly take the liberal project upon themselves—creates an innumerable amount of feedback loops, generating and regenerating suspicion culture. Paranoiac flows of panic and doubt; schizophrenic fears of scrutiny and insufficiency; nervous twitches and anxious sputters violently bursting back and forth at dizzying speeds; mad solipsistic projections and naive erotogenic broadcasts; one persecutory phantasy after another, until the end of time. All of it true and all of it false (worse still, the question of truth itself subsumed into the necessity of function and the ruthlessness of pragmatism): this is the meaning of hypermodern suspicion and the culture it generates.

Legitimate and Illegitimate Suspicion

Having provided the necessary theoretical framework for understanding conspiracy theories (and the broader generative processes responsible for creating them) we arrive at what probably seems like the most important question to be answered by any investigation into suspicion culture: how do I know what is true and what isn't? Or more specifically, how do I adjudicate a given conspiracy theory? When it comes to knowing what to doubt and what to believe, or when to prod and when to pull back, the only answer is that there can be no simple answer. This is not to sidestep the question entirely, but rather to acknowledge the awful challenge of articulating the folk-account of history. One heuristic that is undoubtedly of paramount use to us in these efforts, it should be said, is whether one's investigation drives one further into productive activity or towards paralysis. We presume, of course, that the point of entering into suspicion discourse is to reveal the agents operating behind some injustice and to discipline them. It follows then that our theorizing ought to lead us to some proper course of action; investigations which do not are therefore deemed illegitimate.

Every investigation inevitably stalls, regresses, moves in circles, or hesitates—this is not the meaning I intend when I speak of paralytic suspicion discourses. However, some discourses lead the inquirer down conceptual labyrinths too murky and ill-defined to ever escape from. Dead ends, trapdoors, distractions, and derailments—these are the crooked treasures which await the vast majority of the conspiratorially minded. Faced with such a challenge, less diligent folk-historians will satisfy themselves with clichés, non sequiturs, and prejudices while the truly exceptional ones remain rational, seeking substantiation of their suspicion, not merely satisfaction.

Do our findings push us deeper into abstraction or towards the concrete? When stepping into a discourse of doubt, we must guard ourselves against the dangers of conceptual unconsciousness. Weaker thinkers will interrogate neither the meaning of nor the role played by the concepts which they employ in their investigations and in their discourses. "The New World Order," "capitalism," "the globalists," "the communists," "White Supremacy," "the Jews," "the Jesuits," "patriarchy," "the Marxists," and so on and so forth. Do we entertain conspiratorial ideation simply for amelioratory and therapeutic reasons? This is not to denigrate the profound need to make sense of our world experience, a need in which all participate. Many folk-accounts serve just this role (and an important role, at that). However, it is when we wish to challenge hegemonic history with our own that the standards and methodologies by which an investigation into suspicion culture is conducted must be elevated. The mission (that of justice) demands a greater rigor and lucidity that, were we to operate without, would thrust us deeper into cynicism and hypermodern utilitarianism (not simply the reduction to a function, but the reduction to a functioning for oneself). If we conduct ourselves within the mode of cynical reason, suspicion discourses quickly descend into naive tribalism and vulgar Manichaeism, which is to say, truth becomes subordinated to the principle of "victory." What does that victory look like, and how will we know when we have achieved it? We cannot say what the answer to either question is, only that such pursuits seek to win retributive justice (punitive/vengeance against our enemy) and not restorative justice (inquisitive/the strengthening of our community). Retributive justice tends toward the re-perpetuation of cycles of animosity, offering neither side an opportunity to bring the rivalry to a close; while it achieves the goal of disciplining a rival, it pays little or no regard to the larger goal of restoring and elevating the community. Restorative justice, on the other hand, seeks the rectification of the community, thereby ending troublesome and intractable periods of strife and discord. This mode includes the disciplinary function, only here it is sublimated to the larger intentions of integrality and holism (the basic tenets of any restorative mode of justice). Restorative justice is a disciplinary inquisition intended to help the community achieve a collective self-overcoming, thereby discarding the habits and modes of being characteristic of (or acquired by) the communal organism which precipitated the conflict in the first place.

This is one half of the answer to the question posed earlier (one which we will reformulate again here, namely the question of "how does one enter into a suspicion discourse?"), and should we falter at this first step then all subsequent inquiries shall inevitably falter. (We inquire so that we may overcome.) The second half of the answer, and a rather anti-Popperian one, is that if we wish to know how to uncover a conspiracy, we must re-learn to privilege teleological thought.

A widely practiced heuristic of postmodern suspicion culture—"follow the money!"—served as a precursor to the very principle we have just established. As a foundational axiom for entering suspicion discourse, however, we must say that it failed. Being overly materialistic (specifically its dogmatic reliance on the primacy of the profit motive) and cynical, ultimately the principle lacked imagination. In its failure to unveil the true agents of destruction and defenestrate them, this heuristic-turned-cliché demonstrated itself to be subordinate to the liberal theory of mind and thus lacking revolutionary potential. The liberal theory of mind says that individuals have a coherent and "free" self-concept which finds itself acted out rationally according to a tangible, logical self-interest. Economism of this kind is really liberalism-in-disguise, mutated and vulgarized over time.

If we presume a conspiracy, then we also presume conspirators. Having presumed conspirators, we must then presume agency and purposiveness. Following this, we must ask: agents of what (or whom)? For what purpose was this action intended? Rational and actionable advances made toward uncovering these ends may be considered legitimate lines of inquiry (or as we have so termed them thus far—legitimate suspicions). Legitimate suspicion validates the folk-account of history, guiding us in uncovering the relevant authorities (or sovereignties) operating at the center of a given social field. Our inquiry may remain rational and productive so long as we always keep in mind the following questions:

1) Which interests—given our understanding of the relevant social field(s)—are implied by a given event (and especially, by its political consequences)?
2) Which sovereignties are implied (or even identified) by these interests?
3) What adjacent sovereignties or networks of sovereignty are implicated by the preceding inquiry?
4) How do these authorities, or networks of authority, operate, and how extensive might their operations become?

We might also consider the following questions, which, depending on the circumstance, might take precedence over those inquiries we only just established:

5) What is the jurisdiction of the relevant authorities and what are their duties?
6) Under what circumstances might they deviate from standard procedures?
7) How would we know if they were acting out of error or incompetence (as opposed to malediction)?

The question of legitimacy and illegitimacy in suspicion culture can be reduced to the question of, "Who is in charge?" and, following that, "What are they in charge of?" We might also frame these inquiries as, "Who here desires?" followed by, "And who has the means to realize their desire?" The telos of postmodern suspicion was economic, and to a lesser degree, ideological (naive tribalism, as in the competition for

CHAPTER I   83

resources and territories), and now, in our present hypermodern era, it is world-historical (grandiose Manichaeism, the assent of the individual or his community over and against rival legacy-makers). We cannot answer the questions posed above without first comprehending the driving motives behind hypermodern suspicion culture.

It is from here that we can adjudicate what is and what isn't grounds for conspiratorial ideation; or, having already undertaken the preliminary phases of investigation, what is a productive forward path of inquiry and what isn't. To illustrate this distinction more succinctly between legitimate and illegitimate suspicions, let us put these concepts to work.

Consider these notions with respect to the attacks which took place on September 11th, 2001, in the United States. Do note, however, that our use of this example does not demand a thorough relitigating of the event, and as such I will not be providing a definitive account of what transpired (or what I believe to have transpired). We are interested in the meaning of the event, though, specifically its meaning with relation to our notion of hypermodern suspicion discourse. An analysis of the 9/11 attack (let us not forget to include in our analysis its antisocial and dysgenic political consequences), presents a clear opportunity to implement some critical concepts we have thus far introduced, such as the Patriot Act as PSoE (the evolving use of the term "domestic terrorist" and its constantly mutating political application; the Department of Homeland Security and the Transportation Security Administration as "forever institutions," long outliving the so-called War on Terror, etc.); the resurgent patriotism on both the right (concrete and primal; both pro-Bush and pro-America), and the left (abstract and yet ambivalent; pro-civil liberty, and obviously, the open society) as nR; the international condemnation of U.S. military conduct in Iraq as AoP (domestically, too, for instance the controversy at Abu Ghraib); the anti-war left as proto-"hot politics" (and the patriotic right as a "cold" political entity, unshakeable until 2015, when Donald Trump declared his presidential ambitions). The turn of the century signaled the shift in American teleology, and so the application of these concepts to this example is more than apropos. They were the inspiration of this very text.

In tandem with the only-then emerging internet, 9/11 coronated this new age of American imperialism and the period we have been calling hypermodernity. The two are inexorably linked: the attacks themselves ushered in a new epoch of doubt and paranoia within the lifeworld, while in the nascent hyperworld of the internet, this new medium proved its efficacy in fomenting suspicion culture by disseminating early conspiracy theories about the 9/11 attacks (e.g., the films *Zeitgeist* and *Loose Change*). Utterly unthinkable, and in fact, probably the most unthinkable event to transpire on North American soil since the assassination of John F. Kennedy, the 9/11 attacks shattered the sense of a unified American consciousness in ways quite like that of the Kennedy murder (e.g., racial unrest, political polarization, domestic violence, and the like all following in its wake). But unlike that event, the American public now had the technological means with which to make up their own minds as to what had transpired on that day. And just what did they do with that power?

It is my view that this hybridized social phenomenon (of internet access and 9/11 theorizing) created the conditions for a synthesizing of the dominant strains of American suspicion culture. Suspicion of Abrahamic religion met with a suspicion of institutional medicine and science, leading to a resurgent interest in holistic remedies, mysticism, psychedelic drugs, and anti-vaccination advocacy. Suspicion of the financial system and its dominant economic paradigms led to self-sufficiency movements, the ascendance of the "sovereign citizen," the Occupy Wall Street movement, and a renewed interest in libertarian notions of sound money (and a little later, cryptocurrency). America's perennial race conflict found its way into virtuality as well, producing hypermodern ethno-metanarratives compromised by solipsism and grandiosity (e.g., the Negro as the secret engine behind American exceptionalism, the second Great War as an impassioned defense of the Jewish underdog, and so on). Amidst all this noise was a pulsing instinct for truth and community (but also for novelty and comfort) that persisted, enduring throughout the years, and eventually culminating in an undifferentiated mass of alienated and latent social power capable of being marshalled on a moment's notice.

(The ever-escalating incomprehensibility of American social life has eroded the boundaries which would have kept the various sub-communities siloed and thus incapable of communication with one another, coded as they once were along conventional—but, as we are now seeing, also highly contingent—demarcations of status and identity.[47] This erosion served to catalyze cognitive dissonance, revealing that the categories and concepts deployed by hegemony increasingly lack their explanatory and predictive powers, and that ultimately the only barrier to participating in suspicion culture or discourse, is dependence on and enmeshment with hegemony itself.)

Different aspects of this unformed mass have seen their ranks mobilized over the years, to varying degrees of success (in terms of political mobilization, we may look to Obama's initial presidential run, as well as both Trump's 2016 and 2020 bids for the presidency as examples of this mass coming to life), never fully satisfied, and yet never put to rest, either. This mass persisted then, as it does now, a necro-schizoidal crowd of alienated hypermodern Americans. As we noted earlier in my work *UCT* (and are restating now, once more), this schizoidal tyranny remains as one of the few pastimes in which Americans of all backgrounds may partake: conspiratorial ideation now has become a social mode, a lingua franca, and a common reference or point of entry to some kind of degraded intimacy or worse, further estrangement (a risk which often cannot be mitigated in advance). Hypermodern suspicion, even in its authentic and legitimate mode, is nonetheless born of this para-solipsism, arising from the atomized individual engaging noncontextually with the social and historical fields, an autism of wholly political origination which continually imperils the truth-function of his or her doubting. All subsequent suspicion discourses (e.g., Occupy Wall Street, "Birtherism," Flat Earth theory, et cetera) cannot be properly understood unless placed in this context of cascading suspicion of and estrangement from the American lifeworld (complemented by a submersion into the virtuality of the internet).

As for the September 11th attacks themselves, the truth movement which emerged in its aftermath, and 9/11's role as case study of legitimate/illegitimate suspicion in our current discussion, we will turn to the words of a well-known and highly respected investigator of the 9/11 story: Christopher Bollyn, a journalist and investigative reporter best known for his comprehensive inquiry into the 9/11 attacks, who echoed

---

[47] Nominally right-wing, anti-capitalist, or anti-free-trade sentiment, for instance.

a similar sentiment to our own as regards the proper method of inquiring into conspiratorial events. According to Bollyn, the true path to uncovering conspiracies may be found through an examination of the social and juridical discontinuities committed during and in the aftermath of an event, for targeting technical inconsistencies only delays the moment of justice. This isn't the same as saying that such inquiries are fruitless: Bollyn's own investigation into the meaning behind 9/11 began with an inquiry into the collapse of the towers themselves. It was only until after his investigation was already well under way that the scope and direction of his inquiry began to change.

In an interview conducted a few short years ago, Bollyn shared his view on how to enter into suspicion discourse:

> How the deception was contained, by the destruction of evidence and the coverup. And that's really important, like Nixon said it's not the crime that gets you, it's the coverup. In the coverup you see all the key players, they have to reveal themselves. It's like the media. The media has been complicit in the 9/11 coverup. It will take some real investigation to find out who put the nanothermite in the World Trade Center. Where the nanothermite was made, etc., finding the fingerprints of the actual criminals involved in the crime, that's harder to do. But the people who are involved in the coverup, and the deception, and in taking the country to war based on the lie, that's very clear. So what we really need is a huge investigation in this country in which all the people who are involved in the 9/11 crime and coverup are arrested and charged and investigated thoroughly to find out who was calling the shots, and to connect the network. That will require no less than a political revolution in this country, because it would stand the entire power structure on its head.[48]

As a matter of inquisitive fact, the how of the collapsing World Trade Center could only have preceded the why. But it must always have given

---

[48] Bollyn, "Man Who Solved 9/11."

way to the why, as well. Many participants in 9/11 suspicion-discourse did not successfully make this transition, however, a development which frustrated the broader 9/11 truth movement (which for a time was an energetic and effective thorn in the side of liberal hegemony, along with the advocacy movement for first responders—the neglected heroes of the event). Efforts by those, like the Architects and Engineers for 9/11 Truth for instance, were crucial in articulating early on the case for a legitimate suspicion of the 9/11 narrative. This laid critical groundwork from which later (legitimate) suspicion discourses would emerge. Technically minded, rational, and genuinely scientific, the rigor of these early efforts gave credence to the folk-historian account of the 9/11 event. The later, less rational entries into this discourse (e.g., lasers, holograms, miniature nuclear bombs, et cetera), however, frustrated the growth of the movement, thereby demonstrating all too clearly what illegitimate suspicion looks like in practice.

The speed (and, frankly, flimsiness of pretense) with which the 9/11 attacks paved the way for another Middle Eastern military expedition was the trigger which shifted many inquirers (like Bollyn) from how to why. Now there was a broader context and a political significance which deepened the meaning of the 9/11 attacks and provided them, for the first time, with a directionality. Curiosities and incongruities abounded from the start, to be certain, though they would only make inductive sense later (once the war machine began roaring to life). The most coherent account of the 9/11 attack belongs to Mr. Bollyn, I believe, for his explanation offers a thorough, detailed, micro-and-macro level analysis of the event (and the guiding intentions behind it). As I have already said, I will not be diverging from our own discussion to examine the particulars of specific conspiracy events, but suffice it to say, Bollyn convincingly implicates the state of Israel in orchestrating the 9/11 attacks using precisely the teleological method we have been advocating throughout. Interested readers may take it upon themselves to examine the case further, but in my estimation Christopher Bollyn's account is a prime example of a competently prosecuted and legitimate suspicion.

Partisan suspicion discourse from the anti-war left resulted in polemical attacks on then-President George W. Bush which were quickly forgotten once the man left office. Not only were the accusations forgotten, but Bush and other members of his cabinet were later rehabilitated by the liberal press in service of their anti-Trump, anti-populist agenda during the late 2010s and early 2020s. Some pointed to members of W's cabinet, such as Dick Cheney, and to their associations with the military-industrial complex, while others pointed to their cozy relations with those in the oil industry, suggesting that the event was profit-driven. This too was quickly forgotten; more importantly, it was never meaningfully substantiated, either. America notoriously failed to secure a majority stake, much less a complete monopoly on Iraqi oil: in the immediate aftermath of the Iraqi invasion, Norway, China, France, and Russia all received major contracts with only ExxonMobil securing an American contract. What often goes unremembered about that time was that American oil companies in fact lobbied to lift sanctions, out of a concern over falling profits.[49] (So yes, profit was a motive—just not in the way liberal consensists assumed.) Partisan accusations such as these demonstrate all too well the principle of illegitimate suspicion, as not only were the accusations inaccurate, but they were also impotent. No meaningful political action was taken against the establishment, and in fact, the supreme overconfidence of left-liberalism during this time led to the moral castration of the American left during the following administration. Left-liberal entries into 9/11 suspicion discourse would eventually crumble, dissipating in the face of liberal egotism and prejudice. Because left-liberal America had been imbibing a steady diet of self-disgust-inducing entertainment and education, its cognitive strength had waned, regressing into solipsism, but also aggrandizement and debasement. We have seen the trajectory of left-liberalism over these past several decades toward a madness of reason, one that teetered for a long while before eventually falling into hateful incoherence. That the thrust of left-liberal 9/11 suspicion aimed indistinctly back at America itself before losing interest in the pursuit altogether, in my view, illustrates the illegitimacy of this suspicion discourse.

    A methodology of legitimate suspicion provides us with directionality and intent, with authorities and networks of authorities, all the while resisting the temptation to slide into clichéd and unjustifiably

---

[49] Postel, "It Wasn't about Oil."

prejudicial thinking. Illegitimate suspicion on the other hand, whether organic or orchestrated, is tantamount to self-sabotage. Folk accounts that trade in illegitimacy return us, in the end, to hegemony. At best, illegitimate folk accounts reward their participants with self-satisfied apathy.

As detailed in this chapter, the invocation of conspiracy (within the context of a commoditized hypermodern suspicion culture, specifically) is a call to mystification. When everything in existence is itself already in doubt, and Man happily makes himself the executor of an Enlightenment will to demystify, the peculiar sight of a well-documented and well-lit conspiracy theory serves to direct attention away from actually-existing-networks-of-influence (themselves eager to maintain their clandestine operation). That merchants encourage us to doubt a given practice, person, tribe, institution, or event should, itself, raise the alarm.

II

CONTRA HAIDT: REBUTTING THE MORAL FOUNDATIONS THEORY

ARE LIBERALS REALLY LESS MORALLY ROBUST THAN CONSERVATIVES?[50]

Mea Culpa

Before detailing my primary critique of Jonathan Haidt's book *The Righteous Mind*, I would like to offer a *mea culpa*. This essay was intended to be a refutation of the book's main finding, but in conceiving how best to convey my disagreement I have found it more necessary to qualify Haidt's thesis rather than outright deny it. In the near decade that has passed since first reading Dr. Haidt's book, my feeling that his "3v6" model of political morality was flawed has never waned; I simply struggled to articulate why I thought it was wrong. I had to change how I thought about his argument (and further my own political education) before I could begin to work out my own counterargument.

It is not on psychological—nor even, strictly speaking, scientific—grounds upon which I feel Dr. Haidt's theory fails, but rather the deeper commitments, unconscious or otherwise, which frame the scope and schema of his investigation. Hyperattention to the content of his theory (as opposed to its form, and perhaps, even origin) led to a theoretical stalemate from which, for a long time, I was unable to recover. Only by

---

[50] Originally published in November 2023 in *The Unz Review*.

overcoming this initial hurdle was I finally able to reach the conclusion I will be presenting here.

Haidt offers us a story of political morality, that liberals are less morally integrated than conservatives, but does not attempt a further account of this finding. Therein lies the problem: we assume, because of Haidt's formulation, that liberals are somehow morally defective. The heavily evolutionist framing utilized throughout the work primes the reader to essentialize Haidt's finding: liberals are moral inferiors. What I believe amounts to pseudo-conservative apologia, the legacy of which has essentially proven to be "libs are bad," nonetheless offers valuable insight and did create a liberal-skeptic space to discuss political psychology (without which my own theoretical writing would not be possible). Unfortunately for Dr. Haidt, his story just doesn't hold up.

With regards to political psychology, it is the former which I will be addressing throughout my critique, and not the latter. I will also be challenging the philosophical, or shall we say paradigmatic, grounding from which Dr. Haidt's inquiry stems. The conservative intuition ("something is wrong with liberals"), validated by Haidt's Moral Foundations Theory, correctly identifies a social problem which sadly has been obfuscated by Haidt's ideological framing (ideological in the sense of obscuring power relations). For readers unfamiliar with Haidt's work, I will provide as thorough (and hopefully brief) a primer as I can before moving swiftly into my counterargument. While I am similarly committed to Dr. Haidt's goal, that being the improvement of America's political fortunes, I do not share his desire to fortify partisan Democrat political strategy.

Dr. Haidt's work sought to elevate liberal political rhetoric while validating conservative political sensibilities, a worthwhile goal perhaps, but not one that I wish to pursue here. Nonetheless, we are all aided by elevating our understanding of the political circumstances at hand and their downstream psychological consequences (and by offering a few significant qualifications of Dr. Haidt's theory will achieve, I hope, just that).

A Righteous Find

The driving insight which motivated Jonathan Haidt to publish *The Righteous Mind*, its central conclusion, and the *raison d'être* for Dr. Haidt's political activity is the notion that left-liberals (progressives) are less morally robust than right-liberals (conservatives). As for what exactly that means, for the moment it is enough to simply say that psychologically speaking, progressive moral reasoning operates on fewer axioms (in Haidt's terms, "foundations") than those of conservatives.

Challenging this idea—or, at least, significantly qualifying it—will be the goal of this essay, though before we do, a few things must be said in praise of Haidt's work. It may be that we are dealing with a case of "directionally correct, factually incorrect" more than outright falsehood, for Haidt's error surreptitiously ushered in America's cultural rightward turn. This alone is a significant accomplishment, as it represents a major concession on behalf of the Liberal establishment towards those populations it had spent so much time and effort denigrating. *The Righteous Mind* was an important book for me personally, as it set me on the path of taking my psychological training in a more political and philosophical direction. No doubt it had the same effect on countless others. Right or wrong, Haidt proved to be the canary in the coal mine for the coming conservative intellectual revolution.

Published in March of 2012 some eight months ahead of then President Barack Obama's successful re-election bid, Haidt's book gave a scientific voice to the growing dissatisfaction with progressive liberalism's cultural hegemony. Dr. Haidt walked a very fine line by affirming dangerous scientific and philosophic heresies (e.g., group selection, "irrationalism," etc.) while upholding enough doctrinal liberal social theorizing (e.g., secular humanism, mass democracy) to get his ideas through the gate. Bemoaning conservative underrepresentation in the academy, Haidt followed up his publication by co-founding the Heterodox Academy, a non-profit advocacy group dedicated to restoring intellectual and political diversity on college campuses. Just a few short years later we would get Brexit, Trump, the Intellectual Dark Web, Joe Rogan as the voice of the common man (set against the dominance of liberal culture), and the emergence of a new center-right economy whose sole unifying principle was an ever-intensifying rejection of the liberal arrogance which had obnoxiously sauntered its way into American culture beginning in 2009. Haidt didn't start the fire, but the Moral Foundations Theory was his attempt to fight it.

The Righteous Mind served not only as a genuine advancement of social theory (specifically within the discipline of moral psychology), but as an autobiographical documentation of its author's own rightward drift. Haidt began the book with an examination of his exuberant youthful liberal priors only to note in the final chapters his shocking discovery that it is in fact conservatism which best provides those things he valued so dearly as a devout liberal. Conservatism, Haidt tells us, is responsible for providing the greatest happiness for the most, while liberalism overreaches, changing too many things too quickly, thereby inadvertently lowering the stock of "moral capital." Moral capital, in Jonathan Haidt's words, refers to,

> the degree to which a community possesses interlocking sets of values, virtues, norms, practices, identities, institutions, and technologies that mesh well within evolved psychological mechanisms and thereby enable the community to suppress or regulate selfishness and make cooperation possible.[51]

Progressive liberalism, for all the good it may have brought us, Haidt argued, is now tearing us apart from the inside. Haidt's political career, which had begun all the way back in 2004 during the time of John Kerry's abysmal presidential bid, had brought him over a decade later to the following fact: conservatism operates, just as liberalism does, within the paradigm of Enlightenment thinking, and, in fact, conservatism is the true ideological progenitor of the West's ever self-refining moral tradition. Haidt's wish to expand the liberal "moral matrix," thus helping the Democrat party better reach the American people, now required him to convince his partisan fellows to start seeing conservatives more humanely. Though it does not appear that the DNC has quite received Haidt's good-faith message (despite the many "post-left"

---

[51] Haidt, *Righteous Mind*, 341.

movements which have arisen in recent years), his psychological research has nonetheless contributed to a growing conservative (or rightist) movement—a contribution which we should all feel indebted to.

The Foundation of Haidt's Moral Foundations Theory

Let's take a moment to briefly summarize the main points of Jonathan Haidt's book. Before sharing the findings of his research into our moral foundations, Dr. Haidt lays out a handful of axioms (taken from other disciplines: anthropology, philosophy, and sociology) which are intended to contextualize his research, providing a framework with which to make sense of his own original discoveries. In the introductory chapter Dr. Haidt declares:

> If you think that moral reasoning is something we do to figure out the truth, you'll be constantly frustrated by how foolish, biased, and illogical people become when they disagree with you. But if you think about moral reasoning, as a skill we humans evolved to further our social agendas—to justify our own actions and defend the teams we belong to—then things will make a lot more sense.[52]

As we will soon see, morality is (in Haidt's account) a feature of human life which serves multiple masters.

Dr. Haidt wants to answer the following question: is morality the byproduct of our intrinsic biological condition, or does it emerge due to our cognitive efforts? He begins his answer with the following history lesson: prior to 1987, questions of moral cognition were relegated to the discipline of developmental psychology, to which most researchers interested in the subject fell into either one of two camps: nativism (moral knowledge is pre-given) and empiricism (the theory of a cognitive blank slate). But then a tidal wave of rationalism emerged to break the stalemate, demonstrating rather convincingly that moral cognition

---

[52] Ibid., 20.

is a progressive faculty which develops in tandem with our physical maturation, resulting in a cognition that is self-constructed. Jean Piaget, the progenitor of this style of thinking, developed a series of widely reproduced empirical measures which opened an entirely new space for empirical psychology, what Haidt terms "psychological rationalism." This initial groundwork was later completed—and in effect, consecrated—by Lawrence Kohlberg, a moral psychologist and Piaget's most prominent ideological successor.

Dr. Kohlberg further developed Piaget's theory by building it into a complete moral-psychological paradigm, one that happened to be fully consistent with the secular liberalism of his time. As a result of his experimentation, Kohlberg postulated a moral-cognitive system which validated Piaget's findings but then went a step further: claiming a progressive development of the individual's moral reasoning abilities, Dr. Kohlberg declared its culmination in what he termed "post-conventional" (PC, henceforth) moral reasoning. At this stage, individuals can trade in Kantian categorical imperatives or Kierkegaardian suspensions of the ethical in pursuit of establishing their own internally consistent and individualistic moral weltanschauung.

Kohlberg, as was true of Piaget, felt that formal authority stifled the individual's moral development, a prejudice which came to define his theory of moral reasoning. Of this Haidt says, "[B]ut by using a framework that predefined morality as justice, while denigrating authority, hierarchy and tradition, it was inevitable that the research would support world views that were secular, questioning, and egalitarian."[53]

Elliot Turiel, Kohlberg's protégé, further narrowed the Western scientific conception of morality thanks to his own research. According to Turiel, children recognize that rules which prevent harm ("moral rules") are categorically different from "conventional rules" (rules about clothing, food, etc.) which are arbitrary and expendable. Important to note is that Turiel defined rules as being related to "justice, rights, and welfare pertaining to how people ought to relate to each other."[54] Children seem to grasp early on that rules which prevent harm are "special, important, unalterable, and universal." Dr. Turiel claims this realization is

---

[53] Ibid., 10.
[54] Ibid., 11.

the foundation of all moral development: children construct their moral understanding on the basis that harm is wrong. Specific rules may vary across cultures, but in all the cultures Turiel examined, children still made a distinction between moral rules and conventional rules. "Turiel's account of moral development differed in many ways from Kohlberg's, but the political implications were similar: morality is about treating individuals well. It's about harm and fairness; hierarchy and authority are generally bad things."[55]

This picture of morality as portrayed by twentieth-century social scientists is indeed a queer one, fixed almost entirely on abstract reasoning. Recognizing this, Haidt invoked the acronym "WEIRD" (Western, Educated, Industrialized, Rich, Democratic) to describe our moral sensibilities (largely limited to the "ethic of autonomy"), eventually placing them in stark contrast to those outside of the West's purview (which are broader, including the "ethics of community and divinity"). Dissatisfied with where his own psychological training had brought him, Dr. Haidt turned to other scientific disciplines for aid in excavating the origins of human morality.

University of Chicago anthropologist Richard Shweder's work highlighted this very dichotomy. Shweder argued that different societies all come to their own conclusions about how to order society, and how to balance the needs of the individual against those of the group. Dr. Shweder's work showed that outside of the West, moral dilemmas are resolved by more than just appeals to fairness and harm reduction (a finding that Dr. Haidt was able to replicate as a graduate student), and that there were in fact a wide range of "moral intuitions" which guide our thoughts and judgements. Haidt's own experimentation (intended to settle the dispute between Turiel and Shweder, that is, between WEIRD victimology and sociocentric views of morality), demonstrated that Westerners often struggled to articulate why a given scenario was morally impermissible absent a clear victimological framework, though they were clearly in the grips of a moral judgement. Findings such as these demonstrate that morality, Dr. Haidt tells us, is a post hoc justification of our immediate (and visceral) emotional

---

[55] Ibid., 12.

experience. They also tell us that intuition is an important feature of human cognition.

Drawing from Sir Edward Evan Evans-Pritchard's research on the Azande tribe of Sudan, Haidt came to a functionalist/evolutionary understanding of morality and religion. According to Pritchard's work, the Azande believed that witches were just as likely to be men as they were women, thus the fear of being called a witch made the Azande careful not to anger or induce envy in their neighbors. "That was my first hint that groups create supernatural beings, not to explain the universe, but to order their societies," Haidt says.[56] Renato and Michelle Rosado's seminal work on the Ilongot tribe of the Philippines provided Dr. Haidt with another crucial insight. The young men of the Ilongot tribe gained honor by beheading their rivals. Some of these beheadings resulted from revenge killings, but many of these murders were committed against strangers who were not involved in any kind of feud with the killer. It has been suggested that these killings are intended to channel the resentments and frictions of young men within the group into the formation (and subsequent strengthening) of hunting parties. "This was my first hint that morality often involves tension within the group, linked to competition between different groups."[57]

Haidt provides us with a clear picture of human nature: we are tribal, hive creatures, adapted to our surroundings by generation after generation of group selection. Following from this, he argues that our moral reasoning largely works to fortify our tribe. Important to note, however, is that our moral reasoning is often a servant of moral intuitions. As such, these moral intuitions (or emotions) are critical to human cognition and therefore, must necessarily be understood before throwing oneself into social engineering as a means for resolving man's political woes. Perhaps, in misunderstanding our nature as moral animals, we misunderstand the nature of the problems we face, Haidt suggests. "Morality binds and blinds," he says. Upon this foundation, Dr. Haidt erected his own theory of moral reasoning, positing six basic moral intuitions: care/harm, fairness/cheating, liberty/oppression, loyalty/betrayal, authority/subversion, and sanctity/degradation. Secular Western

---

[56] Ibid., 13.
[57] Ibid., 14.

moralities—which is to say, progressive liberal morality—broadly attempts to stimulate only a few of these foundations (care/harm, fairness/cheating, liberty/oppression), a psychological and political reality which Dr. Haidt has since devoted himself to changing. "We're born to be righteous, but we have to learn what exactly people like us should be righteous about."

Three to Six: Deficiency or (Over)Refinement?

A liberal's moral palate, Haidt argues, largely draws upon the following three foundations: care/harm, fairness/cheating, and liberty/oppression, while that of the average conservative's is informed by all six, including loyalty/betrayal, authority/subversion, and sanctity/degradation. These foundations, or intuitions, arose out of an originary social scene which we have since "evolved" out of—though we are still triggered by contemporary equivalents of those same challenges (now provoking us through increasingly surrogate and abstract formulations). Citing the work of neuroscientist Gary Marcus, Dr. Haidt qualifies his evolutionist framework: our intuitions are *pre*wired and not *hard*wired; biology is the first draft, while our lived experience serves as the chief editor of human psychology. Over the course of a lifetime, we construct our own moral worldview.

Haidt observes a further challenge: depending on one's political orientation, our intuitions are held with contrasting semantic values. For instance, "fairness" implies equality to liberals but proportionality to conservatives. While both sides value fairness to one degree or another, they tend to evaluate the meaning of the word differently. Said simply, not only do liberals and conservatives generally formulate their moral evaluations based on different intuitions, but in those instances where their intuitions overlap, they often intend different meanings. "Sanctity" is another such intuition wherein liberals and conservatives differ radically, though not for semantic reasons but ideological ones. Conservative applications of the "sanctity" intuition reflect their commitment to traditional institutions and norms, whereas it manifests among liberals according to their secular humanist worldview (decrying sanctity when it comes to conventional sexual mores and biomedical issues, but valuing it, for instance, when it comes to matters of environmentalism and spirituality). Not only do we evaluate moral challenges based on differing intuitions, but we also mean different things when we say we hold a certain moral intuition. Furthermore, even when we apply the same intuitions we tend to apply them differently (for instance, applying the same intuition but to entirely different—and in many cases competing—domains of life).

Allegiance to one intuition may impair allegiance(s) to others. Haidt says that the liberal's "loyalty" foundation is impaired both by their commitments to universalism, as well as to the "care" foundation, making them less likely, to use an example Haidt himself provides, to support American foreign policy initiatives. Liberal equalitarianism, derived as we have noted from their commitment to "fairness," compromises their ability to appeal to the "authority" intuition as they are reflexively anti-authoritarian (after all, an end to authority and hierarchy also means an end to oppression, and therefore, the emergence of a truly "fair" society). At least this is the picture as presented by Dr. Haidt. It would seem then that ideological anti-hierarchism results in moral anarchy, such that the liberal individual's moral schema undermines its own function.

But why? How did liberal moral reasoning become so tortured? And what is it about conservatism that preserves a holistic moral palate? Furthermore, are we certain that what has been measured is, in fact, a fundamentally psychological phenomenon? (More on that in a moment). Haidt acknowledges that progressive liberalism has an intrinsically corrosive effect on the social order before begrudgingly affirming the wisdom of classical liberalism (conservatism), however his prescription does not appear strong enough. We should affirm and own our essential tribe-centered self-righteousness and learn to get along, Haidt suggests (the Gene Roddenberry recommendation, in effect). We can transcend our inner chud-simpleton (or conversely, overcome the inner soy-libtard) and soar to ever greater heights of intergalactic pluralism! But can we? Not if we operate under the same premises as Dr. Haidt.

If the events of the 2016 presidential election have taught us anything, it is that we cannot all get along. Moreover, it taught us that "we" are not a "we" at all, and that there is no grand "Us"; rather, we are truly composed of pockets of existential cohesion which find themselves inexorably in conflict with one another. So, the first problem which strikes us is the erroneous presumption of homogeneity. If liberals and conservatives are not part of this "grand Us," then who are they and from where do they originate? The problem of "liberal deficiency" derives, as we will see, from this mistaken belief in a common unity.

To address both items simultaneously (i.e., the moral deficiency of liberals, and the presumptive psychological homogeneity of Americans), let us instead presume the following: expressions of liberal and conservative moral intuition are not mere psychological phenomena reducible to the inherited and acquired conditions of the individual person's existence, but instead are the result of specific modes of political organization (both of which are historically contingent in their founding and are presently in conflict with one another). Haidt repeatedly evokes Darwinian theory throughout his work, suggesting even that we might underestimate the speed at which evolution occurs, but I do not believe that the difference between liberals and conservatives at present is an essentially genetic one, but rather a political and technological one (though it should be said that this bifurcation may, in the end, become inexorably genetic if it hasn't already).

Although Haidt made the transition from a liberal worldview to one that is more conservative, his location of the two as operating, essentially, within the Enlightenment paradigm is ultimately fatal to his analysis. Remaining as committed to his secular humanism now as in his youth, Haidt pins both the origins of political dysfunction—and their solution—inappropriately on the individual person. As I will soon demonstrate, our challenges are political-civilizational and not private-psychological. And while Haidt never explicitly states as much, his evolutionist framing when combined with his goal of helping liberals to rhetorically close the gap on what he calls "the conservative advantage" suggests that the liberal person's moral cognitive ability is in some fundamental way, deficient.

While it is certainly not Dr. Haidt's fault that popular perception has caught up with decades of conservative talk radio rhetoric (consider Michael Savage's famous catchphrase: "Liberalism is a mental disorder!"), thanks to the sheer volume of studies released in the years following his book's publication—all of which paint an unflattering picture of liberal mental health (e.g., higher rates of psychoticism and neuroticism, greater instances of depression, greater likelihood to seek psychotherapeutic and pharmacological interventions, et cetera)—the received wisdom of this book has been "libs bad." The imploding credibility of formerly well-regarded "liberal" institutions has also contributed greatly to the notion of a dysfunctional liberalism. Ultimately, Haidt's image of the "morally deficient liberal" was simply one more brick in the conservative rhetorical wall. Regardless of how this misconception first arose, it requires correcting. It follows from the argument which I will now present that this peculiarity of liberal moral cognition is not a failure of individual character or even partisan political strategery, but the logical outcome of a system of political organization staked on differing foundational axioms than the one which preceded it.

The core confusion which muddles Dr. Haidt's finding may be attributed to what Paul Gottfried has termed "the semantic problem of liberalism." Published in the final year of the preceding millennium, Gottfried's work *After Liberalism* argued that, conceptually speaking, liberalism as a coherent tradition struggles with two problems: 1) that it has been denied a specific meaning; and 2) that is has taken on a polemical sense which overshadows any previously understood positive denotation.

Many of the political developments deemed unfavorable to today's American right have been misattributed to liberalism writ large, when it is in fact more accurate (and conceptually edifying) to regard them as products of a distinct, discrete, political epoch. Proper identification of the liberal tradition is not possible so long as, domestically, there are active rival political organisms each claiming a singular legitimacy. Our failure to make note of such finer details, one which Dr. Haidt has contributed to, remains the leading obstacle to a holistic understanding of the contemporary political scene.

Political and technological crises in the nineteenth and especially twentieth century prompted much debate within liberal circles about the future of their Enlightenment ideology. The emergence of a mass society and all its attendant consequences weighed heavily on the bourgeois liberal elite of old, giving way ultimately to the socialism of mass democracy. The move from bourgeois liberal capitalism to technocratic social democracy (necessitated by the dual challenges of mass and scale, to borrow a phrase from Sam Francis) threatened the integrity of a coherent liberal self-concept, as the liberal societies in which these transformations were occurring suddenly had to contend with a previously unimaginable plurality of desires and demands. Quoting from his book *Leviathan and its Enemies*, Sam Francis is an adroit observer of this phenomenon:

> At the end of the 19th century, liberalism underwent a dramatic reformulation carried out in England by TH Green, JA Hobson, Leonard Hobhouse, and various socialist thinkers in the United States by the writers and activists associated with the progressive movement. The new liberalism of the late 19th century was in many respects a direct response to the impact of the revolution of mass and scale on the political, economic, and social life of the industrialized societies, and represented an effort to discipline and reform the breakdowns that the revolution caused. The reformulation of liberalism consisted primarily in a retreat from or abandonment of the individualism that characterized bourgeois liberal ideology and a new emphasis on the social and collective nature and duties of human beings.
>
> Since society and its political organ, the state, are in this view prior to the individual, this reformulated version of liberal thought rejected the classical liberal view that restrictions on the activities and functions of the state liberated and assisted the individual.[58]

The transition was not strictly a matter of ideology; rather, it represented a hyper-stratification of society such that an entirely new elite sphere sprang up, physically displacing those who previously held favor. Quoting again from the same text by Sam Francis,

> There is a combined shift: through changes in the technique of production, the functions of management become more distinctive, more complex, more specialized, and more crucial to the

---

[58] Francis, *Leviathan and Its Enemies*, 201.

whole process of production, thus serving to set off those who perform these functions as a separate group, or class in society; and at the same time, those who formally carried out what functions there were of management, the bourgeoisie themselves withdraw from management, so that the difference in function becomes also a difference in the individuals who carry out the function.[59]

These "processes of production" are quite numerous and include, for instance, the process of producing knowledge, art, poetry, and entertainment just as much as they mean flat screen TVs, ballistic missiles, and computer chips. In this way, the managerial revolution (as James Burnham termed it) affected large sectors of the population simultaneously, across the various disciplines and domains of social life. Such a transition could only be considered evolutionary in a metaphorical sense (more will be said on this later).

Ideological (or classical) liberalism should then be understood, borrowing Mosca's language, as the political formula of a historically contingent entrepreneurial class and the institutions and networks of influence which it once commanded (and to varying degrees and extents, still does). This is the source and origin of our contemporary conservative moral intuitions. Understanding political conservatism as a defeated or, less hyperbolically, usurped mode of political organization should give us insight into conservatism's present-day status as the battered and beleaguered housewife of liberal progressivism (which we ought to understand as being synonymous with socialism and the mass democratic society).[60]

---

[59] Ibid., 112.

[60] I will leave it to historians and other scholars to demonstrate otherwise, but it appears to me that socialism is a necessary byproduct of industrialization, of the technological society (and of managerialism), and therefore attempted to answer the challenges posed by mass and scale. Given the absolute failure of its stated goal (socialism as "the public ownership of the means of production"), I can only conclude that what socialism really is, is simply another political formula whose primary function is to validate the desire for certain ascendant groups to seize power. Assuming this to be true, I propose a different, more accurate definition: in the same way that capitalism is a form of oligarchical control by those with a monopoly on the accumulation and allocation of capital (i.e.,

Consider Haidt's characterization of contemporary conservative morality in view of the following excerpted passage, taken again from Sam Francis. Do the values of bourgeois entrepreneurial liberals not harmonize with the conservative psychology presented in Haidt's work? Quoting Peter Berger, Francis shares the following:

> [T]he bourgeois believed in the virtue of work, as against the aristocratic idealization of (genteel) leisure . . . in Protestant countries it tended toward a style of inconspicuous consumption. . . . The bourgeois emphasized personal responsibility ("conscience," especially in its Protestant form) . . . [B]ourgeois culture was individuating at the core of its moral worldview. Also, the bourgeoisie went in for "clean living" both in the literal and the derived moral sense. This theme (epitomized in the maxim that "cleanliness is next to godliness") carried into the minutia of daily conduct—the manners of dress and speech habits of personal hygiene, the appearance of the home.[61]

This competition between "liberal" values (care, fairness, liberty) against "conservative" values (loyalty, authority, sanctity) ought to be understood as resulting from a particular group of elites arising organically and in opposition to the hegemonic order of their time. Entrepreneurial bourgeois capitalism overthrew the old aristocracy just as therapeutic social progressivism has now overthrown the preceding "conservative" political order. While vestigial "psychological conservatism" exists in many places as something cultivated (in the form of mass propaganda) while in others as something of a holdout (a pocket of existential cohesion, as invoked earlier), it should primarily be

---

money power), socialism is a form of oligarchical control by those with a monopoly on the accumulation and allocation of human bodies and those social forces which organize them (i.e., people power). Emerging as a strain of liberal thought during a time when progressivism was on the rise and the managerial apparatus was slowly coming together, socialism required a class of technical experts who were capable of administering over the population (e.g., organizing them, propagandizing them, disciplining them, etc). Socialism, therefore, is the political formula which made managerial mass democracy operative.

[61] Ibid., 31.

understood as the downstream consequence of a previous elite's self-justifying political formulation.

Mass democratic society, or socialism if you prefer, being founded on secular rationalism and a commitment to the scientific view of the world should be understood as the progenitor of progressive liberalism and its overemphasis on the "care," "liberty," and "fairness" intuitions. Care, liberty, and fairness, in this sense, are not strictly psychological phenomena but are ideological ones applied in service of the now hegemonic managerial state. Therefore, it is an institutional-structural phenomenon primarily, and not an individual-psychological one singularly. "Progressive liberal morality" is merely the psychological consequence of the political formula we call "socialism."

I will invoke Sam Francis once more, here, as his depiction of the transition into managerial democracy highlights the historical contingencies responsible for provoking this overemphasis on Haidt's care, liberty, and fairness intuitions. Quoting Daniel Bell, he says:

> The real social revolution in modern society came in the 1920s when the rise of mass production and high consumption began to transform the life of the middle class itself. In effect the Protestant ethic as a social reality, and a lifestyle for the middle class; was replaced by materialistic hedonism in the Puritan temper by a psychological eudaemonism ... [T]he claim of the American economic system was that it had introduced abundance, and the nature of abundance is to encourage prodigality rather than prudence. A higher standard of living, not work as an end in itself, then becomes the engine of change. The glorification of plenty, rather than the bending to niggardly nature becomes the justification of the system.[62]

A transformative social reality (access to abundant material resources) led to a transformative psychological one (ravenous pursuit of material and egoic desires), of which modern day progressives are merely the beneficiaries. Occurring against the backdrop of an intensely self-

---

[62] Ibid., 34.

scrutinizing liberal discourse, this thumotic surge would be wedded to the equalitarian interpretation of liberal philosophy which, as we can all plainly see, eventually won out. The resulting metaphysical avarice is yet another bit of progressive inheritance. As such, the supposed moral "deficiency" of today's progressive elites is no deficiency at all, but rather, a mode of self-differentiation. More significantly, it is a means by which they may wage war against—and more fully extirpate—the remnants of the old bourgeois order. Importantly, Francis highlights the natural antagonism between managerial democracy and bourgeois liberalism:

> The managerial elite of the mass corporations thus has a group interest in destroying the individualism and diversity of the bourgeois order through its collective discipline and homogenizing processes. It also subverts the bourgeois work ethic and its derivative values through its promotion of mass hedonism and consumption.[63]

Our present-day self-concept as a "liberal democracy" is merely another political formula by which the elites may tether what remains of the preceding regime to that which exists today. Neoliberalism, then, may be seen as a synthesis of the bourgeois entrepreneurial order with the contemporary therapeutic-managerial state.

Having explained this supposed psychological difference between modern conservatives and liberals from the point of view of political economy, there yet remains an unaccounted-for element of the mystery. As such, folding a sociobiological view into this managerial revision of the Moral Foundations Theory is prudent, particularly if one seeks to explain the dramatic leftward turn that the United States took following the postwar period (and, especially, in the years since "the Great Awokening," beginning roughly around the time of the first Obama presidency). Without incorporating this view, we certainly could not understand the extreme partisan morality displayed by progressives over the last two decades.

---

[63] Ibid., 35.

As Sam Francis has argued, the reach of the managerial revolution has been exponential: technocratically escalating along the dimensions of mass and scale further into populations that were previously not as well represented among prior generations of elites, the twentieth century became what has been termed descriptively (and sometimes pejoratively) "the Jewish century." And while this generation of managerial elites presently looks to be at its nadir, it nonetheless remains well entrenched and capable of significant action. The new political formula, generated specifically for the purposes of postwar governance, represented best among such figures as Leo Strauss, Karl Popper, and Richard Hofstadter (differing in methodologies but always converging in aims) as well as institutions like the ADL (though its origins technically prefigure this new formulation) presented a refortified version of liberalism, Americanism, and the Western canon more broadly, which dogmatically stressed empathetic and equalitarian approaches to political and social problems.

America's descent into cruel, shrill, racial distortion must be understood as the hideous love child of Gentile equalitarianism and Jewish Machiavellianism. In the years following the Second World War, our nation's superego bent suspiciously in the direction of partisan self-preservation, funneling all moral discourse through an imperceptible filter: Jewish interest. Racial supremacy was re-institutionalized through the veiled language of universal dignity and human rights. Taking again from his book *After Liberalism*, Paul Gottfried is again prescient:

> Behind this rhetoric, however, it is possible to discern other far-reaching projects, some of which this book has outlined. All of them have pertained to a specific form of rule and combined a public charge with generally ill-defined but expanding control. The administrative state, as it advances into its therapeutic phase, has refused to recognize its coercive reach or whatever advantages accrued to it from those tasks it has gladly assumed. By concealing its operation in the language of caring, it has blinded us to the truths enunciated by Cicero, Hobbes, Weber, Schmitt, and other past political analysts. Potestas [power, legal authority], as Cicero explained, is given to increase one's dignity; it

allows one to punish wrongdoers and to exercise magisterial authority, while becoming a means for preserving and securing a greater sufficiency of its own resources.[64]

Far from being some harebrained antisemitic conspiracy, the last eighty or so years have born witness to an unprecedented flourishing of Jewish political privilege inside the United States (see both Samuel G. Freedman's *Jew vs. Jew: The Struggle for the Soul of American Jewry* and J.J. Goldberg's *Jewish Power: Inside the American Jewish Establishment*), and with this flourishing (as Gottfried has pointed out) an accrual of advantages. But these "accrued advantages" ultimately are to the detriment of all. Managerial responses to the dual challenges of mass and scale have struggled (and failed) to account for the endless influx of racially alien populations while still maintaining a privileged standing for America's Jewish citizenry. The untenability of such a prospect has quickly become apparent to all, spurring dramatic change not only in the U.S., but around the world. We are seeing very clearly, thanks to the recent conflict in Gaza, just how badly the managerial regime has degraded and even, how it may fall. We are also seeing the moral and cognitive bankruptcy of its fundamentally downstream psychological consequences, which will surely recede into marginality once the forthcoming political paradigm fully instantiates itself.

We cannot understand the self-loathing psychology of today's self-avowed liberal man and woman without first apperceiving the preeminence of political Judaism throughout America's most influential institutions. One half technological (the erection of the managerial state) while on the other half sociobiological (the unceasing surge of Jewish political control), so-called "liberal moral psychology" is in fact the by-product of highly contingent circumstances and is not, as Dr. Haidt has argued, resulted exclusively from individual self-construction.

So it is not the case that we are observing a deficit, so much as we are observing an extreme process of moral refinement. If we are to be charitable and accept Haidt's hypothesis, it is necessary to modify it. The left-liberal's diminished moral palette is a consequence of the

---

[64] Gottfried, *After Liberalism*, 141.

compounding political pressures imposed upon America due to its ever-expanding and diversifying population, in conjunction with the erosion of previously normative moral and social boundaries caused by our ever-advancing program of technological progress. By virtue of occupying densely populated urban centers and taking up employment in advanced technical fields, left-liberal psychology appears less able to exploit all six of Haidt's moral foundations. This is not, however, a primarily psychological phenomenon but an expression of the bifurcation of American political economy (i.e., entrepreneurialism versus managerialism). Left-liberal morality is an expression of institutional conformity (which is true, as well, for right-liberals) before it can be declared a matter of evolutionary development or individual self-construction.

If we accept Haidt's claim, then we must understand this difference in psychology as resulting from a political and technological process of overrefinement (as in, the whittling away of a once robust moral faculty). To be less charitable to Dr. Haidt, there is good reason for rejecting his claim that left-liberals are less morally adroit than right-liberals simply by observing their moral messaging over the last half-decade or so (e.g., the Black Woman as a sacred object of worship (sanctity); the physician and the scientist as unimpeachable arbiters of truth (authority); skeptics of anti-Putinism as disloyal traitors to America (loyalty); etc.). Even more damaging to Haidt's hypothesis, however, is the fact that the full range of left-liberal moral justification was visible to us during the 00's and 10's—the years during which Haidt was busy collecting data for his hypothesis (e.g., advocacy for the working class (loyalty); opposition to Big Pharma (sanctity); etc.). But Haidt himself observes that left-liberals apply their moral foundations differently from right-liberals—an observation which, while posing a major problem for his theory has nevertheless managed to go unnoticed in the years since his book was published. Haidt wishes to bridge a gap that is not merely psychological, or even ideological, but is in fact sociopolitical and economical (which is to say, structural). However one wishes to view Haidt's hypothesis, we may only make concrete sense from it by stepping outside of the atomic, individualistic, psychology which produced it in the first place.

Conclusion

Trump's 2016 campaign was, by most accounts, an unforeseeable event. At the very least we must admit that its consequences were rather shocking indeed. What has been interesting to see was the eruption of liberal chauvinism that emerged in response to Donald Trump. An immune response was provoked, resulting in an uninterrupted wave of cultural and political lib-imperialism even more daring and egotistical than what America witnessed during the Obama years (the previous high-water mark of progressive cultural tyranny—one many, including myself, thought impossible to surpass).

The picture of liberal moral reasoning as seen in the post-Trump era looks markedly different from the one presented by Jonathan Haidt, which to my view only reinforces the necessity for a political critique of his political psychology. A victim of his own ideological commitments, and perhaps as well to a certain self-forgetting of identity, Haidt's Moral Foundations theory provides us with an incomplete (though nonetheless compelling) account of man's moral psychology. Psychologically speaking, Haidt's social intuitionist model—the basis for his MFT—is sound. However, it is the predilection for liberal pluralism and an over-reliance on evolutionary thinking which ultimately weighs down his otherwise novel and insightful psychological findings. For all his criticisms, Haidt is nevertheless a victim of Western WEIRD morality, too. Despite his shortcomings, it is as I said in the beginning: Haidt's publication served as a mighty warning shot. Now, a full decade after its release (and bearing recent events in mind), it is obvious that *The Righteous Mind* precipitated a revolution of thought which reshaped Conservative politics in America (and, indeed, around the world). Which brings me to the last remaining thread yet unpulled: the century-long process of social engineering, as executed by the managerial elites, has undoubtedly had a destabilizing effect on the American gene pool. We are already several generations into a process of familial and social planning which selects against illiberalism writ large. While the origins of this revolution were not genetic in a strong sense, American survival will be predicated on genetic and cultural changes in the population which select for strength, courageousness, and self-sufficiency. The civil war will, in the end, be a genetic one.

III

CONFORMITY AND POLITICAL ECONOMY

ANSWERING THE QUESTION: HOW DID IT GET THIS BAD?

Corrosion of Conformity

In the 1990s and 2000s (the decades of my youth), to call someone a "conformist" was about the most cutting insult you could possibly offer. Rather ironic, seeing as the development of this slight could only be achieved through the very act of conforming. Without fail, targets of this smug and self-satisfied brand of mockery fit a certain stereotype, including but not limited to: 1) adherence to some religious order (typically Christianity); 2) support for the military; 3) support for the State (especially, if not exclusively, rightist regimes); and 4) approval of parochialism (or formality) of any kind.

Anti-conformists often found themselves (and each other) by rallying around the emerging forms within popular culture (e.g., stand-up comedy, punk rock, pop science), and to a person, imagined themselves as free-thinking and independently minded (blithely ignorant of, it would appear, the medium responsible for transmitting these extreme individualist messages: the institutions and apparatuses of the mass society these so-called anti-conformists so ostentatiously detested). Resulting from this process of enlightened identification, then, came estrangement. Unable to feel their own roots, these anti-conformists turned to any number of hyperobjects—a nonlocal object the mind can imagine (e.g., a distant endangered species, the threat of a climatological apocalypse, etc.)—from which they could draw meaning and identification. Despite eventually finding a home for themselves (either in a niche subculture or through the freshly mutated mass monoculture), these anti-conformists endured psychic wounds so profound, the possibility of rehabilitation (or even redemption?) strikes us as remote. Undoubtedly this development ought to alarm us, as the intention of conformism is to bring individuals closer together, but this new conformism has largely done the opposite.

Fast-forward a few decades later and it appears as though these self-styled individualist anti-conformists have in fact become arch conformists (or perhaps have simply revealed themselves to have been as such all along). Whereas many of the old guard conformists (think of the coalition which voted W. Bush into office twice and supported the Mid East military campaign of the early 2000s) have since begun singing a different tune, the new conformists have only reinforced and re-fortified their prejudices. What is remarkable about these younger generations is that against conventional wisdom, they are not aging out of their firebrand liberalism but doubling down on it.[65]

The estrangement suffered by these new conformists quickly festered into a seething and barely restrained hostility; even as a younger person, it was not uncommon to observe displays of caustic and para-moralistic outbursts out on the streets or inside the shopping centers and malls. Coconuts, a once commonplace entertainment retailer (one which I frequented in my teenage years), was home to such explosive fits of youthful indignation. And in response, the store manager (a quiet and professional but obviously fed up middle-aged Black man) would mock these anti-conformists for their painstakingly meticulous outfits, hairstyles, and mannerisms: "Oh yea, you guys are real individuals! Just like the rest of us!" The irony would play itself out in the following way: every few weeks, a different group of teenagers would come in—either to loiter or jeer at the staff—dressed in the finest Hot Topic had to offer, only to be summarily thrown out of the store (occasionally being forced to evade the portly enforcers of mall security on their way out).

---

[65] Mahdawi, "Millennials Aren't Getting More."

Mocking the staff for wearing their company uniforms, destroying displays of (at the time) popular musical artists like Britney Spears or Sisqo, and generally making a nuisance of themselves while signaling to anyone within earshot how much cooler and more refined in taste they were than everyone else, they were, as the exasperated retail manager would have said, "real individuals."

But it wasn't just young age which kept these individuals from recognizing the deep irony which had overtaken their lives. They were simply doing what came naturally to them—to all of us—something that celebrated psychologist Gerd Gigerenzer considers to be an indispensable element of human cognition and social organization: conforming to the dominant social paradigm (in this case, the paradigm of the mythologized individual).

Automatic tendencies such as those which comprise conformism fall under the broader category of human cognition known as intuition, while the specific methods responsible for guiding such behavior Gigerenzer refers to as "rules of thumb" or "heuristics." According to Dr. Gigerenzer, these rules/heuristics are foundational elements of human cognition, not merely quirks or biases which must be overcome or micro-managed; they are the very real grounding which make all manner of decision-making possible (whether simple or complex).

Over the course of his long career at the Max Planck Institute for Human Development, Dr. Gigerenzer has argued that the dismissal of intuition in favor of a more formal and systematic kind of logic has been mistaken, and that these rules (or heuristics) are typically at least as good as the models and techniques employed by technical experts of decision-making. Contrary to the prevailing wisdom, we needn't abandon or replace them; now, more than ever, we must affirm them. At least, that's what the good doctor from Wallersdorf, Germany recommends.

In Gigerenzer's view, rationality is an adaptive tool, one which does not conform to the rules of logic as understood by experts and technocrats and, as such, uncertainty and unpredictability are ontic realities which we must accept. According to Gigerenzer, human logic (intuition) is entirely prepared to meet this challenge. While human logic is not equal to the formally existing abstract systems of logic, it is far from deficient and in many cases produces outcomes nearly as accurate as those generated by experts. Understand that Dr. Gigerenzer is no enemy to the credentialed class. Rather, his work is intended to aid professionals and experts in their decision-making process where it matters most: in the wild (Gigerenzer's phrase for the unstable and uncertain real world where we don't always have access to the necessary data, and yet must act nonetheless).

Gigerenzer has made bounded rationality (the fact of decision-making operating under unavoidable constraint) his expertise, and his career has demonstrated that the "rationality as optimization" view or notions of a "perfect rationality" are not only technically wrong, but a hindrance to health, success, and understanding. Rather than an "optimizing" decision-making process, Gigerenzer opts for a "satisficing" rationality, which based on his laboratory work has helped (and continues to help) others make better (and happier) choices.

And when it comes to moral decision-making, well, our intuitions are just as indispensable. Gigerenzer argues that, "[H]umans have an innate capacity for morals just as they do for language," and "[T]hat in the same way that native speakers can tell a correct sentence from an incorrect one without being able to explain why, the set of rules underlying the "moral grammar" is typically not in awareness."[66] Dr. Gigerenzer's analogy of a "moral grammar" is intended to highlight the intuitive way in which we arrive upon moral judgments. This moral feeling, to us, is second nature. Gigerenzer grounds his theory of moral intuition in the following three principles:

1) Lack of awareness: a moral intuition, like other gut feelings, appears quickly in consciousness, is strong enough to act upon, and its underlying rationale cannot be verbalized.
2) Roots and rules: the intuition is attached to one of three "roots" (individual, extended family, or community) and to an emotional goal (e.g., prevent harm) and can be described by rules of thumb. These are not necessarily specific to moral behavior but underlie other actions, as well.
3) Social environment: moral behavior is contingent on the

---

[66] Gigerenzer, *Gut Feelings*, 185.

social environment. Some moral disasters can be prevented if one knows the rules guiding people's behavior and the environments triggering these rules.[67]

The interesting thing about both the churlish teenagers who frequented my neighborhood Coconuts store, as well as the benighted adults who usually worked there, is that both parties had conformed to the American ideal of the individual, though unbeknownst to them, the precise meaning of that commitment had been altered. Older generations of Americans had conformed (in one way or another) to the entrepreneurial notion of individuality, while the generations that had grown up under the postwar consensus (such as my own) had conformed to a teleologically distinct iteration of the idea. Framing this development using Gigerenzer's language: the social environment had changed, and with it changed the roots and rules which bind our moral intuitions. And just like our moral intuitions themselves, those who were unfortunate enough to live through this transition similarly lacked an awareness of the transformation (or, at least they could not articulate its nature or the extent of its success).

This shift in conception occurred, in part, because of changes in political economy moving the United States away from bourgeois or entrepreneurial liberalism and towards mass democratic socialism, vis à vis what James Burnham called the managerial revolution. Prior to this transition, notions of the individual were bound up in related notions of duty and responsibility, which is to say that the average man was not committed to a solipsistic or self-referential idea of personhood, but a better integrated and more communally oriented one. Similarly, the freedoms and liberties he cherished proved wildly different from those of his twenty-first-century progeny. Negative liberty ("freedom from X," e.g., freedom from religious persecution) quickly gave way to a decadent positive liberty ("freedom to do X," e.g., freedom to undergo sexual reassignment), and by securing these necessary metapolitical changes also secured future generations of "anti-conformists."

Before this postwar consensus, a man was a "free individual" insofar

---

[67] Ibid., 186.

as he was permitted to labor and build towards his own ends, unencumbered (relatively speaking) by the will of another. In other words, he was "free" to make it on his own, effectively. People maturing through this period of American history were acculturated to much stricter and more constrained notions of "the self," "freedom," "the individual," and so on. For those who have grown up in the wake of the postwar consensus, however, these concepts have become much broader in scope, more therapeutic in nature, and therefore have enjoyed a more seductive effect on the development of the individual personality.

Propagandizing the population into this new economy required transforming the human psyche into a playground of discrete spaces and terrains (the frontier now turned inward: sexuality, for instance, becomes a new continent to colonize—not with sadistic and violent racism of course, but instead masochistic legalism). This was achieved through the joint efforts of the culture industry and the universities to great effect. America's domestic economy was also reconstructed, obviously, seeing as women were now joining the labor force in droves. Faced with new financial pressures, diminished social resources (e.g., support from family and friends), and harebrained psychological advice from the latest generation of scientific experts, new families struggled greatly. With dysfunction now the norm and not the exception, young people maturing through these times endured attachment-related challenges which no doubt only reinforced this tendency towards an aggressive and neurotic conformism.

Consequently, individuals and their para-communities became depoliticized (e.g., lost their agency); this "new" individual was effectively de-individuated, made into a dividual (or multiplicity of persons), thus rendered pliable, inert, and only capable of mobilizing him or herself to avoid pain—never to crawl out of the hole again. Upon this social foundation, the political economy of the twenty-first century was erected—one capable of subordinating people to it regardless of its aims (such as creating the legal and medical horror Mary Rice Hasson of the EPPC famously termed "The Trans-Industrial Complex").

Hyperconformity and Its Consequences

One paradoxical aspect of this new political economy is the manner in which, at the microscopic level, individuals are mired within—even subsumed by—irrationalism (caught within the tug of war between desire and prejudice), while at the more macroscopic levels (e.g., the level at which managers, credentialed experts, and technocrats alike operate), our entire civilizational enterprise appears fixated on the elimination of the irrational: reducing uncertainty, managing risk, fending off populism, algorithmically stamping out emotions like hatred, and so on (all manifestations of human irrationality, *especially* the desire to *eliminate* irrationality). Further examination of this dichotomy is beyond the scope of this essay; however, it must be noted that the psychic toll for those stewing in this artificially fomented micro-irrationalism has only continued to accrue for each passing generation, and now appears to be a greater potential catastrophe than any nuclear holocaust or climatological apocalypse could ever have hoped to be.

In fact, it is the core demands which individuals must conform to that are killing society, America, Western Civilization, etc., and all the scapegoats which currently absorb discursive attention are simply red herrings. The fertility crisis comes to mind. Or the panic over chronic and long-lasting hormone disruption. In fact, health-related anxieties almost universally tend to be attempts to deny the underlying political and existential factors at work. I must admit again, we are at an inopportune moment for fuller elaboration (that will come in my next essay); however, the issue must be raised now since I have just invoked "the existential." The life offered to us by mass democratic society strikes us as anti-human, which is because the logic of mass democracy (and industrial society writ large) is, in a psychic sense, anti-human.

Industrial society, and the political forms expressed within it, have their own logic, what French sociologist Jacques Ellul called "technique." Technique denatures life, subjugating man and the world around him and enforcing upon him both the cruel reign of productive efficiency and perpetual change. Technique is as insatiable as it is thorough, operating without a concern for the humans executing it (hence we say it is anti-human). Psychologically, this circumstance is untenable (the proof of which is all around us in the form of drug addiction, suicide, mental illness, and so on). I believe Ellul's account provides us with a complementary explanation for the extremism of twenty-first-century conformity: the demands which technological society places on us (e.g., continual advancement in all fields of human endeavor, tolerance of a permanently volatile economy, unquestioned allegiance to technique and the fruits of the technological society—even in the face of clear political abuses of human innovation) strain the limits of human intuition and social organization. We are more dependent on others because of increasing conditions of uncertainty (and the existential crises provoked by them), but we are also less able to connect and communicate with them (hence the conformist's reliance on vulgar dogmatism).

I have spoken a great deal about the ways in which these political and technological developments have disempowered us, but in other ways, they have empowered us too (just not in the manner one might prefer). Over the course of the last century, "the self" has accumulated a kind of centripetal power, empowering the individual towards both tremendous and terrible acts of grandiose vacuity. In my view, the rapid pace of technological development over the last twenty years has sped up, intensified, or "hotted up" (to borrow one of Marshall McLuhan's coinages) the psychic and social forces of conformity, producing a kind of hyperconformism—one ill-suited for thriving in a political climate of insipid technological growth, economic decline, and demographic collapse. Under such conditions, few can aspire to anything beyond milling around as human livestock. Ill-suited as it is, it appears to most to be the only way to live (certainly it is the only way to stay in the good graces of the consensus). Accordingly, a "consciousness of alternatives" is as inaccessible to the average person as a "consciousness of what-it-was-once-like-to-have-been-such-a-person" is to those who manage to psychically escape such paradigms (a fact which is and will continue to be the primary obstacle to any mass psychological transformation). A necessary consequence of conformism is the handicapped capacity to see beyond a paradigm—or peer back upon one only recently abandoned. ("It is easier to imagine the end of the world than it is to imagine the end of capitalism," says the neoliberal conformist.)

Under conditions of hyperconformism, the self becomes overrefined in its pursuit of influence and social dominance. Overrefinement—the process of individuating into social and reproductive impotency—does not blunt the self's imperial desires, though it does diminish recruitment of technical skills sufficient for realizing such aims. Those especially lacking in natural endowments (e.g., charisma, intellect, beauty) must rely on indirect and passive-aggressive methods of social dominance (the conduct we've observed on American campuses over the last decade being a prime example). Even in their antagonism, their conduct assumes a co-dependence (with the sole aim, invariably, of restoring the confidence or primacy of group consensus). I invoke Christopher Lasch's notion of the self here, one which borders on a kind of psychological totalitarianism: Lasch's self is both terrifying and infantile, capable of tremendous para-moralistic feeling and posturing. Victimological thinking derives from this psychic condition, too, since at this level of self-absorption, personal dissatisfaction takes on a cosmological significance. Inconveniences are perceived as personal slights, just as disagreements easily devolve into bitter rivalries.

It appears as well, at least to me, that the personal and moral failings of the average person syncretize with those of the managerial elites (and their superiors), suggesting even further that the fundamental values to which the whole of society attempts to conform are fraudulent if not outright malevolent. More strongly intuitive individuals will perceive a metaphysical condition at work, and increasingly, culture and policy makers seem willing to oblige this sentiment. For all we know, they are correct. (Ellul's description of technique, to my eye, certainly reads like a disembodied will.)

The individual of the nineteenth or even early-to-mid-twentieth century did not operate from this axiomatic narcissism in the way that the individual of the late twentieth and twenty-first centuries does, for today's individual is a fanatic while yesterday's individual was merely a cynic. And yet, while we do perceive a distinction between the two, structurally (that is, psychologically) such a distinction does not quite exist, for the same rules are still at play. Once more, Dr. Gigerenzer's work assists in our analysis. According to Gigerenzer, the prime heuristics for conformity are as follows: 1) don't break ranks; 2) if there is a default, do nothing about it (the default rule);[68] and 3) do what the majority of your peers do.[69]

We are wired for simplicity, so Dr. Gigerenzer says, and so the rules of thumb which guide our social habits are appropriately simplistic: Do what you're told; do not attempt to alter the established norms or consensus; do what those around you are doing. These are the fruit of Gigerenzer's human logic—three simple rules for intuitively navigating social uncertainty.

With all this in mind, it should be easier to understand, empathize with (and a little later, organize politically), the eighteen-year-old girl who goes off to college, joins a sorority, and embraces feminism ("don't break ranks"). We might understand further, why she started binge-drinking ("do what the majority of your peers do"), or how she came to engage in degrading and promiscuous acts to the point of enduring sexual violence. We might also understand why she never did anything to change her course of action ("the default rule"). If we were able to understand all these things, then we would bring a sense of urgency and necessity to our political cause for we would understand that: 1) most people are powerless to do anything else (much less to develop a consciousness of what goes on around them); and 2) as such they need to be defended by those who can.

We might also understand why the thirty-two-year-old man, who, at the age of eighteen joined the military ("do what the majority of your peers do"), witnessed or perhaps even participated in behavior he knew was wrong ("don't break ranks"), which he attempted to cope with before falling into drug abuse and taking his own life ("the default rule").

Or, consider the twenty-six-year-old couple who despite being raised Catholic, nonetheless apostatized—sought wisdom from ethnic and spiritual strangers—without first attempting the barest understanding of the faith they inherited. By reckoning with the primacy of human intuition, we would attain a greater understanding of the extent to which the consensus victimizes all who encounter it. These hypotheticals are, perhaps, somewhat dramatic and salacious, but the real challenge is recognizing these patterns in the countless (and seemingly

---

[68] Ibid., 181–182.
[69] Ibid., 191.

inconsequential) exchanges you observe daily, and to overcome the egotism bias which forces you to morally bind individual with circumstance.

Reinforcing the egotism bias (shall we call it), disempowers one from perceiving the embedded relations and influences which bear down upon the individual—suggesting and seducing him or her into a specific habit of life. We look at others and try to understand their failures and foibles—or their internal mental condition—and often we judge them too harshly, for we are participating in the egotism bias by mistaking others and their actions as wholly and rationally self-constructed.

Proper moral accounting requires us to determine where conformity ends and true agency begins, not only for our own well-being, but also so we may properly ground a revolutionary political movement. We are never just fighting for ourselves—that is, the ones "in the know"; rather, we are fighting for everyone else. Mostly for people who will never "know," as if it matters whether or not they do. This is sage advice for any person, but particularly for the aspirant radical, for failure to do so hinders or even precludes the possibility of social change.

A sharper understanding of our essential conformism would produce two necessary and beneficial changes: 1) it would give us a greater understanding of political economy (its formation and maintenance); but also 2) allow for greater recruitment of psychic resources, let's call it "using the dark side of the force," i.e., using otherwise negative or unpleasant emotions like anger and fear towards productive ends.

Without this understanding we can only recede into private prejudices, and in doing so, descend willingly into our own graves.

IV

KAHNEMAN, ELLUL, AND "TECHNOCRATIC PSYCHOLOGY"

DECONSTRUCTING THE NOBEL PRIZE-WINNING BEHAVIORAL ECONOMIST'S CELEBRATED WORK, *THINKING, FAST & SLOW* WITH THE HELP OF PHILOSOPHER JACQUES ELLUL AND PSYCHOLOGIST GERD GIGERENZER

Technocracy and Its Discontents

The question concerning technology, as Martin Heidegger so long ago termed it, puzzles us still to this day. Not because we suffer from a lack of answers, mind you, for many thinkers and theoreticians have answered that call (some more constructively than others). No, the problem is far more troublesome than that. Qua Heidegger, we no longer ask what technology is, what it may reveal, or how (or if) it relates to truth; rather, we wonder instead how it may bring about our salvation.

The skepticism of the twentieth century has waned, and in its stead has arisen the sycophancy of the twenty-first. At our wits' end with the limitations of mankind and its troublesome psyche (or soul), we have come to regard technology as a panacea capable of rescuing us from this impasse. As a result, we have become entirely dependent on what Jacques Ellul called "technique" and its medium, what I am calling "technical logic" (the meaning of which shall be elaborated by the end of this essay). But matters are worse still, for even in resisting the awful reign of technocracy we find ourselves nevertheless bound by fidelity to the awesome might of technique and thus unable to approach the challenge rationally.

Perhaps it seems odd to have suggested that we are currently being irrational with regards to technology, for after all, isn't technology (and those social forces which bring it about) the epitome of human rationale? Aren't the technologists themselves the most rational among us? My answer is no, judging by the "normative" standard technocrats declare for themselves (the meaning of which we shall also explore). It becomes clear, then, that the notion of rationality itself must be highly qualified if we are to continue this investigation. By the end of this essay—aided by this notion of "technical logic"—I will have achieved as much.

Our circumstances being such as they are, we remain trapped in the vice-like grip of an awful paranoia, unable to either extricate ourselves or improve our position. Though many fear the looming technological apocalypse (whether expressed in terms of artificial intelligence, automated labor, gene editing, etc.) and the consequences it will have for the economy, the labor force, and the population size, the technocratic class themselves pay this anxiety no mind, choosing instead to antagonize the population for their inadaptability and surplus-ness. Transhumanist and technocratic thinker Yuval Noah Harari put it blithely when asked what will be done about the mass of people displaced by automation and artificial intelligence: "drugs and computer games." This circumstance has gone largely unchanged for decades, and now, we find ourselves forced—with little alternative—to accept the future designed for us. Aided by a proper understanding, however, we may just find a way out yet.

Despite describing technocrats as belonging to a "class," I do not encourage any Marxist pretenses; I do intend, however, a distinction between the people who comprise the technocracy and those they rule over, for the former are, in fact, distinct. This distinction, as will become clearer over the course of the discussion, is primarily biological and metaphysical (rather than economic or ideological). The final goal of this essay will be to analyze these metaphysical and biological differences, and ultimately, to devise a portrait or profile of the technocrat himself.

From the point of view of the technocrat, most human life is simply not worth consideration. Not even the best humans can offer is good enough for the technocrat, as it is the very definition of "human" which requires changing if we are to facilitate the next stage in the development of the technological society. According to the technocrat, humanity is our problem while technology is the solution. Technocrats therefore place themselves on the side of technology, as midwives to the birth of the tech-revolution. They are a kind of collaborator class, effectively, traitors to man, while dutiful allies of technique. We will, over the course of this work, come to a psychological understanding of this rivalry using Jungian archetypal thought.

Today's technicians are yesterday's magicians, as Ellul observed, and while the modes of social and political organization productive of technocracy have grown more complex since the times of tribal magic, the underlying psychology has not. In at least one crucial way, it has in fact regressed (but I'll save that for the end).

While our discussion is indeed a philosophical one, I do not intend to prosecute the matter abstractly—at least, not entirely so. To that end, I would like to frame the subject within the context of a long running debate occurring in the cognitive sciences stretching back some thirty or more years between the German Gerd Gigerenzer and the Israeli Daniel Kahneman. Gerd Gigerenzer and Daniel Kahneman both spent their careers studying uncertainty and decision-making (e.g., human cognition), contributing to what has come to be known as the "probabilistic revolution" within psychology. And while their findings have intersected nearly as often as they have run afoul of one another, the pair made for a heated academic rivalry (one which I intend to use toward our own ends here). The exact relationship between *their rivalry* and *the nature of Ellulian technique* will be detailed once I have provided both a summary of their individual views as scientists as well as the content of their disagreement.

The exact nature of the disagreement will be elucidated in the following section, though I can at least draw the battlelines now. For our purposes here, Gigerenzer's work will be used to support the folk psychology of what he calls "human logic" in contrast with the technocratic psychology of Kahneman's "technical logic" (again, my own language). It is still necessary to disentangle the desirable results of technological innovation from the deterritorializing aspects of technique itself to better fortify a political resistance against the technocratic class. Thus, Gigerenzer's critique of Kahneman will help lead our investigation as well as guide us towards a psychology of the twenty-first-century technocrat.

Gigerenzer v. Kahneman

Let us begin by first introducing the thought of Gerd Gigerenzer. Our German friend opens his 2007 publication titled *Gut Feelings* by declaring, "A beneficial degree of ignorance can be valuable."[70] He uses an experimental test of "the recognition heuristic" to demonstrate this: a group of American college students and a group of German college students are asked whether Detroit or Milwaukee had a larger population. Almost half of the Americans (40 percent) guessed Milwaukee, which was incorrect, while nearly the entire class of Germans guessed correctly. Gigerenzer argues that, relative to these Germans, the Americans knew too much about their country's geography, its history, its culture, and were therefore unable to deduce the answer. Something appears to happen in the mind when it needs to make a choice or undertake some action but is beset by large amounts of discrete (and often conflicting or contradictory) information.

I've written about this phenomenon in my first book, *American Extremist*, where too much information impairs decision-making, but with regards to the recognition heuristic specifically, Gigerenzer's point is that models of human cognition which presuppose complex calculations struggle time and time again to substantiate themselves, both in the lab and "in the wild" (Gigerenzer's term for the world of unstable and unpredictable human relations).

More simply stated, the sweet spot between human thought and action is one wherein we are not repeatedly prompted to engage in a sustained process of strenuous and exacting mental labor. His dichotomy is between that of maximizers and satisficers, as in those whose cognitive style exhaustively searches for the precise solution, versus those whose cognition operates according to the dictum of "good enough." According to these maximizers, "The mind solves a complex

---

[70] Gigerenzer, *Gut Feelings*, 8.

problem by a complex process,"⁷¹ an explanation which is not supported by the available data, Gigerenzer swiftly informs us. What the data shows is that cognition operates based on "heuristics" and "rules of thumb," and not complex and immediate mathematically-informed calculations (which can somehow be activated consciously, spontaneously, by human thought). Human cognition is made possible by simple rules which are "less prone to estimation or calculation error and [are] intuitively transparent."⁷²

Gigerenzer offers us the example of Dan Horan, a police officer whose job it is to spot drug couriers. Puzzled by Officer Horan's accuracy in picking couriers out from crowds of several hundred, Gigerenzer could not get an explanation from the man for his methodology. It was simply a "hunch." Of this, Gigerenzer says:

> Although many judges may condemn police hunches, they tend to trust their own intuition. As one judge explained to me, "I don't trust the police officers' hunches, because they are not my hunches." Similarly, prosecutors show little hesitation in justifying to themselves a peremptory challenge against a potential juror because she's wearing gold jewelry and a T-shirt, or does not seem too bright, given that her hobbies are eating and doing her hair and watching Oprah. However, the issue should be neither hunches per se nor the ability to come up with reasons after the fact while hiding the unconscious nature of hunches. To avoid discrimination, the legal system instead needs to survey the quality of policemen's hunches, that is, a detective's actual success in spotting criminals. In other professions successful experts are evaluated by their performance rather than their ability to give post-hoc explanations for their performance. Chicken sexers, chess masters, professional baseball players, award-winning writers, and composers are typically unable to fully articulate how they do what they do. Many skills lack [a] descriptive language.⁷³

---

[71] Ibid., 10.
[72] Ibid., 12.
[73] Ibid., 16.

Whether we call it a "gut feeling," an "intuition," or just a "hunch," the fundaments of cognition (which are expressed through heuristics and rules of thumb) comprise Gigerenzer's "human logic," a form of bounded rationality which he argues in favor of based on ecological considerations. According to Gigerenzer, man does not suffer from systematic cognitive biases; rather he suffers from mismatches between his psychology and his ecology (e.g., social and natural environments). Gigerenzer is careful to define his terms, characterizing these gut feelings as,

> judgment(s) that 1) appear quickly in consciousness 2) whose underlying reasons we are not fully aware of and 3) [are] strong enough to act upon.... Their rationale consists of two components: 1) simple rules of thumb which take advantages of 2) evolved capacities of the brain.[74]

Evolution provides us with capabilities which over time become capacities; the simple rules of human logic (e.g., heuristics, rules of thumb) deliver on our capacities by only considering the most important information, thereby enabling swift action. Heuristics are, in this way, *fast* (not reliant on heavy calculation) and *frugal* (selecting only for important available information).

Skewing towards simplicity (a cognitive first principle in Gigerenzer's model), fast and frugal heuristics are robust in the face of environmental change and benefit from generalizing to novel circumstances. Critics of this view (such as Kahneman and Tversky) hold that fast and frugal heuristics don't conform to the normative test of logical coherence, and therefore produce "biases" and "systematic errors." We will explore this disagreement more fully at the end of this section, but for now it suffices to say that we are dealing with a difference of paradigms, not empirical proofs. (As in, a difference between *human* logic and *technical* logic).

Beneath the dim light of conscious awareness, pattern matching marries the correct rule to the proper circumstance. As a result, "biases"

---

[74] Ibid., 16–18.

and "systematic errors" may arise due to the improper pairing of a given rule with some environment. They are therefore not shortcomings of the mind but obstacles of an entirely ecological nature. Other limitations of the mind such as forgetfulness, in this view, are not bugs of human cognition but features: forgetfulness is but one of the many mechanisms (according to Dr. Gigerenzer) by which the brain controls the information equilibrium, enabling it to act reliably and swiftly: "I called this an ecological question because it is about how cognition is adapted to its environment."[75]

Having provided a theoretical and empirical basis to ground his thesis, Gigerenzer then provides several compelling examples of simple human logic matching, even outperforming, the complex logic of technical experts. Human logic's satisficing methodology can provide competent solutions and does so quickly. Overdeliberation, the result of a prejudice for cognitive complexity, does not universally produce superior outcomes to those derived from simplicity. A memorable line from *The Empire Strikes Back* captures the spirit of Gigerenzer's position well: "Never tell me the odds!"

Gut feelings are neither good nor bad—that is, not necessarily so. We judge them as irrational solely because we cannot articulate how they come upon us or where they come from. In a prejudicially rational world this becomes a grave problem, for we are always expected to provide a reliable accounting of ourselves. From this "normative" view, such limitations of the mind are a liability (though this is also not necessarily the case). Intuition is often the cause for sound judgment, and where it isn't, this is often due, as we have said, to ecological challenges—mismatches between the mind and social environment. Dr. Gigerenzer offers a further clarification to explain those circumstances where simplicity outperforms complex calculations (as well as the other way around):

> Intuitions based on only one good reason tend to be accurate when one has to predict the future (or some unknown present state of affairs), when the future is difficult to foresee, and when

---

[75] Ibid., 25.

one has only limited information. Complex analysis, by contrast, pays when one has to explain the past, when the future is highly predictable, or when there are large amounts of information.[76]

It is not that Gigerenzer is arguing for the superiority of simplicity in absolute terms; he is merely trying to rescue the baby of simplicity from the bathwater of complex calculations. His criticism of Daniel Kahneman's theoretical work (one which I share as well), is rooted in Kahneman's fundamental dismissal of simplicity, and importantly, of the ecologically situated basis for human cognition. Of the logic employed by scientists like Daniel Kahneman and Amos Tversky, (what I am calling technical logic), Gigerenzer says, "Logic is the ideal of a disembodied system, the proper yardstick for deductive arguments that concern the truth of propositions, such as in a mathematical proof."[77]

While logic is disembodied, humans are not. Therefore, we must not make the error of condemning too harshly the "mistakes" of human logic, for it is far from necessarily true that the means with which intuition operates are, themselves, faulty.

Perhaps this overestimation of technical logic emerges from the native condition of the scientist who operates in a maximally controlled space, one ripe with easily accessible information, as well as the resources with which to analyze it. While I intend to offer an entirely different explanation a little further on in this work, it is worth considering the disjunction between the tightly controlled and high-information space of the cognitive researcher with that of the anarchic and data-diffusive space of the cognitive actor (i.e., law enforcement, medical professionals, investors and traders, et cetera). The real world, as Gigerenzer observes, is filled with situations where,

> rules are only partially known, can be overthrown by a powerful player or are kept intentionally ambiguous. Uncertainty is prevalent; deception, lying, and lawbreaking possible. As a consequence, there are no optimal strategies known for winning a

---

[76] Ibid., 151.
[77] Ibid., 102.

battle, leading an organization, bringing up children, or investing in the stock market, but of course good enough strategies do exist.[78]

Having briefly summarized the major strains in Gigerenzer's thought, let us move on to the work of Daniel Kahneman and Amos Tversky. Responsible for popularizing investigation into the heuristics and biases (systematic errors) of the mind, the two worked together for decades, with their academic partnership culminating in critically lauded *Thinking, Fast & Slow*, the text I am here to critique. At the start of the book Kahneman describes his relationship with Amos Tversky thusly:

> We once discovered with great delight that we had identical, silly ideas about the future professions of several toddlers we both knew. We could identify the argumentative three-year-old lawyer, the nerdy professor, the empathetic and mildly intrusive psychotherapist. Of course, these predictions were absurd, but we still found them appealing. It was also clear that our intuitions were governed by the resemblance of each child to the cultural stereotype of a profession. The amusing exercise helped us develop a theory that was emerging in our minds at the time about the role of resemblance in predictions, and elaborate that theory and dozens of experiments as in the following example: an individual has been described by a neighbor as follows: "Steve is very shy and withdrawn, invariably helpful, but with little interest in people or in the world of reality. A meek and tidy soul, he has a need for order and structure, and a passion for detail." Is Steve more likely to be a librarian or a farmer?
> The resemblance of Steve's personality to that of a stereotypical librarian strikes everyone immediately, but equally relevant statistical considerations are almost always ignored. Did it occur to you that there are more than 20 male farmers for each male librarian in the United States? Because there are so many more farmers it is almost certain that more "meek and tidy" souls will

---

[78] Ibid., 91.

be found on tractors than at library information desks. However, we found that participants in our experiments ignored the relevant statistical facts and relied exclusively on resemblance. We proposed that they used resemblance as a simplifying heuristic (roughly a rule of thumb) to make a difficult judgment. The reliance on the heuristic caused predictable biases (systematic errors) in their predictions.[79]

Their partnership led them to develop a list of heuristics and biases, such as representativeness and availability, which itemized the various types of errors in human judgment. According to Kahneman and Tversky, our predisposition for intuitive thought leads us to concoct "cognitive illusions"; that is, errors of judgment which may be explained empirically by the activity of limited heuristics and faulty biases. A significant part of their research program was based on generating logical puzzles (e.g., the Linda problem, the hospital problem—we will discuss them further in the next section) which could highlight the illogical and anti-probabilistic tendencies of folk psychology (or human logic).

Part of the problem (that being faulty human judgment) may be accounted for by our reliance on heuristics and the inevitably of cognitive biases, but Kahneman and Tversky believed another factor was also at play. Adopting the language of psychologists Keith Stanovich and Richard West, the team of Israeli researchers proposed that human consciousness functions via the interplay of two distinct systems: "system 1" and "system 2."

System 1 operates automatically and quickly, with little or no effort and no sense of voluntary control. System 2, on the other hand, allocates attention to the effortful mental activities that demand it (our aforementioned "complex calculations"). The operations of system 2 are often associated with the subjective experience of agency, choice, and concentration. Of the relationship between our cognitive illusions and the s1/s2 model of consciousness, Dr. Kahneman says the following:

---

[79] Kahneman, *Thinking, Fast & Slow*, 6–7.

The question that is most often asked about cognitive illusions is whether they can be overcome. The message of these examples is not encouraging. Because system 1 operates automatically and cannot be turned off at will, errors of intuitive thought are often difficult to prevent. Biases cannot always be avoided because system 2 may have no clue to the error. Even when cues to likely errors are available, errors can be prevented only by the enhanced monitoring and effortful of activity of system 2. As a way to live your life, however, continuous vigilance is not necessarily good, and it is certainly impractical. Constantly questioning our own thinking would be impossible, tedious, and system 2 is much too slow and inefficient to serve as substitute for system 1 and making routine decisions. The best we can do is a compromise: learn to recognize situations in which mistakes are likely and try harder to avoid significant mistakes when the stakes are high. The premise of this book is that it is easier to recognize other people's mistakes than our own.[80]

Cognitive illusions, according to the duo, are simply unavoidable. Kahneman and Tversky offer further elaborations on this model: system 1 cognition is affected by our mood, so if we are uncomfortable or unhappy then our intuition is no longer of service to us.[81] System 2 controls our thoughts and behaviors, though it is plagued by feelings of uncertainty and doubt.[82] Owing to the "law of least effort," we prefer minimal exertion—both physically and cognitively—and so Kahneman and Tversky tell us that "laziness is built deep into our nature."[83] Already we see a picture of human consciousness that is more stark and pessimistic than the adaptive optimism of Gigerenzer's model.

Back to the dynamic duo. The glue of psychological coherence which holds together the many aspects of Kahneman and Tversky's model is a principle they call "What you see is all there is," or WYSIATI for short. In their words:

---

[80] Ibid., 28.
[81] Ibid., 69.
[82] Ibid., 41, 80.
[83] Ibid., 35.

WYSIATI facilitates the achievement of coherence and of the cognitive ease that causes us to accept a statement as true. It explains why we can think fast and how we are able to make sense of partial information in a complex world. Much of the time, the coherent story we put together is close enough to reality to support reasonable action. However, I will also invoke WYSIATI to help explain a long and diverse list of biases of judgment and choice, including the following among many others:

1) Overconfidence: as the WYSIATI rule implies, neither the quantity nor the quality of the evidence counts for much in subjective confidence. The confidence that individuals have in their beliefs depends mostly on the quality of the story they can tell about what they see, even if they see little. We often fail to allow for the possibility that evidence that should be critical to our judgment is missing—what we see is all there is. Furthermore, our associative system tends to settle on a coherent pattern of activation and suppresses doubt and ambiguity.

2) Framing effects: different ways of presenting the same information often evoke different emotions. The statement that "the odds of survival one month after surgery are 90%" is more reassuring than the equivalent statement that "mortality within one month of surgery is 10%." Similarly, cold cuts described as "90% fat free" are more attractive than when they are described as "10% fat." The equivalence of the alternative formulations is transparent, but an individual normally sees only one formulation, and what she sees is all there is.

3) Base-rate neglect: recall Steve, the meek and tidy soul who is often believed to be a librarian. The personality description is salient and vivid, and although you surely know that there are more male farmers than male librarians, that statistical fact almost certainly did not come to your mind when you

first considered the question. What you saw was all there was.[84]

Human logic, in Kahneman and Tversky's paradigm, is strongly biased towards causal explanations and does not deal well with "mere statistics."[85] The predictions it generates must be corrected because they are not regressive, and thus are biased.[86] Our reliance on the heuristics of human logic is not statistically optimal, for even when they do hold some validity, intuitive predictions still lead to sins against statistical logic.[87] Kahneman and Tversky go as far as to recommend "thinking the opposite" (engaging in persistent and deliberate self-contradiction of the mind's natural insights and predictions) to negate the "biased recruitment of thoughts" that produce these effects.[88]

Before detailing the nature of their disagreement, it is worthwhile taking a brief inventory of the facts as I have presented them. Gigerenzer's ecological model of bounded rationality situates human logic within a space of uncertainty where adaptation helps to marry human psychology with social (and natural) ecologies. Errors of judgment are not limitations of the mind; instead, they represent an incongruity between, or a misunderstanding of, mind and environment. Kahneman and Tversky's heuristics and biases program, on the other hand, offers us a model of the mind divided. Human judgment derives from the interplay between system 1 and system 2 consciousness, each with its own limitations. The glue which holds these systems together is simply a principle, WYSIATI, which is a way of describing human psychology as essentially and hopelessly egotistical. Cognitively this results in a comedy of errors, the culprits of which are our heuristics and biases.

And now, on to the debate. Gigerenzer argues that the so-called "errors" of Kahneman and Tversky's heuristics and biases program do not in fact violate probability theory, and moreover, may not even constitute errors in the first place. He attributes the existence of these

---

[84] Ibid., 87–88.
[85] Ibid., 182.
[86] Ibid., 190.
[87] Ibid., 151.
[88] Ibid., 127.

"errors" to a "very narrow normative view" which ignores conceptual distinctions such as the difference between single-cases and relative frequency.

Contemporary psychology, Gigerenzer says, is the offspring of the probabilistic and cognitive revolutions which took place in the preceding century. As a result, "probabilistic and statistical concepts were piggybacked onto cognitive concepts." He gives the example of Harold Kelley's proposal that "the layperson attributes a cause to an effect in the same way as a statistician of the Fisherian school would, by (unconsciously) calculating an analysis of variance." This led to a reification of the individual within psychology, as social cognition became the domain of the individual (a reflection, Gigerenzer points out, of statistics: "statistical calculations are those of an individual statistician"). Under this paradigm, human motivations and personalities became reducible to "passionless information-processing errors, due to basic shortcomings in intuitive statistical reasoning."

Summarizing his rivals in their own words, Kahneman and Tversky's model assumes that,

> in making predictions and judgments under uncertainty, people do not appear to follow the calculus of chance or the statistical theory of prediction. Instead, they rely on a limited number of heuristics which sometimes yield reasonable judgments and sometimes lead to severe and systematic errors.[89]

The success of this program was widespread, expanding beyond the confines of psychology, becoming influential in law, economics, management science, medical diagnostics, and behavioral auditing, to name just a few disciplines. Of Kahneman and Tversky's program, Gigerenzer says:

> [T]hey see the study of systematic errors in probabilistic reasoning, also called "cognitive illusions," as similar to that of visual illusions. The presence of an error of judgment is demonstrated

---

[89] Gigerenzer, "How to Make Cognitive."

by comparing people's responses either with an established fact (e.g., that the two lines are equal in length, as in the case of the famous visual Muller-Lyer illusion) or with an accepted rule of arithmetic, logic, or statistics.[90]

This accepted rule is known alternatively as the normative theory of prediction, and the normative principle of statistical prediction, and refers to the practice of affirming a rule's use "when there is a consensus among formal scientists that the rule is appropriate for the particular problem." Gigerenzer argues that the working assumption behind the normative model presumes the existence of only a single correct answer to any of the numerous logical problems posed by Kahneman and Tversky (e.g., the cab problem, engineer-lawyer problem, Linda problem, et cetera), for if there weren't only a single correct answer then there would be no reason for cataloguing the number of "errors" and "illusions" generated by attempts at solving them. (The correct answer, of course, being determined by credentialed mathematicians, statisticians, and probabilists.) Gigerenzer proceeds, then, to demonstrate the folly associated with this line of research, giving special attention to the overconfidence bias, the conjunction fallacy, and the base-rate fallacy.

The overconfidence bias emerges by testing an individual's general knowledge and then assessing his or her confidence in the answer provided. One example of this test looks as such:

Which city has more inhabitants?
a) Hyderabad, b) Islamabad
How confident are you that your answer is correct?
50% 60% 70% 80% 90% 100%[91]

Typically, subjects who assessed a 100 percent confidence rate had a relative frequency of correct answers at about 80 percent; subjects who self-reported a 90 percent confidence rate had a relative frequency of correct answers of 75 percent. A similar ratio persisted at each level of confidence with this asymmetry between confidence and relative

---

[90] Ibid.
[91] In Ibid.

frequency understood as "overconfidence."

Arguing that probability theory is interested in frequencies instead of single events, Gigerenzer says that any comparison between the two amounts to a difference between apples and oranges. An apples-to-apples comparison, instead, would compare one's estimated relative frequency of correct answers to the true relative frequency of correct answers (at which point the overconfidence "bias" disappears, as demonstrated in experiments run by Hoffrage, Kleinbolting, and Gigerenzer himself).

Comparing estimated frequencies with actual frequencies makes overconfidence disappear, since the experimenter's normative confusion between single events and frequencies has been eliminated. Gigerenzer's main rebuttal here is that discrepancies between probabilities of single events (confidences) and long-run frequencies should not be framed as errors, and furthermore, that judgments need not be explained by the presence of fundamentally flawed cognitive operations.

On to the conjunction fallacy. The conjunction fallacy emerges from the kinds of logic puzzles Kahneman and Tversky have become famous for. One such example is the Linda problem, which goes as follows:

> Linda is 31 years old, single, outspoken and very bright. She majored in philosophy. As a student, she was deeply concerned with issues of discrimination and social justice, and also participated in antinuclear demonstrations. [Which is more probable?] Linda is a bank teller (T) [or] Linda is a bank teller and is active in the feminist movement (T&F).[92]

Out of 142 subjects, 85 percent chose T&F, which according to Kahneman and Tversky, is incorrect because "the probability of a conjunction of two events, such as T&F, can never be greater than that of one of its constituents." This fallacy arises due to the presence of the "representativeness heuristic," which is to say that the test subjects' judgments were based on the similarity or representativeness between the description of Linda and T&F. Because the description calls to mind images

---

[92] In Ibid.

associated with feminism, T&F appears to be the obviously correct answer.

The problem with Kahneman and Tversky's experiment, once again, is the confusion between probabilities of single events (that Linda is a bank teller) and those of frequencies. Such judgments, Gigerenzer says, "should be treated in the context of psychoanalysis, not probability theory." Tests of the conjunction fallacy have one advantage over tests of confidence in that they compare subjective probabilities to other subjective probabilities, whereas confidence tests compare them to frequencies. Gigerenzer concedes that the conjunction fallacy "is a violation of some subjective theories of probability, including Bayesian theory," but does not violate probability as such (at least, not from a frequentist's point of view).

Kahneman and Tversky's "conjunction fallacy" mostly disappears when the question is posed along frequentist lines (as opposed to single event probabilities). The frequentist version of K+T's test looks like this:

> There are 100 persons who fit the description above (i.e., Linda's). How many of them are:
> a) bank tellers
> b) bank tellers and active in the feminist movement. [93]

The frequentist view assumes the layman's basic competency in distinguishing between single cases and frequencies, and when the problem is framed in such terms, test subjects rarely disappoint.

Of the Linda problem, Gigerenzer says that its "rigid, logical norms" overlook that intelligence must "operate in an uncertain world, not in the artificial certainty of a logical system."[94] Human logic operates under conditions of simplicity, and in particular relevance, especially when it comes to conversation. In the case of the Linda problem, it is in fact logical to assume the relevance of the information provided, though this clearly contradicts the normative (in our terms, technical) view of the matter.

---

[93] In Ibid.
[94] Gigerenzer, *Gut Feelings*, 94.

Human logic also interprets the meaning of "probability" not exclusively in terms of mathematical possibility, but also in terms of "plausibility," "believability," and "whether there is evidence"; that the conjunction fallacy mostly disappears when the language is changed from "probable" to "how many" demonstrates the layman's understanding that sets cannot be smaller than subsets.[95]

Consider the following question:

If a test to detect a disease whose prevalence is 1/1000 has a false positive rate of 5%, what is the chance that a person found to have a positive result actually has the disease, assuming you know nothing about the person's symptoms or signs?[96]

Of the sixty students and staff at Harvard Medical School who answered this problem, "almost half of them judged the probability that the person actually had the disease to be .95 (a modal answer)" while "18% of participants responded .02." The average answer was .56 while .02 was the correct answer according to the study's authors. Kahneman and Tversky argue that these results are proof of "the base-rate fallacy," which is the tendency to underemphasize or even ignore the base rate (general underlying probabilities) of an event in favor of specific, individuating information.

As we have seen with the other examples, once the base-rate fallacy is put through a frequentist lens, it suddenly appears less fallacious. This problem is unique, however, as Gigerenzer contends that while it does not pose a problem for frequentists (in terms of probability theory), there are multiple possible answers, complicating a Bayesian interpretation. "One piece of information necessary for a Bayesian calculation is missing," Gigerenzer argues, and that is "the test's long-run frequency of correctly diagnosing persons who have the disease (admittedly a minor problem if we can assume a high true positive rate)." He also points out that the medical diagnosis problem is unclear as to whether the person was "randomly drawn from the population to which the base rate refers."

---

[95] Ibid., 95.
[96] Gigerenzer, "How to Make Cognitive."

A frequentist version of the medical diagnosis problem (published in 1990 by Cosmides and Tooby) takes the following form:

> One out of 1000 Americans has disease X. A test has been developed to detect when a person has disease X. Every time the test is given to a person who has the disease, the test comes out positive. But sometimes the test also comes out positive when it is given to a person who is completely healthy. Specifically, out of every 1000 people who are perfectly healthy, 50 of them test positive for the disease.
> Imagine that we have assembled a random sample of 1000 Americans. They were selected by a lottery. Those who conducted the lottery had no information about the health status of any of these people. How many people who test positive for the disease will actually have the disease?[97]

Inputting the missing information (and re-framing the problem in terms of frequencies) dramatically reduced the so-called base-rate fallacy: drawing from a pool of Stanford undergraduates, 76 percent of subjects gave the Bayesian answer of .02 (or, one out of 50 or 51). When Cosmides and Tooby re-ran the original single-event iteration, the Bayesian answer was given only 12 percent of the time.

Based on these results, Gigerenzer confidently declares that the mind is, in fact, a frequentist—that is, it can distinguish between single events and frequencies in the long term just as probabilists and statisticians do. Kahneman and Tversky's heuristics and biases program does not acknowledge this distinction, opting instead to apply their "normative view" to logical problems. Gigerenzer argues that this approach expects subjects to routinely and mechanistically apply Bayes' theorem to any given probabilistic question. On this point he asks, "Is the structure of the problem the same as the structure of the statistical model underlying the formula?" to which the answer, he tells us, is a resounding "No."

---

[97] In Ibid.

Gigerenzer closes this salvo by accusing Kahneman and Tversky of distorting the original understanding of the heuristic, moving it further away from the notion of "selecting the first option available that meets minimal standards" to a catch-all concept by which to explain away the "failures" of human cognition. Kahneman and Tversky claim that heuristics can provide us with accurate judgments, but as their research program has borne out, heuristics are only ever invoked in the negative. Gigerenzer contends that despite the enthusiasm for and volume of research conducted in this vein, virtually none of it has deepened our understanding of human logic (or psychology in general).

In opposition to Kahneman and Tversky's "heuristics and biases" program, Gigerenzer endorses the theory of probabilistic mental models (PMM), which integrates this frequentist philosophy with the notion of mental models. PMM theory posits that we construct some mental model—consisting of a reference class and a list of probability cues—to solve a given problem. "Probability cues are hierarchically ordered according to their (subjective) cue validities," at which point we scan for probability cues that can be activated.

> Once a cue is found that can be activated for the problem under consideration, the judgment is made accordingly and the subject's confidence in this particular judgment is determined by the cue validity of the activated cue; since cue validities are learned frequencies of co-occurrences, PMM theory explains single-event confidences [via frequentism].[98]

Because natural environments often have "surplus structure," we cannot merely rely on using the structural properties of a given statistical model to understand its structure. Surplus structure includes "space and time, cheating options, perspective, and social contracts" among others. That the heuristics and biases program relies on the notion of "structural isomorphs" (i.e., using a given model or principle to construct problems with identical formal structures but differing contents) fails, Gigerenzer tells us, is because it does not account for surplus structure

---

[98] Ibid.

and therefore inappropriately identifies "errors."

Gigerenzer expounded on the problem of probability just a few years later in a publication by Routledge.[99] Citing frequentists like Richard von Mises and Jerzy Neyman, Gigerenzer again argues that probability theory concerns itself with frequencies, and "not degrees of belief in single events" which, thanks to the Bayesian renaissance, appears to have shifted the meaning from this earlier conception.

Arguing on evolutionary grounds, Gigerenzer states that statistical reasoning of the variety espoused by Kahneman and Tversky took "millennia of literacy and numeracy to evolve," and that owing to the historic illiteracy of mankind, information representation instead took the form of "frequencies of events, sequentially encoded" and containing "information about the sample size which allows one to compute the ambiguity or precision of the estimate" (Gigerenzer gives the example of the following input representation: three out of twenty as opposed to 15 percent or P = .15). The frequentist view, so Dr. Gigerenzer claims, offers us a more cognitively meaningful way of thinking about, and ultimately acting upon, the information we are exposed to. He clarifies further, saying "one cannot speak of a probability unless our reference class has been defined. Since a single person is always a member of many reference classes, no unique relative frequency can be assigned to a single person."

His defense of the PMM continues in this paper: probabilistic mental models are well adapted, such that although the individual's knowledge of a given domain may be insufficient, this insufficiency does not speak to a systematic bias. While individual validities "roughly correspond to ecological validities," this does not imply that the individual has knowledge of the relevant cues. Of this, Gigerenzer says:

> If the general knowledge questions were a representative sample from the knowledge domain, zero overconfidence would be expected. ... Selecting difficult and misleading questions decreases the number of correct answers, and "overconfidence bias"

---

[99] Gigerenzer, "bounded rationality," 284–313.

results as a consequence of selection, not of some deficient mental heuristic.

Gigerenzer's critiques did not go unanswered. Kahneman and Tversky wrote their response, published in *Psychological Review*, addressing the most significant charges levied against them by the German scientist. The pair defended their research program on the following basis: that 1) the study of "judgmental or perceptual biases" are "of interest in their own right"; 2) on account of their "practical implications" to "clinical judgment [and] intuitive forecasting"; and because 3) by studying systematic errors we can uncover "the psychological processes that underlie perception and judgment."[100]

The pair restate their belief in the usefulness of heuristic-based thinking, even going so far as to concede that "although errors of judgments are but a method by which some cognitive processes are studied, the method has become a significant part of the message." Consequently, they lament the perception of their research program as "[portraying] the human mind in an overly negative light."

Demonstrating that they understood the basis of Gigerenzer's critique, Kahneman and Tversky repeat the disagreement between the Bayesian and frequentist views of probability, though they do not challenge Gigerenzer's claim that the assertion of Bayesian normativity on the part of the Israeli researchers is indefensibly arbitrary. It is precisely the point that this (seemingly arbitrary) commitment to Bayesian probability is in fact the source of intuitive misjudgments observed in K+T's "heuristics and biases" program. Instead, they argue that Gigerenzer's critique does not apply to the whole of their laboratory efforts. On this point, Kahneman and Tversky declare:

> The reader of Gigerenzer's critique is invited to believe that the heuristics and biases approach was exclusively concerned with biases in assessments of subjective probability, to which Gigerenzer has had a philosophical objection. However, much of our research has been concerned with tasks to which his objection does

---

[100] Kahneman and Tversky, "Theoretical Notes," 582–591.

not apply. Our (Tversky & Kahneman) 1974 Science article, for example, discussed twelve biases. Only two (insensitivity to prior probability of outcomes and overconfidence in subjective probability distributions) involve subjective probability; the other ten biases do not. These include the effect of arbitrary anchors on estimates of quantities, availability biases in judgment of frequency, illusory correlation, nonregressive prediction, and misconceptions of randomness. These findings are not mentioned in Gigerenzer's account of heuristics and biases. Inexplicably, he dismisses the entire body of research because of a debatable philosophical objection to two of twelve phenomena.

Charging Gigerenzer with misrepresenting their views (e.g., that judgmental heuristics are "independent of context and content" and that "mathematically equivalent information formats must be psychologically equivalent"), Kahneman and Tversky argue the contrary: their work has always recognized that "different framings of the same problem of decision or judgment can give rise to different mental processes." The duo then takes the opportunity to go on the offensive, conjecturing that Gigerenzer deliberately put forth inaccurate criticisms so that the positions being attributed to K+T therefore "could be discredited." That cognitive illusions could be made to disappear through assessing frequencies over subjective probabilities betrays "a surprisingly selective reading of the evidence," the two argue, as "most of our early work on availability biases was concerned with judgments of frequency, and we illustrated anchoring by inducing errors in judgments of the frequency of African nations in the United Nations." Citing Slovic, Fischoff, and Lichtenstein (1982), K+T declare the righteous empirical basis for systematic biases in judgments of frequency, as the Israeli duo are not the only researchers to have identified the phenomenon.

Following this, the two take aim at Gigerenzer's frequentism:

> The relation of correspondence or similarity between events, we reasoned, is largely independent of their frequency. Consequently, the base rates of outcomes are likely to have little impact on predictions that are based primarily on similarity or representativeness. We have used the term base-rate neglect to

describe situations in which a base rate that is known to the subject, at least approximately, is ignored or significantly underweighted. We tested this hypothesis in several experimental paradigms. Gigerenzer's critique of base-rate neglect focuses on a particular design, in which base-rate information is explicitly provided and experimentally manipulated.

Remarkably, they argue against Gigerenzer's request for formal definitions of heuristics like representativeness or availability, saying:

> This objection misses the point that representativeness (like similarity) can be assessed experimentally; hence it need not be defined a priori. Testing the hypothesis that probability judgments are mediated by representativeness does not require a theoretical model of either concept.

I am not quite sure how one can experimentally test a concept that has not been formalized in any meaningful way beforehand, but I digress.

Unless I misunderstand them, they appear to affirm Gigerenzer's critique of subjectivity as though it were the point of their experimentation:

> The heuristic analysis only assumes that the latter is used to assess the former and not vice versa. In the outcome-ranking paradigm, representativeness is defined operationally by the subjects' ranking, which is compared to an independent ranking of the same outcomes by their probability. These rankings of the outcomes rely, of course, on subjects' understanding of the term's probability, similarity, or representativeness. This is a general characteristic of research in perception and judgment: studies of loudness, fairness, or confidence all rest on the meaning that subjects attach to these attributes, not on the experimenter's theoretical model.

It is unclear to me how anything could be meaningfully said about human intuition given this approach. Moreover, this response appears to confirm Gigerenzer's claimed reification of individualism within psychology following the probabilistic revolution (which K+T played a not insignificant role in perpetuating).

Perhaps Kahneman and Tversky (both now deceased) misunderstood, or else did not fully appreciate, Gigerenzer's argument for a frequentist view of probability when they claimed that:

> The refusal to apply the concept of probability to unique events is a philosophical position that has some following among statisticians, but it is not generally shared by the public. Some weather forecasters, for instance, make probabilistic predictions (e.g., there is 50% chance of rain on Sunday), and the sports pages commonly discuss the chances of competitors in a variety of unique contests. Although lay people are often reluctant to express their degree of belief by a number, they readily make comparative statements (e.g., Brown is more likely than Green to win the party's nomination), which refer to unique events and are therefore meaningless to a radical frequentist.

Gigerenzer argued strenuously that the mind appears to cohere with frequentist ideas of probability and statistical judgment and is thus capable of automatically understanding the difference between single-events and frequencies, and as such, can provide appropriate judgments. K+T's argumentum ad populum does little to fortify their position, here.

Similarly, their closing remarks do little to deter the reader from sympathizing with Gigerenzer's critique. They protest the fact that Gigerenzer attributes unmade assumptions to them ("that judgmental heuristics are independent of content and context") even though Gigerenzer doesn't claim that they believe this explicitly, rather that this error arises through the application of their theoretical framework. (It is conceivable that a scientist might misunderstand the nature of his own work.) "There is less psychological substance to his disagreement with our position than meets the eye," K+T declare, as though Gigerenzer didn't begin his critique by grounding it in philosophy. The "terminological question," as the duo puts it, while not the entire substance of the debate is nonetheless critical to Gigerenzer's view; for all Kahneman and Tversky's bluster that the German ignores inconvenient data, they never even attempted an objective formulation of concepts like "error" and "bias." It isn't a concern for their program, and they were not willing to investigate the possibility that it could be.

Having summarized this disagreement I must disclose that it is far from a complete overview; after all, I am not a subject matter expert. Nor is this essay the appropriate place for a full examination of the matter. I have provided as thorough an overview of the researchers in question, their individual views, and the nature of their conflict as is necessary for broaching the larger issue I aim to present.

It is not necessary to get lost in the details, as we only need to demonstrate the paradigmatic differences between the two. I broadly agree with Gerd Gigerenzer's critique of the "heuristics and biases" program and seek to use his criticism as a means for drawing out the metaphysical differences between Gigerenzer and Kahneman even further. An exchange of empirical proofs may in fact support one view or the other (though I admit to finding Gigerenzer's experimental proofs convincing), but it is not empirical proofs which concern me. I am concerned by the a priori psychological commitments which inform the scientific process as carried out by researchers like Daniel Kahneman and Amos Tversky, who, while far from the worst offenders, are nonetheless influential and thus worthy of critique.

Technique and "Technical Logic"

Having competently discussed their differences, perhaps we ought to change gears and highlight points of agreement. Gigerenzer and Kahneman are both interested in decision-making. Both researchers understand the importance of intuition to our general psychological makeup, and both seek to improve man's capacity for judgment by exploring the processes through which he arrives upon these judgments. Perhaps most importantly of all, they both see a tension operating inside this phenomenon. The critical point of departure arises here, as the two differ wildly in locating that tension. For Gigerenzer, that tension occurs between man and his surroundings, while for Kahneman it takes place between man's left ear and his right.

Kahneman's psychology is akin to Freudian thinking in the way that it posits an essential self-denying opposition at work in the mind. Accepted as artful metaphors, "system 1" and "system 2" (like Freud's id, ego, and superego) do conjure a specific picture of the mind—and a seductive one at that—but as Gigerenzer himself points out, K+T's image of the mind ultimately lacks meaningful explanatory power. What Kahneman and Tversky do achieve, however, is a reification of observed cognitive processes which are then pathologized (again, not unlike certain Freudian concepts). This betrays an inappropriately individualistic and atomized view of cognition and the social sciences that I believe is both self-imposed and self-refuting. Whatever the virtues of the heuristics and biases research program may have been (it certainly generated a lot of novel academic work), the practical benefits are difficult to see amidst the fog of prejudice.

So, if I am correct in assuming that it is prejudice which explains K+T's failure to deliver a comprehensive picture of man's cognitive processes, the question which must necessarily be asked is this: what is the nature of this prejudice? Extrapolating from K+T's maximizing perspective on human cognition, one which ruthlessly scours the mind in search of flaws like a computer performing a virus scan, we get an image of efficiency not unlike the one presented to us by Jacques Ellul. I will soon direct your attention to Ellul's notion of "technique," but for the moment, let us take a broader view of Kahneman's work.

There is a curious overlap between 1) those who emphasize the fundamentally flawed nature of humans and human cognition; 2) those who want to transcend biological consciousness; and 3) those who want to censor human consciousness (the true dark triad of pathological personality types).

We call such people technocrats. A critical reading of *Thinking, Fast & Slow* offers a glimpse into this cross-section, for Daniel Kahneman belongs to that rare class of blissfully transparent social theorists whose work allows us to peer back at him, rather than simply analyze ourselves. Taking into consideration his social theoretical doctrine, his patronizing support of libertarian paternalism,[101] his career working in the IDF, and his close relations to figures like Cass Sunstein (e.g., adopting

---

[101] Kahneman, *Thinking, Fast &* Slow, 411.

his rhetorical language, endorsing his "nudge" policy,[102] etc.) it appears that Kahneman's allegiance (as is true for the rest of his ilk) is to the technocracy, the managerial state, and the censorship regime.

Because we are Humans (i.e., logically inconsistent and therefore rationally incoherent), and not "Econs," who are the model of logical coherency and consistency (Sunstein's dichotomy of rational actors), it is only proper that we subject ourselves to the Econs' program of "choice architecture" and staff of "nudge units." After all, it's for our own good.

(As a brief aside, upon seeing the political ramifications of K+T's social theory it should be easier for the reader to accept critical aspects of Gigerenzer's critique, as Kahneman's prejudices are more obvious when viewed through the lens of public policy.)

Cass Sunstein, as I have written about in both *AE* and *UCT*, uses this social doctrine to justify waging his own information war against Americans who fail to accept the waning legitimacy of liberal democracy and its open society (goals which, one can only presume, Kahneman himself considered noble and therefore shared). Sunstein is motivated in no small part by Americans' increased skepticism of Israel, which his essay on conspiracy theories (co-authored by Catholic legal scholar Adrian Vermeule) clearly demonstrates. Hopefully you see how this is no longer a mere academic dispute, but a matter of grave political consequence. Econs, as representatives of Ellulian technique and practitioners of technical logic, are themselves the predators which Kahneman warns Humans need defend themselves against.

What began as a misunderstanding (i.e., the difference between mistakes of social organization and mistakes of human psychology) is now, in truth, a humanitarian and civil rights crisis, as countless millions of Americans (indeed, humans the world over) are psychologically manipulated and politically persecuted so that Econs may pave the way toward a technological utopia. Understanding this, I believe now is the time to delve further into the meanings of technique and of technical logic.

The major issue with Kahneman's work (and by extension the work of technocratically minded scientists) is neither its psychological

---

[102] Ibid., 412.

accuracy nor its scientific validity, as I hope these last few paragraphs have demonstrated. Kahneman, like every other scientist before or since, holds certain metaphysical commitments which distort his science. In this case, Kahneman and his technocratic colleagues take their presuppositional marching orders from the metaphysics of technique, Jacques Ellul's term for the ethic of efficiency which was once locked within the domain of productivity but has now colonized all fields of human endeavoring. And so, to complement the human logic of Dr. Gerd Gigerenzer, we may now present Dr. Kahneman's technical logic (but not without first explaining what Ellul meant by technique).

Of all the supposed evils in the world (capitalism, Marxism, colonialism, fascism, atheism, etc.), it is remarkable that technique should emerge as a philosophical concept so late in the game despite predating and even serving as the impetus for a great number of these other presumed evils. What critics claim to hate about the rapaciousness of capitalist economics, or the soullessness of ideology, is true tenfold of technique in its purest form, so Ellul tells us. In fact, it was the increased prestige of and reliance upon technique which made these other social phenomena possible to begin with.

Like the work of Marshall McLuhan (who in his own way emphasized the need to look past the machine itself to understand the meaning of technology), Ellul places the emphasis not on technology (or the machine), but the process generative of technology—a process which he calls technique. Technique replaces everything with itself, allowing all things to be bent to the will of efficient progress alone. Of course, on the way toward mass spiritual enslavement (a process several centuries in the making), technique offers us all manner of liberation from the horrors of our natural and social confines. Air conditioning, birth control, high-speed internet, the electric guitar, penicillin, the super-sized double cheeseburger—all gifts to man bequeathed by the ascent of technique and of the technological society.

It is easy to understand the appeal of this, Ellul says himself in *The Technological Society*, and as such, those who find this arrangement disagreeable tend to make themselves enemies of the whole species—such is the seductive persuasion of technique. Within the realm of production (which is now rather vast), technique's ever-refining efficiency yields outstanding results to the approval of most. Where it falters, we tend to look the other way.

This is not to suggest that no one has ever run afoul of technique before, rather that technique (and its consequences) has differed throughout history, and therefore played a smaller (or less transparent) role in human dissatisfaction. It is only following the eighteenth century, Ellul argues, that technique takes on a life of its own. In prior historical epochs, technique served masters other than itself—often with wildly differing results.

The difference between technology (or the machine) and technique is the difference between manual activity and intellectual activity, insofar as the latter precedes the former. Technical progress often awaits the precise historical circumstances with which it may be converted into a material reality (a fact which speaks to its essentially non-economic character). Ecologist and philosopher Chad Haag describes technique in the following way:

> Productivity is not the purpose of technique, as technique also generates destruction (consider the hydrogen bomb). Technique can be understood as teleology plus method, where technical forms replace spontaneous forms to better facilitate efficiency and adaptability.[103]

Through this process, the particular is made into a universal, the unconscious is brought to consciousness, and ultimately, embodied intuition transforms into disembodied rationality. Technique is therefore the desacralized, acivilizational, and homogenized expression of human creative prowess, premised on 1) objectivity; 2) principles of self-development and self-augmentation; 3) monism, as in the singularity and unimpeachability of technique (and therefore, its uses); 4) co-extensivity, or centralization of technique(s); and 5) autonomy, as in the promulgation of an expert class to administer technical matters ultimately to the detriment of society itself (i.e., technocrats).

Consider the problems of 1) cratering birth rates; 2) the proliferation of novel sexual identities; and 3) the collapse of romantic love and

---

[103] Haag, "Philosophy of Jacques Ellul."

sexuality, which in fact all arise due to our ever-expanding technological society. Intimate social relations have declined mightily due to the proliferation of technique, as people no longer meet and respond to one another as men and women, but instead as practitioners of rational and autonomous technical self-augmentation. Instead of family formation, men and women (under the thrall of technical logic) pursue those things which more effectively satisfy their lustful desires. Though human sexuality, too, is a "domain of production," man is no machine. Supplanting the human logic of social relations with technical logic leads to an overrefinement of the population—the result of which, as we can clearly see, could only have ever been demographic collapse.

Of all the purported causes for the ongoing fertility crisis—and there are many—the root cause is fundamentally metaphysical, which is why the paradigm of technique is unsustainable: it operates at the deepest levels affecting human psychology: the existential. Men and women do need access to affordable housing, health and childcare, time away from work, and so on (that is if they aspire to parenthood); however, what they need even more is liberation from technique and the oppressive psychology it imposes upon them by virtue of its invisible and ubiquitous nature.

Technical solutions may only compound problems, especially if those problems are rooted in the uncritical application of technical logic. Ellul himself defined technique as the "totality of methods rationally arrived at and having absolute efficiency (for a given stage of development) in every field of human activity."[104]

The technological society which emerges from this process is rife with division and iconoclasm, as the proliferation of technique renders all non-technical forms of life illegitimate. This was not true of prior eras, as technique was demonstrably restricted to philosophical aims (as with the Greeks), social aims (as with the Romans), and religious aims (during the Medieval period), thereby preventing technique from freeing itself and running amok. This remained as such even through the seventeenth century, Ellul claims, following the Protestant reformation (though it would not persist for much longer).

---

[104] Ellul, *Technological Society*, 25.

The discovery of technique as a discrete transformative power was delayed, unsurprisingly, by the inability of the emergent technocratic order to see past itself. Consider Max Weber and his famous assertion that "the Protestant work ethic" drove capitalist success and excess. Ellul argued the contrary, claiming instead that the centuries which followed the Protestant reformation were in critical ways less technical, as evidenced by the tendency for scientific treatises of the time to be "open-ended reflections" rather than formalized technical tracts. If this sublimated religious paradox was in fact active in a significant way, then we would have seen large-scale technical systematizing emerge as a result. This was not so, Ellul tells us.

Interestingly, such errors demonstrate a common tendency among social theorists of the nineteenth and early twentieth centuries: the commitment to a kind of Type II metaphysical error. For Weber, the roots of modern industrial society were to be found in Protestant theology, while others (as we shall see in a moment) sought differing metaphysical grounds on which to base modern man's destructive conduct. Despite Ellul's contributions, the same prejudice persists to this day.

Ludwig Klages, the influential German psychologist, once made a similar error when he declared:

> It is monstrous folly to suppose that the civilized man of today is of the same material as man during the periods of the Caesars or of a St. Catharine, St. Cecilia or St. Lidwina, when one glance at the condensations of consciousness in buildings, pictures, and costumes could teach us that the mankind of heathen temples and festivals, of Gothic cathedrals and glowing twilights, of pomp of robes and sounding organs is finished, and has given way to a generation which manifests itself in the Stock Exchange, Wireless, Aeroplane, Telephone, Cinematograph, factories, poison gases, instruments of precision, and newspapers.
>
> The pilgrim's path has its stations, which end at Golgotha, and similarly the path of Spirit in European man has its main chapters, which may be headed as follows: war of body and soul—decorporization of the soul, or condemnation of joy, or paralysis of creative force—extinction of the soul in body, or blinding of intuition, or, the body machine—man as the instrument of the

will to power—in place of the soul, soul mimicry, the phantom, or Mask. But, if it should seem altogether too strange that a mere mental discipline should strike at the germ-cell and should, as generations succeed one another, produce new varieties, then it must be remembered that Spirit, if not consciousness, is a metaphysical power—that each new change of mankind is accompanied by changes in economic conditions which make servants of former masters, and produce a bloodless and gradual extinction of all who cannot adapt themselves to this new mode—and finally, that the selection is aided and completed by simultaneous intervention of most ruthless force.

We only mention the slaughter of the Knights Templar, Stedings, Hussites, etc., the Inquisition with its burning of witches and Auto-da-fe, a St. Bartholomew's night, the horrible religious wars, not to speak of the French Revolution. Such feasts of death are biological necessities, and are chiefly directed against those who embody and will not relinquish old substances.[105]

Klages is correct to identify the distinctly metaphysical ailment responsible for modern man's ceaseless suffering, however he errs by applying his private prejudices to the unveiling of the culprit (opting instead to revive the ancient rivalry with Spirit vis-à-vis Nietzsche). This is in fact a common error made by thinkers willing to confront the metaphysical dimensions of human misery; often we will hear how Christianity, universalism, or Gnosticism (as examples) are the root cause of decline and decay. Klages certainly gets nearer than most when he bemoans the effects of Spirit on man and as well upon his generative capacities. When he describes the declining state of man and of human innovation, which nevertheless bedazzles the soul, enslaving him, he is similarly speaking to the phenomenon which Ellul has termed technique, that being the formalized consciousness of efficient development (and subsequent enslavement by it). For Klages, our present circumstances share continuity with the great woes of human history, while for Ellul, the

---

[105] Klages, *Science of Character*, 172.

emergence of our technological society is discontinuous with the deep past (having only emerged in the last few hundred years).

While this is a slight tangent, it is worth taking a detour to correct Klage's error on the way to correcting the larger Type II metaphysical error. Carl Jung, the Swiss psychiatrist (and contemporary of Klages) saw Spirit differently:

> It seems to me, frankly, that former ages did not exaggerate, that the spirit has not sloughed off its demonisms, and that mankind, because of its scientific and technological development, has in increasing measure delivered itself over to the danger of possession. True, the archetype of the spirit is capable of working for good as well as for evil, but it depends upon man's free—i.e., conscious—decision, whether the good also will be perverted into something satanic.[106]

Spirit (or mind, intellect, consciousness, the metaphysical, etc.), while not the operating force responsible for elevating technique, is nevertheless the medium by which technique enters human affairs. Jung, in my view, corrects Klages' error, though his contribution does not shed further light on the genesis of technique or the technological society itself. For that, we must return to Ellul himself.

Having spoken at length about Ellulian technique, let us say a few words about its cognitive apparatus: technical logic.

Technical logic is the cognitive style endemic to technocrats, and the rival of intuition (human logic); it is the medium through which technique perpetuates itself, using humans like fungible midwives for the realization of a perfectly technical world. Whereas human logic is temporal and local, technical logic is neither bound to a single individual or community nor a given epoch. Fundamentally desacralizing, technical logic denatures its object, making it more like itself (as is true, broadly, of technique as such).

Human logic is spontaneous, improvisational, and associative, while technical logic is iterative, clinical, and tightly regimented. Technical

---

[106] Jung, *Archetypes*, 253.

logic is ends-oriented while human logic is means-based. Human logic is contemplative and profound, while technical logic is total and uncompromising. Technical logic is defined, as well, by its uniformity and strict coherence, and as such is "the proper yardstick for deductive arguments that concern the truth of propositions, such as in a mathematical proof," as Dr. Gigerenzer says, but utterly inappropriate when applied to the social and natural realms. Coherency and consistency are the ruling orders of technical logic, which seeks to apply the same uniform approach to all social and natural problems it attempts a solution for.

Practitioners of technical logic naturally find uncertainty, ambiguity, and multi-facetedness psychologically intolerable, and in fact, the inability to ward away these demons with technical thinking is, for them, a source of tremendous stress. Technical logicians prefer automated solutions because, in most cases, they are rather shallow and incurious people. Or rather, their curiosity is reserved for entirely conceptual and abstract matters. Time spent reflecting on the nature of something (or someone) else is wasteful and inefficient. In this way, technical logicians are among the most prejudicial of all, for they operate under a strict mandate of conformity (that is, conformity to technique and its attendant logical apparatuses).

Parochialism is their bane, just as novelty is their muse. Technical logic requires a strong egoic force to house it, for cognitive apparatuses such as this can only function in a blinkered, confined environment. For technical logic to be operative, it must ignore or dismiss "complicated data" (e.g., social facts which highlight technical logic's limitations). This requires an untrammeled ego so strong it borders on the psychopathic. Technical logicians are, as a result, typified by a certain kind of urgency, or nervous restlessness. Not the restlessness of youth, for example, eager to test itself against the challenges of life. Nor, even, the urgency of the ego, which senses the finite nature of existence and wishes to declare itself before time runs out. By this kind of urgency or restlessness, I mean something closer to that of an addict, or of a man desperately running to escape an assailant.

For the technical logician, the human condition far too closely resembles a prison. This antagonism does not arise purely from psychological conditions, nor from mere adherence to technical logic (although, like Tolkien's ring, uninterrupted use will corrupt); rather, this condition of mind is primarily a biological condition—that is, a typological condition. I will elaborate this further in the following section.

There is no satisfying technical logic, for the parameters given to human life are always insufficient. Technical logic, as with technique proper, constantly seeks new horizons and new territories to overtake. Old ways of doing things (i.e. traditions) crumble in the face of technique and technical logic (unlike its pre-modern equivalent, magic, which Ellul says is definitionally temporal and therefore bound to a people and a place). Magic, or rather, the particularist logical understandings of specific people-groups, die when they do, unlike technique, which lives on even after separating from the bodies which propagated it. Technical logic is the cognitive means by which embodied knowledge loses its particularity and temporality, for it constantly seeks to strip knowledge of its embeddedness by formalizing and replicating it.

The explosion of technique and technical logic arose, as has already been noted, during the eighteenth century, though Ellul refrains from telling us why. During this period, governmentality all around the world broadly moved in a scientific, centralized, and more technical direction, so it is plausible that technique formalized out of necessity. Social democracy and mass society were made possible by the kinds of things (i.e., individualism, materialism) that technique also drew its strength from. While this is not the place for further speculation, it is worth noting that Robin Robertson wrote a fantastic book about mathematics and psychology which, if read from an Ellulian point of view, accomplishes much in illuminating the question of technique's liberation.[107]

His book analyzes the relationship between mathematics, logic, and consciousness, culminating in a discussion of Carl Jung and Kurt Godel. Newly emerging possibilities of self-concept have, throughout history, played a role in expanding man's mastery over the world; Robertson traces the changes of mind which may very well have contributed

---

[107] Robertson, *Jungian Archetypes*.

to the present-day rule by technique. If nothing else, it is a highly satisfying work to read.

Psychology of a Twenty-First-Century Technocrat

At this time, it must be said that Jacques Ellul himself thought the reign of technique would be so complete that in the future, there would no longer be an interest in decision-making, for the procession of technique required only technicians, not thinkers. The technological society of the future would have no need for it, or so he predicted (bear in mind that Ellul's book first appeared in the mid-1950s).

This has proven not to be the case, for not only did the "probabilistic revolution" of the twentieth century completely change the direction of the social sciences (psychology chief among them), but the ongoing experiment McLuhan called "the global village" has similarly demonstrated Ellul's error: thirty years of internet access have only intensified the interest in decision-making. In fact, mankind has seemingly never been more invested in the magic of human cognition (mostly for occultic purposes). Even though the public's enthusiasm for tech-optimism has waned, there have never been more well-to-do technocrats walking around, dreaming up ever more novel ways of technologically abasing the psyche.

Perhaps it is worth pondering the reason why Ellul's prophecy failed to come true. It may well be that the thousand-year Reich of technique was declared too early, for while technique may function as though it does not need mankind, in truth it *does*. The political reality of technique, such as it is, requires a stable human regime to give it life. Technique's only weakness appears to be this fallibility of human regimes, for its true limits are identical to the political and psychological limits of its chief technicians. Politically, its limits are defined by how adroitly human regimes can wield technique against enemies, and whether they can hoard this strength, keeping it safely out of distance from potential rivals. Psychologically, its limits are identical to the strengths and weaknesses of its individual practitioner's constitution.

Cthulhu does not swim left; rather, it is untrammeled technique and technical logic which drags us into biological irrelevancy. Political formulations abound to justify this arrangement, though the general trend has been anti-human for some time. Our contemporary formulation, however, is distinguished by its nervousness; twenty-first-century technocrats are an anxious bunch, terrified by the prospect of having to govern. So let us say a few things about the psychology of the technocrat, and of his strengths and his weaknesses, so that we may better understand not just the allure of technique, but the allure of the technocrat, whose hypnotic rhetoric and high esteem still hold sway over the ruled.

As to the typology of the technocrat, Carl Jung is once again highly instructive. In his *Archetypes and the Collective Unconscious*, Dr. Jung elaborates on a historical figure—that of the archetypal trickster—whose essential characteristics vividly call to mind the twenty-first century's technocratic types. Of this type he says:

> A curious combination of typical trickster motifs can be found in the alchemical figure of Mercurius; for instance, his fondness for sly jokes and malicious pranks, his powers as a shape shifter, his dual nature, half animal, half divine, his exposure to all kinds of tortures, and—last but not least—his approximation to the figure of a savior. These qualities make Mercurius seem like a daemonic being resurrected from primitive times, older even than the Greek Hermes. His rogueries relate him in some measure to various figures met with in folklore and universally known in fairytales: Tom Thumb, Stupid Hans, or the buffoon-like Hanswurst, who is an altogether negative hero and manages to achieve through his stupidity what others fail to accomplish with their best efforts.[108]

Considering Jung's description, who comes to mind?

For me it was people like Mark Zuckerberg, Bill Gates, and Steve Jobs; specifically, I recalled a segment Alex Jones of *InfoWars* used to do where he would mock "globalist technocrat demons like Bill Gates" for their inoffensive outfits, their sweaters and socks, and their glasses,

---

[108] Jung, *Archetypes*, 255.

pantomiming their body language by affecting an effete posture and prancing behind the desk of his home studio. Especially in the world of social media (where we know the managerial class deliberately uses their power to demobilize demographic groups they feel threatened by), Jung's attribution of maliciousness rings true. The buffoonishness of a Gates or even a Warren Buffett, who present as unassuming while feverishly working behind closed doors to radically restructure economies and ecologies the world over, rushed immediately into my awareness. Even Elon Musk, a veritable hero to some these days, bears shades of the trickster with his cloyingly sentimental and self-effacing mannerisms, as well as his juvenile humor.

Remarkably, consider the folk heuristic used in conspiracy theory circles about "lizard people." Jung himself highlights the half-animal aspect of the trickster, a charge which fits all too neatly. Alex Jones also used to describe technocrats as "interdimensional vampires," speaking to Jung's identification of the trickster with divinity. Even if only superficially, the contemporary technocrat harkens back to an ancient type.

Interestingly, I did not think of a Henry Ford or Howard Hughes type. WEF came to mind, not the 1964 World's Fair. Technocrats of the twentieth century do strike us as characteristically different from the ones still delivering Ted Talks today. As Klages said, it is difficult to imagine these two types as consisting of the same material. Something has changed, but what? Earlier I suggested that the essential psychology of the creator has not changed, but rather only regressed. Today's technocrat is lost to his shadow, to borrow another Jungian coinage, and this darkness is made evident whenever he (or she) articulates his worldview. I shall elaborate this more fully, but for now, let us first heed Dr. Jung's words.

Returning again to the archetypal trickster, Jung shares the following:

> His universality is co-extensive, so to speak, with that of shamanism, to which, as we know, the whole phenomenology of spiritualism belongs. There is something of the trickster in the character of the shaman and medicine man, for he, too, often plays

malicious jokes on people, only to fall victim in his turn to the vengeance of those whom he has injured.[109]

The trickster is connected, therefore, to the shaman and the magician, an association that often finds itself expressed today via the technocrat's interest in occultism. Technocrats turn inward, hoping to call upon the mind's psychic energy, a practice which often drives them to megalomania. Especially amongst today's ruling technocratic elite, savior complexes run rampant. Shamans live on the edge of consciousness, and as a result possess the power of life over death. Today's technocratic elite oscillate between harassing the peasants and exalting the transformational power of their technology to solve intractable political conflicts. They want to save the human species nearly as much as they wish to destroy it.

Jung later says:

> He is a forerunner of the savior, and, like him, God, man, and animal at once. He is both subhuman and superhuman, a bestial and divine being, whose chief and most alarming characteristic is his unconsciousness. His original nature is as a creator. . . .
> According to the old view, Mercurius is duplex, i.e., he is himself an antithesis. Mercurius or Hermes is a magician and God of magicians. As Hermes Trismegistus he is the patriarch of alchemy. His magician's wand, the caduceus, is entwined by two snakes. The same attribute distinguishes Asklepios, the God of physicians.[110]

The trickster archetype is psychologically given to mania and grandiosity, a formula from which the technocrat has always drawn his strength. But, as we have said, modern day technocrats are distinguished by their shadow psychology which dictates their every action. We ought to think of technocrats as belonging to the collaborator class. A quick pop culture reference point: think of the shadowy Syndicate from the X-Files. While not a perfect analogy, as Chris Carter's (creator

---

[109] Ibid., 256.
[110] Ibid., 263–264, 311.

of the X-Files) Syndicate were a true power-elite, as opposed to today's mostly surplus class of actually existing technocrats, in other respects, the analogy holds water, for the psychological basis for their conduct is rooted in fear and awe. It is appropriate to call them "envious elites" or "insecure elites," for their naked power lusting leaves them vulnerable to the energy of naturally stronger and more impressive competitors. Hence, we say they operate from within the psychological shadows.

In a stricter sense, Jung's shadow refers more to psychic unconsciousness, a condition wherein the unacceptable aspects of the personality are forced out of awareness. Though they are not immediately accessible to the mind, they nonetheless drive much of human behavior. It is my view that the fixation on technological progress and technical solutions—to the exclusion of introspective, contemplative, or otherwise psychic means—is further proof of the hypothesis I have put forth here. That which is unacceptable to the individual technocrat himself is thusly projected onto the whole of the human species, a condition which only furthers their genocidally utopian zeal.

Technocrats conform to the shadow-magician archetype, for the technocrat's favored mode of communication is deception. Naturally this implies self-deception, as well, since the technocrat must first be able to fool him/herself about the truth of technique and man's relation to it. Of this archetype, Jungian analyst Robert Moore says:

> The energies of the magician archetype, wherever and whenever we encounter them, are twofold. The magician is the knower and he is the master of technology. Furthermore, the man who is guided by the power of the magician is able to fulfill these magician functions in part by his use of ritual initiatory process. The human magician is always an initiate himself, and one of his tasks is to initiate others.[111]

In its immature masculine form ("the know-it-all"), the trickster,

---

[111] Moore and Gillette, *King, Warrior, Magician, Lover*, 98.

plays tricks, of a more or less serious nature, in one's own life and on others. He is expert at creating appearances, and then "selling" us on those appearances. He seduces people into believing him, and then he pulls the rug out from under them. He gets us to believe in him, to trust him, and then betrays us and laughs at our misery. He leads us to a paradise in the jungle, only to serve us a feast of cyanide. He's always looking for a sucker. He is the practical joker, adept at making fools of us. He is a manipulator.[112]

Elizabeth Holmes, the disgraced fraudster behind fake blood-testing company Theranos, fits this description rather aptly. Furthermore, the know-it-all,

is that aspect of the trickster in a boy or man that enjoys intimidating others . . . He wants [others] to understand that he is more intelligent than they are . . . he is verbally abusive of others, characteristically smug, and often wears a cocky grin.[113]

Again, Yuval Noah Harari comes to mind. But this could just as easily describe any member of the contemporary technocratic class. Of this shadow aspect, Moore says:

Mastery over nature, a proper function of the Magician, is running amuck, and with incalculable results that we are already beginning to feel. Behind the propaganda ministries, the controlled press briefings, the censored news, and the artificially orchestrated political rallies lies the face of the magician as manipulator.[114]

Interestingly, Moore makes the connection for us between the archetype of the magician and those belonging to the class of technocrats by highlighting the propensity for control and domination through

---

[112] Ibid., 28.
[113] Ibid., 29.
[114] Ibid., 111.

technical means (e.g., controlled briefings, censored news, orchestrated political rallies). Moore goes on to say:

> The shadow magician is not only detached, he is also cruel. His interest is not in initiating others by graduated degrees—degrees that they can integrate and handle—into better, happier, and more fulfilled lives. Rather, the manipulator maneuvers people by withholding from them information they may need for their own well-being.[115]

Does this not sound familiar? Does it not strike us as like the various social media tycoons, Silicon Valley gurus, and Ted Talk technocrats whom we have come to know so well? The magician feels a certain sense of election based on his natural virtues, but upon being initiated into the technocratic class, this perception expands into complete delusions of grandeur. Technocrats, as modern-day manifestations of the magician/trickster archetype, excel in precisely this kind of self-absorption.

Now that we have a profile of the technocrat, as well as an understanding of technique itself, what can be done? How can we restore not only our sciences, but our societies?

According to Ellul, the solution to the riddle of technique is found through contemplation and self-awareness, but also through the assertion of a discrete teleology (one which does not subordinate man to the will of technique). "The magician in his fullness," as Robet Moore and Douglas Gillette term it, is one such man capable of carrying that torch (thereby making him the natural rival of the technocrat-trickster, even more so than the man of action whom they allege to be the main source of envy for the trickster-magician).

"The magician in his fullness" presents himself only by stepping out of the shadows, thereby achieving psychological integration, and with it, mastery over his vast psychic power. Technique, as in teleology + method, must no longer be posited as its own reason for being. A rival

---

[115] Ibid.

vision is necessary to disrupt the present culture of creation. So too are rival visionaries.

V

PAUL BLOOM'S RACIST BABIES

DISPROVING THE SCIENCE OF RACIAL EQUALITARIANISM BY CRITIQUING PAUL BLOOM'S LAUDED 2013 PUBLICATION *JUST BABIES: THE ORIGINS OF GOOD AND EVIL*

Ethnoscience as Information Warfare

In its original usage, ethnoscience refers to particularist and tribal methods or techniques of knowledge and power. Reifying the myth of the noble savage, this paradigm nonetheless struck at the heart of an emerging problem: the disintegration of liberal authority and its institutions. A critical discourse at its height, the concept of ethnoscience has since been pacified by integration into the hegemonic neoliberal paradigm.

In my view, this idea did bring about much worthwhile discussion even if its inherently political orientation made it worthy of some derision. I do believe that different groups have different experiences of the world and therefore possess unique understandings and aptitudes. That an individual, having already been acculturated to the paradigms of his people, struggles to assimilate into the folkways of another is simple to understand. People are different and they always have been.

There are other uses of this concept which could bring it back into relevance, thus returning it to its critical beginnings. I am not proposing a dramatic reinterpretation of the concept, merely uncovering a yet unrealized potential application. First, we must affirm the core element of the concept: that all people-groups possess some way of practicing knowledge and power. To put it more precisely (and with greater relevance for this discussion): all people-groups have a manner in which they approach the scientific method, or at the least, some formalized ritual for the discovery or application of power-knowledge. There is more to say on this point, but for now I would like to broaden our perspective.

Earlier in this book (and in previous writings), I have spoken about ethno-metanarratives and their social consequences. By ethno-metanarrative, I mean the narrative or ethical framework of a given people, itself the result of biological and existential impositions made upon said peoples. By "social consequences," I mean the negative externalities of in-group psychosocial mores (as in, their influence on members and institutions of outgroups). I gave the example of Karl Popper to demonstrate how ethno-metanarratives can influence individuals and their work, arguing that his *Open Society and Its Enemies* was not a proper analytical text but rather a sophistic plea for supreme power, showing how ethnic pride often wears the mask of noble social theorizing.

It takes great patience and practice in hermeneutical thinking (or at the least, a gruff disposition) to read a text against its intention and read between the lines presented if one is to understand the text within the text—that is, the author's unconscious or unspoken commitments. Certain threads suddenly emerge that, even if only pulled slightly, immediately spill out with dark secrets.

Uncovering the text within the text can change (though in most cases, *fully realize*) the message presented in bare words. Authors bring a certain character to bear on their writings, whether they intend it or not, and as a result they bring a whole color and life which infuses, or in other cases supersedes, their meaning. Since authors come from communities of other people and possess a history and an inheritance, their writings often come to represent a certain broader and more general tendency or even *will*, which may not always immediately avail itself in a single work (or even a collection of works).

One requires a text of texts to take the necessary step back from an individual piece of writing and apply a critical hermeneutic. That text of texts includes an understanding of the relevant knowledge-domains expressed in the texts, but also an understanding of the context which produces a given work. This is to avoid the risk of taking a given piece of work at face value—that is, to treat a text and its author as faithfully expressing their positions, or goals, as well as their reasons for wanting to express them. This also allows us to avoid making the mistake of assuming the author himself or herself in fact possesses a self-understanding which could articulate all of this in the first place (this is not always the case, even amongst gifted and intelligent writers).

Back to this idea of a work of writing having a character. It would be accurate to describe Charles Darwin as having belonged to a particular milieu and moment, of having a certain perspective which informed his writings. We can easily understand Darwin as being characteristically English in his scientific proceedings. Similarly, one thinks of the transcendentalists like Emerson or Thoreau, or the pragmatists like William James as being particularly American, and more importantly, *Old* American. We understand that it matters who these writers were, where they came from, and what they may have aspired for their writings to accomplish. Their lives were defined, in large part, by their respective ethno-metanarratives (said differently, the mythic self-concepts of a people).

It would be difficult, a challenge at least, to understand Paul Bloom's *Just Babies: The Origins of Good and Evil* any other way than through the method I have just laid out, for his work is so insular and self-referential, as in, designed so as to not invite too fine an inspection into its inner workings, while at the same time adorning itself with paralogical flairs which nevertheless call attention to itself. We should understand in advance that Paul Bloom is Jewish, and as we will see, brings a unique and existential perspective to bear on the question of moral psychology. This is not some harebrained antisemitic interpretation, for early and often Bloom draws parallels to—and bases the justification of his appeals upon—an explicitly particular experience and understanding of history.

Drawing upon his laboratory findings, Dr. Bloom's book asks whether infants have a moral consciousness, and if so, when it first emerges. This investigation is undertaken, seemingly, for the purpose of discovering the origins of (and a solution to) racism. From the point of view of contemporary equalitarian liberalism, this may in fact be a worthwhile investigation to undertake. But from a less servile point of view, the premise is loaded with so many dubious assumptions and constructs as to raise serious questions about the nature or even utility of the investigation. Bloom's investigation specifically suffers from its reliance on dubious social science constructs, though we are already getting ahead of ourselves.

Paul Bloom's work demonstrates itself to be an ethnoscience by virtue of how it reveals the inner workings of its author, rather than anything factual about the external reality which we all participate in. Bloom is like Freud in this regard—not to give Freud short shrift, for his contributions *did* in fact open a new and legitimate conceptual discourse; in the case of Paul Bloom, his book *Just Babies* tells us more about the life and style of a certain kind of middle-upper class Jewish professional than it does the development of moral thinking in infants and adolescents.

So, it is with this view in mind that I wish to launch into a critique of his work, laying my prejudices and priors at the outset with the hope that by sharing my framework, I am at least doing something to illuminate the associations and perhaps even leaps of logic which may appear unjustifiable otherwise. It is a very against the grain reading which I propose here, but in an age of critique there is in fact only one type of inquiry which is not sacralized by mainstream acceptance, and that is criticism of Jewish expertise. Surely, as public figures, their participation in (theoretically) transparent social affairs permits us a say in the matter. Besides, it is America. And after all, considering we live in a climate where racial critiques are quite commonplace, and depending on circumstance or political alignment *encouraged* (e.g., Sino-skeptic sentiment following Covid-19, Russo-skeptic sentiment following the war in 2022, Arab-skeptic sentiment following 9/11, Euro-skeptic sentiment following 1945, and so on), then it is only right to turn our critical eyes towards wherever truth directs them.

Critical to the understanding of *ethnoscience* as will be presented in this essay, is the notion that a given ethnos may use science and scientific knowledge to achieve some ends (typically to cultivate power). This means that we account for the presence of certain social tendencies like cynicism, deception, ignorance, misrepresentation, and so on, and may even anticipate them when analyzing a text. The suspicion directed at Western forms of knowledge (e.g., Big Science), while not undue, has grown impotent over time. There still remain other social powers which have thus far eluded criticism.

And it's not that any sentiment drives this inquiry, least of all a hateful one, for that which has brought me to make this critique is far simpler and plainer than that. Bloom's book is terrible in ways that I had not thought possible from a celebrated Ivy League intellectual. Its core premise is incoherent; the logical arguments deployed in service of its premise are unintelligible; the historical examples called upon to justify his inquiry don't even rise to the level of speciousness; and the blending of personal prejudice with objective science occurs with such frequency as to muddle the entire conversation altogether. What Bloom ultimately provides, in my view, is a clear depiction of Jewish misunderstanding-ness (that is, the will to ignorance). This is, in fact, a significant contribution, as I feel an entire field of scholarly work could be opened simply for the purpose of mining similar contributions by thinkers and writers made since the dawn of the post-war era.

We are awash in a sea of *anti*-knowledge: information which in fact *impairs* cognitive function. In a literate and technological society such as our own, such a development ought to be considered catastrophic, for the entire enterprise of free thought is thereby imperiled. Owing to this, differentiation is necessary if we are to distinguish knowledge from anti-knowledge. Consider this essay as one such attempt to make this needed distinction.

Just Racist Babies

One of Bloom's intellectual hobby horses has been demonstrating that man's predilection for moral discernment is not only baked into the cake, but is also apparent in the behavior of infants as young as the age of one.

A proponent of rationality who has critiqued Jonathan Haidt's work on social intuition in other publications,[116] Bloom argues for the active and constructive process by which even the very young may come to their moral judgments. His laboratory work has demonstrated that

---

[116] Pizarro and Bloom, "intelligence of the moral intuitions."

infants as young as three, six, and ten months old evaluate others based on their social behavior toward third parties,[117] and in the process upset the applecart of Piagetian developmental thought which had previously shown that more taxing cognitive efforts (such as demonstrated by Bloom's babies) only appeared much later during their development. His interest in the subject matter—the presence of so-called "moral" cognitive functioning in early infancy—is summarized best in the following statement Bloom published in an essay for *The New York Times*:

> Socialization is critically important. But this is not because babies and young children lack a sense of right and wrong; it's because the sense of right and wrong that they naturally possess diverges in important ways from what we adults would want it to be.[118]

The natural moral inclination of the young "diverges in important ways" from the desires of adults. An innocuous statement? Perhaps not, although the time is not yet right to enter this portion of the investigation. But clearly, Dr. Bloom wants to understand the ways in which this moral faculty can go wrong.

Questing for a "naive morality," as Bloom says in the same *New York Times* article, is dangerous, for "the existence of a universal moral code is a highly controversial claim; there is considerable evidence for wide variation from society to society."

He does concede the universality of basic moral concepts on the premise that they cohere with the logic of natural selection. Certain functions of the mind, such as compassion, altruism, and empathy, while not strictly moral, nonetheless appear to be innate (again, due to their accord with a certain interpretation of Darwinian theory).

While Bloom struggles to define morality, he argues that "the notion at the core of any mature morality is that of impartiality," an appeal he makes on philosophical grounds, not scientific ones. It is this first unjustified leap which fells Bloom's project. Further in the same article, Bloom says:

---

[117] Hamlin et al., "Three-month-olds show"; Hamlin et al., "Social evaluation."
[118] Bloom, "Moral Life of Babies."

The morality of contemporary humans really does outstrip what evolution could possibly have endowed us with; moral actions are often of a sort that have no plausible relation to our reproductive success and don't appear to be accidental byproducts of evolved adaptations. We possess abstract moral notions of equality and freedom for all. It makes sense to marvel at the extent of our moral insight and to reject the notion that it can be explained in the language of natural selection.

Because very young children—under the age of one—demonstrate kin preference (as opposed to high altruism), we must acknowledge the essentially evolutionary basis for our moral senses. Quoting Richard Dawkins, Bloom is quick to emphasize that biological nature offers no aid to an equalitarian philosophy of life. According to Bloom, we are born to be parochial (a lower morality), but somehow through cultural transmission (Bloom does not even attempt any kind of explanation for the claim), a higher sense which aspires toward an "enlightened morality—one in which all beings capable of reason and suffering are on an equal footing, where all people are equal" emerges, which we should use to "override our parochial impulses."

His 2013 publication *Just Babies: The Origins of Good and Evil* offers an overelaborated version of the case presented above, which can be summarized as follows: how can we justify changing the folk moral psychology of the very young so that we may bring them into conformity with the consensus?

Now, I have used heavily sardonic language here, admittedly, so it is worth addressing the premise at face value. Are there good reasons for correcting bad habits, whether "moral" or otherwise? Naturally, the answer is yes. Is there a formalized set of rules with which the young must be introduced so that they may integrate into society? Also yes. Do we observe the early emergence of tendencies we might discipline harshly if they were observed in an adult? Yes. And should they be addressed in a formal manner? Yes.

Imagine that you were yourself having this debate with a disagreeable other: surely at this point there would be some tension between the two of you, for the other may likely feel as though you've pushed an indulgence too far. The fact of the inquiry itself seemingly cannot be impugned, so why push the matter further?

Here we see, in microcosmic form, the difficulty posed by falsely presumed homogeneity. Any suspicion discourse must first overcome the most important hurdle of all, the apathy or even hostility, of its rival interlocutors. Our concept of an ethnoscience presumes difference *prima facie*, though it is of no value to us now as mere words on a page. Presently, American culture is dominated by skepticism and legitimate paranoia, so in at least one sense, the difficulty posed in raising the question can be mediated by a given zeitgeist. Hoping to be born under more favorable circumstances is no good replacement for actual understanding and strategizing, however. To large degree, any justification given for doubting the motives of a credentialed expert are about as warmly received as justifications for the existence of bigfoot, even during times of hyperpolarization, for people simply dig their heels deeper (or more perversely) into already accepted authorities. So really, the problem merely becomes more tedious as individuals grasp more cloyingly to less and less rational ways of thinking and are far more prone to hysterical outbursts. The assumed gain of "raising consciousness" or "participating in free speech" neglects the phenomenological experience of the individual, who even in today's period of commoditized conspiratorialism by and large struggles silently until a braver person comes into view.

The social element is ultimately the liberating factor, not the information element. Certainly, you need both, but raw data alone does not move consciousness.

So, returning to the question at hand: why push further? What is the reason, effectively, for presuming malice? The simple and rational answer is because the wrong people might take charge of educating and disciplining the young. For our case, the answer is because the author's work is self-discrediting once read critically. Of course this is an argument from hindsight, for we are already familiar with the subject matter, and so that is not helpful for those who are uninitiated. The simple answer, while effective, only raises a further question: why would someone want to do that? (To which the natural reply is, "Because they want to hurt you.")

It is common, even this far into a fair and rational conversation, for the rival interlocutor to continue denying our premise (e.g., that it is worthwhile to read against expertise's grain); really what is needed is an emotionally stirring rebuttal which opens the door to inquiry. During my time as an adjunct, I would show a segment from *60 Minutes* which featured Dr. Paul Bloom and his research on infant morality in which he discussed the very same ideas I have summarized here.

A brief segment, I used it to supplement my lectures on human development. Without fail, the reaction of my students was a mix of curiosity and horror. Curiosity, because by and large none of my students had ever considered a six-month-old child as experiencing anything resembling moral qualia before, and horror, because they were mortified by the thought of objectifying and, in a way, responsibilizing a newborn child. This is to say nothing of the terrifying political ramifications of such research, a subject which also came up because I had shown my students this video (and to which we will return by the close of this essay).

Everywhere I taught, the campus demographics were highly diverse, and so I present this bit of anecdotal evidence with a sense of its generalizability. People of all ages, races, and religions reliably responded in only those two ways, often both at the same time. Which brings us back to the question at hand: how do you burst the bubble of opposition? As I learned from my students, you accomplish this by observing and affirming the (seemingly) superficial revulsions spontaneously provoked by unjustifiable invasiveness. The kinds of revulsions that would be studied by social scientists, eager to popularize a novel paralogical solution to the problems posed by folk psychology.

The very nature of this inquiry is to incriminate the young and still-forming, and to conscript them into the ideological paranoias of their parents and teachers. Does this mean that there is no utility in developing measurements of cognition—even moral cognition—of the very young? The fine line between true knowledge and true power is never well-defined; it's no wonder that so many miss it.

Here we arrive upon one of the earliest conceptual problems with Bloom's work, which is his blending of the social and the moral, treating the elements of mind which detect pattern and difference (as well as show preference for the familiar) as having a superordinate moral dimension to them. If the observed functions are not moral functions of the mind, then they are social functions—or perhaps more accurately, survival functions—and as such there would be no challenge to one's integrity for inquiring into them. There would also, importantly, be no *casus belli* for Bloom either, for there would no longer be any relation between the native dimensions of psychology which he seeks to problematize and the social stigmas he (and the rest of liberal society) considers to be so odious, i.e. racism and anti-Semitism.

Now if it could be demonstrated that these functions *did* hold a distinctly moral dimension (Bloom would first have to operationalize his definition of morality, which he hasn't), and that they *were* malleable through culture (Bloom would have to admit of the mechanisms by which this is achieved, which he doesn't), then there would be serious moral questions about the ramifications of engineering a new "morality" into the minds of very young children.

A more subtle—and ugly—problem now emerges, for while I have been slowly making my case against Bloom and his hypothesis, I must admit that in fact I do agree with a great deal of his hypothesis. Upon filling in some of the details myself, I can agree with the claim that we are born cognitively prefigured and that through medicine, social institutions, and media, we can alter the cognitive functions of the young (of people of all ages, in fact). The problem with affirming all of this is that it amounts to a tacit endorsement of mass scale psychological trauma and brain damage as a means for solving intractable political conflicts. And as I hope to make evident by the end of this essay, Bloom seems to approve of this entirely, so long as no one attempts an articulation of the finer details.

But this, too, is still all inside baseball. Let's bring back our rival interlocutor, what does he have to say? Is it useful and good to study moral cognition in infants or not?

If it could be said that the research would not be conducted in pursuit of better social engineering, then yes, all is fair in scientific research. But then again, that is not the point of the social sciences, particularly not in a technological and democratic society such as ours. So once more we come up against a reason to doubt the intentions of Paul Bloom (and his ilk). The manner of consensus science (or "Big Science") is to separate and instrumentalize all life, and to make life a supplicant to technological power. But there is an alternative power in the folk intuition which says life, especially the life of the very young, is something precious, and that the truth of the world is that it looks to take from young life as early and as often as possible.

And so having provided at least some defense to the skeptically minded person, let us turn to Paul Bloom and his book *Just Babies: The Origins of Good and Evil*, and figure out just what precisely is going on. I have selected several excerpts from his book to aid us in our dissection, and the mode of our inquiry shall more closely take the form of an interrogation.

On the Origin of Good and Evil in Infancy

> I read in the newspaper this morning about a man whose girlfriend broke off the relationship; he later stalked her and threw acid at her face. I remember, as a child, first hearing about the holocaust, of gas chambers and sadistic doctors and children being turned into soap and lampshades. If our wondrous kindness is evidence for God, is our capacity for great evil proof of the Devil?[119]

Man's capacity for magnanimity and malevolence is well documented, and so it is perfectly understandable that a natural curiosity as to the source of man's behavior would persist throughout the ages. The problem with the direction that this inquiry has taken over the last century or less is that it isn't actually interested in any universal concept of humanity, dignity, or morality, and it certainly isn't interested in any kind of eusocial engineering. Hence my notion of an ethnoscience.

Disciplines like psychology have become, in the decades since the emergence of the postwar consensus, an intelligence operation in service of the Jewish intelligentsia. Ethnoscience, as it was dreamt up in the 1960s, amounted to a kind of "science of the native," with the intention being to elevate the epistemology of non-industrialized and non-technological societies. It was concerned with the traditional ways of knowing, we might say. But a critical ethnoscience which examines

---

[119] Bloom, *Just Babies*, 2.

Jewish epistemology and Jewish notions of persuasion reveals that theirs is not a way of knowing, but a way of *undermining* the knowing of others. It is about the appropriation of social forms for the advancement of the Jewish people. Consider the following excerpt in this light, taken again from Paul Bloom:

> We are by nature indifferent, even hostile, to strangers; we are prone towards parochialism and bigotry. Some of our instinctive, emotional responses, most notably disgust, spur us to do terrible things, including acts of genocide. In the penultimate chapter, I show how an appreciation of the moral natures of babies can ground a new perspective on the moral psychology of adults, one that takes seriously our natural propensity to divide the world into family versus friends versus strangers. And I end by exploring how we have come to transcend the morality we were born with—our imagination, our compassion, and especially our intelligence give rise to more insight and moral progress and make us more than just babies.[120]

While it is not immediately apparent from this excerpt (I will slowly tease out the inadequacies of Bloom's ethnologic over the remainder of this essay), Bloom implicitly associates the psychological, sociological, and evolutionary characteristics of the family with persecutory hatred of the other, the unfamiliar. This, for Bloom, comprises the sum of his interest in the question of "morality." (That he opens his book with a discussion of the holocaust tips his hand more than a little bit.)

> What I am proposing, though, is that certain moral foundations are not acquired through learning. They do not come from the mother's knee, or from school or church; they are instead the products of biological evolution.[121]

This poses another strong problem for his program, for Bloom presumes that social dysfunction emerges due to certain cognitive

---

[120] Ibid., 6.
[121] Ibid., 8.

processes—processes which Bloom, as an evolutionary thinker, must assume exist for a critical purpose. His faulty presumption, as we will see, gives us good motivation for doubting this line of research, casting doubt ultimately on whether it is necessary at all.

Bloom struggles greatly with the idea of morality. Though he is certain that our evolutionarily informed parochialism is bigoted (thus immoral and therefore wrong), he nevertheless spends several meandering and non-clarifying pages laboring over what may or may not constitute "moral." Consider the following excerpts:

> What about "morality"? Even moral philosophers don't agree about what morality really is, and many non-philosophers don't like to use the word at all. When I've told people what this book is about, more than one has responded with, "I don't believe in morality." Someone once told me—and I'm not sure that she was joking—that morality is nothing more than rules about whom you can and can't have sex with. Arguments about terminology are boring; people could use words however they please. But what I mean by morality—what I am interested in exploring, whatever one calls it—includes a lot more than just restrictions on sexual behavior.[122]

It isn't clear what the scientific or philosophical value is in such an approach; if no one agrees on what the definition of morality is, and furthermore, some people don't even like using the word, then what is even the purpose in undertaking a moral investigation? Can it even be done? How can there be any moral content or criterion when we are so ambivalent about the concept itself? "Arguments about terminology are boring"—is this some attempt to curry favor with the reader? People come to experts for answers, not to be spun around like a dreidel. Arguments about terminology are crucial, in fact, for without a common basis for understanding, there can be no further attempt at knowledge. We may pursue our own individual and ever-evolving, solipsistic—and ultimately sophistic—understandings, but they cannot be considered

---

[122] Ibid., 9.

legitimate contributions to an objective or universally valid understanding. Which then raises the question: what reason is there to engage in science if not to further understanding?

> Hitting someone is a very basic moral violation. Indeed, the philosopher and legal scholar John Mikhail has suggested that the act of intentionally striking someone without their permission—battery is the legal term—is a special immediate badness that all humans respond to. Here is a good candidate for a moral rule that transcends space and time: if you punch someone in the face, you better have a damn good reason for it.[123]

Let's turn this around on our dear author: if you try to rewrite someone's psychological makeup so that they no longer value their biologically extended kin, you better have a damn good reason for it. But is there ever any reason to do so? Considering Paul Bloom's multiple references to the holocaust, it would appear that his reason has nothing to do with science, philosophy, or the universal process of learning and understanding, but racial violence against Jews.

> Here is a simple example: a car full of teenagers drive slowly past an elderly woman on her way to get to a bus stop. One of the teenagers leans out the window and slaps the woman, knocking her down. They drive away laughing. Unless you are a psychopath, you will feel that the teenagers did something wrong. There are other, less direct, moral violations. The teenagers might have thrown a brick at the woman. Or they might have purposely sideswiped her car, damaging it; this would harm her, even if she wasn't there to witness it. They might've killed her dog. They might have gotten roaring drunk and hit her with their car by mistake—this would be wrong, even if they had no malicious intent, because they should've known better. . . .
> For other types of moral wrongs, the issue of harm is not as clear cut. Think about: bestiality, breaking a promise to a dead

---

[123] Ibid., 10.

person, defacing the national flag, sexual contact with a sleeping child (unharmed and never learned about it), incest between consenting adult siblings, consensual cannibalism (person A wishes to be eaten by person B after he dies, and person B obliges). Now some of these activities may actually be harmful . . . but in many of these cases it's clear that nobody, in a concrete sense, is actually worse off.[124]

Bloom's moral confusion is fully transparent here, placing his judgment on worse than shaky ground. Frankly, such paralogical tendencies ought to disqualify someone from any position of higher learning. The victim and the perpetrator of bestiality are both demeaned by the act, perhaps even traumatized. Patriots are worse off for seeing their symbols of national pride disrespected. It is difficult to imagine any *real* situation where sexual abuse of a minor occurred and *didn't* harm the victim. The family of the incestuous siblings, perhaps even their close friends might be made "worse off" by the revelation of their affair. And while person A technically *desires* to be eaten, and not prematurely mind you, person B (and his or her relatives) are certainly not better off for having been made party to the experience.

Curiously, one wonders why such an effort would be made to undermine a normative notion of morality, why one would seek to equivocate so much between man's many moral challenges, only to then assert the non-negotiable status of racism and anti-Semitism, particularly when Bloom acknowledges that such faux pas were never historically problematic, rather they only recently became so. If they persisted all this time, then surely this was for reasons owing to evolutionary selection pressures. What changed, in evolutionary terms, to make this no longer the case? Dr. Bloom gives us no inkling.

If you think of evolution solely in terms of "survival of the fittest" or "nature red in tooth and claw" then [moral] universals cannot be part of our natures. Since Darwin, though, we've come to see that evolution is far more subtle than a Malthusian struggle for

---

[124] Ibid., 10, 12.

existence. We now understand how the amoral force of natural selection might have instilled within us some of the foundation for moral thought and moral action.[125]

And yet, Dr. Bloom gives us reason to believe otherwise. Citing the work of anthropologist Richard Shweder, Bloom provides a self-contradicting list of things considered morally neutral, laudable, or appalling, depending on the observed society (e.g., masturbation, homosexuality, sexual abstinence, polygamy, abortion, circumcision, corporal punishment, capital punishment, Islam, Christianity, Judaism, etc.), which despite the diversity of material and opinion, he claims, nevertheless points to the existence of certain moral universals. But the only way to know for sure is to "study the minds of babies."[126]

Using a looking-time methodology to measure habituation—as in the length of time an infant will hold his or her gaze on an object before looking away—researchers can gain insight into the mental processes of the very young.[127] The longer an infant maintains its gaze on an object, the more stimulating or interesting the infant finds it. Citing the thought of psychologist Alison Gopnik, because infants are not able to maintain 'effortful control' (i.e., they cannot internally moderate their responses to external stimuli), research methods based on 'looking-time' methods are therefore highly effective at providing us a glimpse into the minds of the very young.[128] This style of research was pioneered by researchers like the Swiss psychologist Jean Piaget who used it to itemize the "naive physics" of human infancy. Using this looking-time research method, Karen Wynn found that not only do infants understand the physics of rudimentary objects just as adults do, but that they are capable of simple arithmetic, too. Bloom details these findings:

> In a classic study, Karen Wynn found that babies can also do rudimentary math with objects. The demonstration is simple. Show a baby an empty stage. Raise a screen in the middle of the

---

[125] Ibid., 16.
[126] Ibid., 18.
[127] Ibid., 20.
[128] Ibid., 21.

stage. Put a Mickey Mouse doll behind the screen. Then put another Mickey Mouse doll behind the screen. Now drop the screen. Adults expect two dolls, and so do five-months-old; if the screen drops to reveal one or three dolls, the babies look longer than they do if the screen drops to reveal two.[129]

These same methods were then used to uncover the naive psychology of early infancy. Bloom describes the logic behind this innovation:

> We've known that babies respond in a special way to other people. They are drawn to them. They like the sound of human voices, particularly those they are familiar with; they like the look of human faces. And they are disturbed when interactions don't go the way they expect. Here's how to freak out a baby: sit across from the baby, engage with him or her, and then suddenly become still. If this goes on for more than a few seconds, with you looking all corpselike, the baby will become upset. In one study, two-month-olds were seated across from a TV screen displaying their mother. When the mother interacted with the babies by means of real-time videoconferencing, babies enjoyed it. But when there was a time delay of a few seconds, the babies became agitated.
>
> The psychologist Amanda Woodward designed a looking-time study to demonstrate that babies know that individuals have goals. First, a baby was placed in front of two objects and watched a hand reach for one of these objects. Then experimenters reversed the objects' locations. Babies expected that when the hand reached again, it should go for the same object, not the same location. This expectation was special to hands; if they saw a metal claw reaching for the object, the result went away.
>
> In another set of studies, the psychologists Kristine Onishi and Renee Baillargeon showed that 15-month-olds can anticipate a person's behavior on the basis of his or her false belief. Babies watched as an adult looked at an object in one box, then

---

[129] Ibid., 22.

observed the object moved to another box while the adult's eyes were covered. Later on, they expected the adult to reach into the original box, not the box that actually contained the object. This is a sophisticated psychological inference, the sort of rich understanding of other minds that most psychologists used to believe only four and five-year-olds were capable of. Early in life, then, we are social animals, with a foundational appreciation of the minds of others.[130]

Bloom's team switched from using looking-time measures to reaching measures on the basis that the latter are better suited for determining what babies themselves prefer. Using three-dimensional geometrical objects (as infants are often unwilling to approach strangers), a helper or a hinderer either aided in pushing a ball up hill or pushing it down; the helper and hinderer were then placed on a tray near the infant to see which it would reach for. Bloom and his team found that, in accordance with their expectations, infants between the ages of six and ten months unanimously reached for the helper. Subsequent iterations of the experiment included a third neutral individual, with the findings turning out just as unanimous: infants reached for the helper over the neutral individual (as well as the neutral individual over the hinderer). When the experiment was conducted again, this time examining the cognition of three-month-olds (swapping out the reaching method for a looking-direction method, with the direction of the infants' gaze being used as a proxy for preference), the results were very much identical.

A follow-up study of three-month-olds was conducted, this time with different results. Returning once more to the looking-time methodology, Bloom and his team found that three-month-olds looked longer at the neutral figure than the hinderer, but did not favor the helper over the neutral figure, thereby confirming in infants the presence of a phenomenon often observed in adults: the negativity bias (man's tendency to focus on "the bad" over "the good").[131]

Bloom concludes from his research that the philosophers of the Scottish Enlightenment (like Adam Smith and David Hume) were

---

[130] Ibid., 24.
[131] Ibid., 29.

correct: rather than being born angels (or devils), we are born with a certain aptitude or capacity to distinguish between "good and bad, kindness and cruelty."[132]

In Bloom's view, not all moral intuitions are biologically rooted, nor are all our biologically rooted moral intuitions worth holding on to. To this point, in his quest to uncover the secret of human morality, Bloom ultimately reveals his progressive liberal priors, declaring that "It's just wrong to establish an inequity when you don't have to."[133] Now this is neither a scientifically nor a philosophically justified position, and furthermore, Bloom doesn't even attempt a logical justification: the best he offers are *ad populum* appeals, such as, "Most everyone agrees that a just society promotes equality among its citizens, but blood is spilled over what sort of equality is morally preferable: equality of opportunity or equality of outcome."[134]

The pursuit of equalitarianism, and along with it, the crusades against racism and anti-Semitism, are by Bloom's own admission recent developments. Presumably he would say that this occurred because of certain cultural interventions though he not only doesn't explain what those may have been, but also fails to detail the kinds of cultural interventions that would be necessary to carry his psychological discoveries out of the laboratory and into the courtrooms and classrooms. Nonetheless, he feels damn strongly about the matter, saying, "Some people are the world to us, and others hardly matter at all. We'll see that it's part of our nature to make such distinctions—even babies do it. But we can also rebel against our parochial biases."[135]

But why should we want to rebel against the winning intelligence of evolutionary selection pressures? Over the last half-century or more, we have given license to this desire and now, all civilized society is going up in smoke. Why should we persist? It is at this point where a legitimate justification is needed that Bloom, rather than providing his own accounting, punts. Though Bloom doesn't have his own explanations, he does have decontextualized and half-assed appeals to biblical and

---

[132] Ibid., 31.
[133] Ibid., 59.
[134] Ibid., 60.
[135] Ibid., 101.

philosophical logic. We see this clearly in the excerpt provided below, where after sharing the parable of the Good Samaritan Bloom says:

> The moral of the story isn't hard to figure out. The Samaritans were despised by the Jews, which might be why the lawyer didn't just answer, "the Samaritan"—he couldn't bear to say the name. Plainly, then, what we have here is an injunction to ignore traditional ethnic boundaries. As the philosopher and legal scholar Jeremy Waldron puts it, "Never mind ethnicity, community, or traditional categories of neighbor-ness"—the point of the story is that the mere presence of the stranger makes him a neighbor and thus worthy of love.[136]

While I don't personally take issue when someone appeals to their religious faith for, shall we say, "extralegal" justifications—as in a leap in logical accounting not otherwise substantiated materially—Bloom's attempts appear to function as a crutch, holding up the shambling and shoddily assorted pieces of evidence, if only limply so. This is made worse with knowledge of Bloom's other works: he famously argued for the "religion-as-accident" theory earlier in his career; if religiosity is just a psychological fluke of evolutionary selection pressures, why should Bloom's readers accept this biblical appeal since he not only isn't a believer, but considers belief of this kind to be categorically illegitimate? Such conduct ought to merit immediate discrediting, for it goes beyond mere bad science (which could be explained through negligence), into ethnoscience (as in the cynical use of the scientific method for ethno-teleological ends).

And then there are bizarre statements like, "Any adequate theory of moral psychology has to explain both our antipathy towards strangers and how we sometimes manage to overcome it."[137]

While it is true that we would want an accurate accounting of all social phenomena, the central relation Bloom creates between morality and out-group ethics is scientifically unjustifiable. Bloom has a particular interest in the relationship between psychology and ethics that he

---

[136] Ibid., 102.
[137] Ibid., 104.

wants to imbed, or covertly introduce into, the idea of morality. And then he wants to cast that into early infancy to justify, one can only assume, a more exacting social engineering program of equalitarianism. Several times over the course of the work, Bloom makes inappropriate reference to the holocaust (the only other example of racial conflict provided was that of the conflict in Rwanda), making another unjustifiable association, this time between the folk psychology of kinship and the specific persecution of Jewish peoples during the twentieth century. This doesn't even have anything to do with science, and furthermore, reads as the pained and contorted post hoc justifications of an ethnic partisan.

Morality is, in Darwinian terms, man's evolved sensibility or capacity for discernment which helps him to succeed in life. But because this function did not come with a philosemitic ethical subprogram, it apparently poses a grave scientific—and ultimately, political—problem to all of us. The problem as Bloom sees it, if I haven't made it clear, is that due to our evolutionarily derived features, we are all potential Hitlers (even as infants).

Another example of Bloom's paralogical ethnoscience, this time referencing a study which demonstrated three-day-old infants' preferences for the sound of their mother's voice, is as follows:

> Since babies can't know ahead of time what their mom looks like or smells like or sounds like, these preferences must be due to learning: babies see and smell and hear this woman who has been caring for them, and this is who they come to prefer.[138]

Bloom's argument befuddles more than it illuminates. Never mind the research which shows the various ways in which newborn infants "prefer" their mothers (including tests of smell using the mother's breast pad) which could hardly be described as an acquired or learned preference, an unnecessary dialectic is imposed between the innate and the acquired, for it is both technically more accurate as well as parsimonious to acknowledge that the voice preference is a consequence of the

---

[138] Ibid., 104.

child's embeddedness within the mother; the mother's body is the context in which the child's learning takes place, just as the mother's body is also the reason for or means with which the child's learning faculties even came into existence.

They (mother and child) are one and the same, and so by uncovering the "flaw" in Bloom's logic we in fact discover a technique of Jewish ethnoscience, which is the artificing of a dialectic to drive the investigation in a predetermined direction. Bloom is slowly building the case for an anti-racist disciplinary science which, though he does not come right out and say it, is necessitated by the evolutionary fact of psychosocial kinship. Bloom's preoccupation with the specter of German persecution seeps into his writing repeatedly, revealing the opaque intention behind his investigation: never again.

Perhaps there is a place for this kind of writing in the world, but that place is not within the realm of scientific inquiry (which is why I designate inquiries like Bloom's as "ethnoscience": it is an attempted prosecution of the hegemonic ethno-metanarrative of Jewish life).

Several times, Bloom veers dangerously close to outright condemning newborn infants as little Hitlers-in-the-making, before finding a way out (one which manages to keep the inquiry on course to its intended destination):

> Babies also share with adults a tendency to look longer at what they like, and we can use this to explore their preferences. It turns out that babies who are raised by a woman look longer at women; those raised by a man look longer at men. Caucasian babies like to look at Caucasian faces, as opposed to African or Chinese faces; Ethiopian babies prefer to look at Ethiopian faces rather than Caucasian faces; Chinese babies prefer to look at Chinese faces rather than Caucasian or African faces. If you saw these biases in adults, you might assume that they reflected a preference for others of their own race. But this isn't likely true for babies. They don't often look into mirrors, and they wouldn't understand what they were seeing if they did. Instead, babies are developing a preference based on the people they see around them. Consistent with this, babies raised in ethnically, diverse environments—such as Ethiopian babies living in Israel—show

no preference on the basis of race.

Racist views get elaborated in the course of development, but the seeds of racism are there from the very start, in a simple preference for the familiar.[139]

Bloom appears to act out the Principal Skinner internet meme (*"No, it's the children who are wrong!"*) before grabbing the intellectual life preserver which will find him sparing little Timmy and tiny Jane from an unavoidable fate as awful, racist, antisemites. I'll share that excerpt next, but before doing so it is worth examining the argument Bloom has presented here more closely.

The apparent preference for one's own race observed in infants is not racial as such, because "infants don't often look into mirrors, and they wouldn't understand what they were seeing if they did." This is a non sequitur, and an obvious one at that. Here we see a second technique of Jewish ethnoscience, which is the implementation of a non sequitur at a critical point in the process of delivering an argument, such as when a hard claim is made and thus requires substantiation. Or, when an incontrovertible truth must be paved over with sophistry. Very young infants would also fail to understand themselves as sexed beings, according to Bloom's argument. Would he then attempt to deconstruct the idea of biological sex? An infant looking at his image in the mirror would similarly lack a concept of being a human—does that invalidate our notion of the human being? Bloom regresses into paralogical thought whenever he needs to finesse the argument, as evidenced above. Infants are capable of perceiving *differences*, of which race is one category by which we designate the differences between various people-groups. It is not necessary for an infant to have a conceptualization of this at first, for as Bloom himself notes, this comes later.

His statement about Ethiopians in Israel is also very odd, especially considering that Israel is infamous around the world for the well-observed mistreatment of its African-Jewish population. Bloom provides neither context nor citation for this claim, or any other made in the book—not a problem for me personally, though the absence is suspicious—and so statements such as this really fail to corroborate Bloom's

---

[139] Ibid., 105–106.

argument except as an argument from authority (as in, "I'm an Ivy League academic who has published several books, accept my words.")

Dr. Bloom does find a way to exonerate the newborns of the world, however, as detailed in the following excerpt:

> In an influential article, the psychologists Robert Kurzban, John Tooby, and Lida Cosmides point out that there is something strange about the triad of age, sex, and race, [the three categories thought to be automatically parsed by humans]. The focus on sex and age makes sense—our ancestors would have needed to appreciate the difference between a man and a woman, or a three-year-old and a 27-year-old, in order to conduct any kind of social interaction, from procreation to childcare to warfare. But race is the odd man out. The physical cues that correspond to what we now see as races are determined by where people's ancestors came from, and since our ancestors traveled mostly by foot, the typical person would never have met anyone belonging to what we would now call "a different race." Kurzban and his colleagues conclude that attention to race per se could not have evolved through natural selection. Instead, they argued that race matters only and so far as a piggyback on coalition.[140]

Dr. Bloom continues, providing a further detailing of this "coalition theory":

> Race becomes important because in some societies people learn that skin color and certain body features indicate which of many conflicting groups an individual belongs to. This is much the same way that we might learn that different sports teams have different colored uniforms; there's nothing inherently interesting about the color of the uniforms—they matter because of what they signal. Racial bigotry develops, then, in much the same way as a child growing up in Boston will come to associate a Red Sox uniform with us and a Yankees uniform with them.[141]

---

[140] Ibid., 107.
[141] Ibid.

Here we see another non sequitur, as different people-groups have been in contact with one another—either via trade or war—for millennia. Literature on group differences comes down to us from the age of antiquity, with Aristotle being merely one such example. So, it appears less the case that Bloom wants to exonerate the young of their racism; instead, it seems as though he wants to reconstitute the factors which coalesce around race and replace it with "coalition theory." In Bloom's view, we unjustly misattribute characteristics to race, an illegitimate category (therefore we are not born racists), and, best of all, we can solve for this problem through better education and social engineering. The duty of moral psychology in Dr. Bloom's mind is, then, to discover how we can educate the young out of their sense of kinship through paramoral reeducation. Bloom attempts another explanation of this great error that our ancestors ignorantly fell into for so long:

> Now there may be other reasons why race is salient. For one thing, our hominid ancestors may have regularly encountered other hominid species. If so, we may well have evolved cognitive mechanisms to reason about these species and may then have applied this mode of reasoning to other human groups within our own species. This would explain our tendency to biologize race, sometimes thinking, incorrectly, of distinct human groups as if they were distinct species, rather than coalitions. Or our interest in race could get a boost as a byproduct of a general perceptual bias to favor the familiar—what is sometimes described as the "mere exposure" effect.
> Finally, a focus on race could be a byproduct of an evolved interest in who is and isn't family. Kin has always mattered; it makes perfect Darwinian sense to favor someone who looks like you, because that individual is likely to share more of your genes. Instead of being a proxy for coalition, then race could be a proxy for kinship.[142]

Bloom's hasbara-as-science attempts to explain away the reality of difference, and when that fails, he retreats into a tendency common among

---

[142] Ibid., 108.

modern psychologists, which is to view the essential operating functions of the mind as "faulty" and "biased." Oscillating between "well, our ancestors might have been wrong," to "well, perhaps we are wrong," Bloom never once acknowledges the basic assumption which supports the argument he is attempting to make. That assumption being, of course, that evolution is doing something wrong. Evolution has done something wrong by giving us reasons to be racist (which is why we need moral psychology to redress this mistake).

It's interesting to consider how it is that a concrete phenomenon, like race, could be a proxy for an abstract one, like coalition. We can observe the phenotypic markers which signify biological difference immediately, but this is not so for "coalition," which is really just a linguistic convention to describe the more generalized phenomenon by which human sorting occurs. How, at face value, could an individual assess meaningful difference (as in, life-and-death differences, the kind of things evolutionary processes would contextually function within) based on coalition theory? Comparing the phenotypic markers of biological difference to a sports jersey, for instance, is a very flimsy bit of equivocation for the contexts (and consequences) implied by each are hardly identical; the similarities are only superficial, and at the level of public education and policy, these differences wash out entirely. If anything, the causality is reversed: coalitions are the technologically and democratically bastardized imitations of primal and actual tribal differences (i.e., categories of ethnicity and race).

Undeterred, Bloom continues arguing his support for coalition theory:

> There is compelling support for the race-as-cue-to-coalition theory. To test their hypothesis, Kurzban and colleagues used a method known as the memory-confusion paradigm. Researchers give people a series of pictures of people's faces, each with a sentence attributed to that person. Later, researchers ask participants to recall who said what. Given enough picture/sentence pairs, participants inevitably make mistakes, and those mistakes reveal what characteristics we naturally encode as meaningful. Kurzban and his colleagues' memory-confusion study used pictures and statements by black and white people, but they added

a clever twist: sorting the people into two groups (with equal numbers of white and black people in each group) and dressing them in distinctly colored basketball jerseys. They found that participants still made mistakes based on race, misattributing statements like "I need to do some stretching" or "I just want to get out and play" but now when people got it wrong, they were most likely to do so based on jersey color, not skin color. To put this in real-world terms, a sports fan—at least when watching sports—is thinking more about team membership than about the skin color of the individual players. This way of making sense of race fits well with the work of the psychologists Felicia, Pratto and Jim Sidanius, who argue that societies form hierarchies based on three factors: age, sex, and a third variable category that is sometimes race, but may also be religion, ethnicity, clan, or any other social factor.[143]

It is odd to say that such an approach "helps make sense of race" when the whole enterprise appears to be premised on the deliberate confusion of consciousness. The presumption, as well, that the participants errors reveal what we "naturally encode as meaningful" perplexes the reader, but without proper context or citation readers cannot decipher the veracity from Bloom's text alone. Kurzban's 2008 publication on the memory-confusion study affirms that kinship is a fundamental social category[144] (kinship, in our view, merely being a synonym for race or racial proximity), but it his 2001 publication where Kurzban and his team point out that a "race-erased effect" is present in environments where other coalitional cues are available, such as sorting groups based on their outfit.[145]

All that this study demonstrates to me is that when an authority 1) attempts to impair an individual's reasoning capacities; and 2) arbitrarily institutes a new social sorting system, then the average person complies. Has race been erased? Well as Bloom points out, no. Participants still occasionally made their categorical determinations based on race,

---

[143] Ibid., 109.
[144] Lieberman et al., "family of fundamental."
[145] Kurzban et al., "Can race be erased?"

only less frequently than they would have if they were left unperturbed. What we observe is the human mind laboring to weigh its natural sorting mechanisms against the unwieldy and arbitrary demands of irrational equalitarians.

Consider this counterargument in light of the following excerpt: after discussing studies which demonstrate the emergence of racial biases by age six, Bloom shares this bit of evidence:

> [Some] studies find that children often favor peers of the same race and think that they are better people—but again this holds mostly in racially homogenous schools. When the studies are run in heterogeneous schools, children don't care about race. . . . Only later racial biases start to creep in, and only for children raised in certain environments. We might have natural biases to favor some groups over others, but apparently we are not natural born racists.[146]

As with the Kurzban studies, race apparently disappears under tightly controlled and highly propagandized social environments where a new social and moral order is imposed upon students and their families by extremist equalitarians (i.e., teachers, administrative faculty, political activists, policymakers, et cetera). So, the support for coalition theory is not found so much in its logical structure or empirical outcomes, but in the fact that powerful people with deep pockets can engineer social circumstances so that they accord with their own private, antisocial and anti-Darwinian prejudices.

Dr. Bloom continues his paralogical hasbara, enjoining us to follow along with him as he exhaustingly lists the reasons why race doesn't matter and doesn't represent a social or cognitive reality, but nonetheless must be eradicated because it is an unacceptable and evil non-phenomenon which drives people to commit genocide—mostly of Jews, or so Bloom intimates throughout the course of his short book:

> If coalition is what matters most, one wouldn't expect children to focus on skin color or any other physical feature. Rather, they

---

[146] Bloom, *Just Babies*, 113–114.

should pay attention to something that is uniquely human—language. Language is a superior indicator of coalition and group membership. Young babies can recognize the language that they have been exposed to, and they prefer it to other languages, even if it is spoken by a stranger. . . .
 What's more interesting, though, is that we see the same effect with accents. Babies preferred to look at a speaker without an accent, even if the speaker with an accent is perfectly comprehensible. This suggests that children's preferences are driven by some degree of cultural identification, conveyed via language, just as predicted by the coalitional theory.[147]

Why would coalition matter most? Because Dr. Bloom would like it to. What makes language a superior indicator of in-group belongingness? While this is a more plausible declaration, it remains a matter of opinion, nonetheless. Linguistic similarity does signal relatedness, however it is a trait or characteristic which can be acquired by non-members and, as we currently see unfolding across the United States, may be shared by individuals and groups who do not actually profess or partake in any greater identification with those they share the language with. While an infant would not have any cognizance of this, from the standpoint of logical coherency this makes no difference. If we wanted to demonstrate the primacy of coalition theory, we would look for those markers which most often, under the greatest number of constraints, signal authentic belongingness.

 I agree that children's preferences are partly driven by cultural identification; however, culture arises from groups of related individuals who participate in the same style of life and draw upon an essential and immutable unity. Coalitional theory does not give us any deeper insight into the nature of human social organization, just as it does not help us understand the individual's cognitive apparatus for social sorting. But Bloom's hasbara runs its course at this point, as he admits that none of the topics he has so tediously deliberated over are even necessary for forming a coalition. Coalitions, the great skeleton key of social

---

[147] Ibid., 110–111.

categorization, can apparently be conjured up arbitrarily by some other party by conjuring up artificial rivalries. Of this Dr. Bloom says:

> Neither race nor language is necessary to sort people into coalitions. There was a large body of research showing that it takes very little to make a coalition that really matters: to establish group loyalty, pit people against one another.[148]

Bloom dismisses the Israeli-Palestinian conflict as being too "long and complex" to aid us in understanding what divides people, perhaps because an examination into the Israeli-Palestinian conflict would implicate Israelis (and Jews more generally) in the same parochial and bigoted conduct as the rest of us. Dr. Bloom opts instead to point to the examples of Muzafer Sherif (a Turk) and Henri Tajfel (a Polish-Jew), a pair of social psychologists whose studies focused on uncovering the ways in which rivalries may be instigated where none had previously existed. Their research, among others conducted in the same vein, demonstrated what has come to be known as the minimal-group standard—that is, the absolute minimum of relevant social cues necessary for stimulating belongingness (and consequently, rivalry). By citing these studies, Bloom does his co-ethnics no favors here in helping them beat the stereotype of being self-interested and clannish interlopers.

This last bit, at least in my view, does major harm to Bloom's argument that "coalitions" are part of the core of human social categorization considering that they can be generated arbitrarily and don't even need to reflect actual social realities or dynamics. Especially when compared with race, which in addition to being composed of linguistic, cultural, and genetic markers, is easily and immediately identifiable to all. Race does what coalitions don't, which is permit us to make immediate and highly accurate intuitive judgments without requiring some special training, esoteric knowledge, or formal authority to adjudicate. So, what Dr. Bloom has really done is take us through a long and winding path of non-arguments which neither elucidate the problem at hand nor lend credence to the positions he attempts to stake, challenging us to

---

[148] Ibid., 115.

CHAPTER V

ask the question: what is the purpose of this book? What essential questions about human nature have been answered by this investigation? The purpose, if it hasn't been made clear yet, is to use the scientific method (in conjunction with the academic and mainstream press) to present an argument for anti-White equalitarian re-education. Bloom doesn't answer any of our burning questions, nor does he pose any interesting new ones. Instead, he is practicing the ethnoscience of psychology with the aim of furthering the political privilege of Jews around the world.

Bloom reminds us that coalitions cannot develop around socially meaningless distinctions, rather they develop based on the realistic generalizations we make about social groups. Dr. Bloom gives the example of writer David Berreby, whose book *Us and Them* opens by asking if it is appropriate to assume that a White adult walking down the street accompanied by a non-White child is the parent, but a non-White adult with a White child is the nanny. According to Bloom:

> [T]he answer might be yes if [Berreby] thought that this pattern had no exceptions—if the idea of a nonwhite adult being the parent of a white child was *impossible*. But Berreby knows full well that it is a generalization, not an absolute rule.[149]

Bloom, eager to provide another example of the potential falsity of reifying generalizations then states:

> One might notice that there are a lot of Jewish university professors. Jews make up between 1 and 2 percent of the total American population and 4 percent of the population in New Haven, Connecticut, the city where I live and teach. I haven't seen any statistics, but I can assure you the proportion of my colleagues who are Jewish is a lot higher than 4 percent.[150]

Another bizarre non sequitur from Paul Bloom. This excerpt only makes sense in the context of the one which follows, but what appears

---
[149] Ibid., 119.
[150] Ibid., 119–120.

obvious at this point (from a critical point of view, at least), is that Dr. Bloom once again wants to protect his people against the natural tendency of the mind to analyze groups, group behavior, and form critical judgments of them based on such observations. Perhaps if people took note of the population size of Jews and their transparent overrepresentation in positions of power, they might draw certain conclusions which politically privileged Jews might not like. Of our tendency to generalize, Dr. Bloom asks:

> So what's not to like? Well, one concern is moral. Even if stereotypes are accurate, it may sometimes be wrong to utilize them. The issues here are subtle: we are not morally bothered by *some* generalizations about people. We are comfortable with laws and policies that discriminate on the basis of age, for instance. This is because we are forced to do so (we can't let everybody drive); because the stereotypes are so clearly rooted in facts (four-year-olds are really too young to drive); because such policies apply to a slice of everyone's lifespan, not to a subset of the population, so they seem fair. Sooner or later, everyone will get his or her chance. As another example, life insurance companies are allowed to make generalizations based on whether a person smokes and how much here she weighs.
>
> But the use of stereotypes on gender, race, or ethnicity is more fraught. This is in part because it can cause suffering—even if the stereotypes are accurate, the costs that are borne by those discriminated against may outweigh the increased efficiency of the people doing the discriminating—and in part because it violates certain notions of fairness. But there are instances where it's just wrong to treat an individual on the basis of the group he or she belongs to; it's better to take the extra time.[151]

According to Paul Bloom, there is nothing scientifically or philosophically (that is, *logically*) wrong with the production or usage of generalizations; rather, the problem is a moral one. It is curious that Paul has

---

[151] Ibid., 122.

no problem using the "m" word here, when it concerns something that he personally cares about, for he has spent page after page problematizing the very notion of a universally binding morality.

Naturally we disagree: the issue is not moral, in fact, but ideological. Morality deals in the ontological difference between right and wrong, good and evil; ideology, on the other hand, deals with the handful of things any individual person may, themselves, arbitrarily consider to be unimpeachable. Bloom is an ideological equalitarian, so therefore the problem with generalizations is that 1) there is an unequal distribution of generalizations about the different people-groups and 2) there is an inequality in how the consequences of these generalizations affect relevant people-groups. So really, morality must be subordinated to ideology, the result of which is the subordination of natural human biology and psychology to the demands of tyrannical social engineers. Evolution shaped us to be efficient thinkers, but because this efficiency may lead us to come to (more or less) accurate judgments about certain legally protected (read: politically privileged) groups, we must abandon evolution altogether (says the alleged evolutionary scientist). To hell with Darwin!

But this isn't even the worst part. Consider the following excerpt:

> College students from North America and Europe may well be the least racist people in the world. Even when tested in the most anonymous of contexts, they tend to be diligently nonracist. In fact, race is a taboo for this population. Children don't start off seeing race as taboo [although] they [do] reach the point in development at which there is a psychic cost to even mentioning race. Indeed, social psychologists find that many of their overly non-prejudiced white research subjects experience a pressing anxiety about appearing racist when interacting with blacks.[152]

This really should be the silver bullet which stops the beating heart of Bloom's anti-racist reeducation dead. Bloom remarks on the fact that the pursuit of anti-racist equalitarianism has led to a circumstance

---

[152] Ibid., 124.

where young White men and women from all around the world singularly and uniquely endure excruciating psychological pain and angst when confronted with questions of race and ethnicity. For a man so interested in understanding and improving human morality, Dr. Bloom does not appear troubled by this picture of human suffering, preferring instead to maintain the cool dispassion of a cultural anthropologist. Perhaps he considers this to be a necessary part of the cultural transmission which helped "elevate" our morality. Clearly, part of this cultural transmission includes terrorizing select members of the population to the benefit of others, thereby enlightening the entire population.

On the other hand, Bloom suggests that this "psychic cost" arises from our development, which only raises further questions such as:

1) At which stage of development does this phenomenon emerge, and at roughly what age?
2) Why do we only observe this phenomenon among Whites? Is it not universal?
3) Shouldn't an investigation into human morality as it pertains to in-group/out-group psychology focus on this finding, possibly even to the exclusion of others?

These are pertinent questions which Dr. Bloom appears unwilling to broach. But perhaps Bloom isn't suggesting that this psychic cost is a normative phenomenon, one which arises organically over the course of human development, but is instead, as we have already mentioned, the result of cultural interference. What this suggests is that at a certain point in a young White person's life, they will be subjected to extreme social pressures disincentivizing them against thinking or engaging in human sorting on a more fundamental and elementary basis.

Dr. Bloom tells us that social psychologists observe this behavior among many of their White research subjects, but what we don't observe in these social scientists is any intellectual or moral curiosity about why this occurs. Presumably it is because they believe this development to be a positive or at least necessary one. Dr. Bloom inadvertently demonstrates that equalitarianism (and its various expressions, such as anti-racism, feminism, the fixation on anti-Semitism, and so on) is simply a disciplinary ideology aimed first and foremost at the White populations of North America and Europe. This, in Dr. Bloom's mind, is the height of morality.

From the point of view of a critical ethnoscience, the entire antiracist enterprise collapses since its practitioners hold neither normative nor formalized standards or definitions for their investigation and perceive the critical impairment of large portions of the population to be representative of a successfully implemented program. Equalitarianism, anti-racism, and anti-Semitism can only be understood as partisan hobby horses for the maladjusted and incompetent. For further proof, at least as regards claims of *incompetence*, Dr. Bloom, astoundingly, cites the junk science of the implicit association test[153] in support of his

---

[153] Developed in 1995 by Harvard social psychologists Anthony Greenwald and Mahzarin Banaji, the implicit association test is a computer-based measure that assesses a user's implicit attitude towards a given item. The two scientists argued that implicit and explicit memory could be applied to social constructs such that if our actions can be informed by unconsciously held information (i.e., implicit memory), then the same could be said for the associations we make. The IAT was therefore designed to help understand those attitudes which cannot be measured by self-reports due to lack of awareness (or other reasons, such as the desire for social acceptability). Participants sort stimuli (both words and images) into categories that combine concepts and evaluations, for example "fat" and "thin" with "good" or "bad." Three years after its initial development, it appeared for the first time in The Journal of Personality and Social Psychology ("Measuring Individual Differences in Implicit Cognition: The Implicit Association Test") and has since been cited over four thousand times across a variety of different fields. The IAT is now used for implicit bias training by corporations and federal institutions alike.

Questions have since arisen about the IAT's validity, however. In a pair of studies, Schimmack (2021) demonstrated the IAT's inability to assess implicit constructs, e.g., self-esteem and racial bias (Schimmack, "Invalid Claims"; "Implicit Association Test"). Blanton et al. (2015) assert that the IAT relies on "the presence of random noise to obtain variability," without which all individuals end up receiving extreme scores (Blanton et al., "Implications of the Implicit"). Their final judgment is that the IAT's D-score (the algorithm used for coding the implicit association test) is an inappropriate tool for formal assessments. In a study from 2018 (also conducted by Blanton and Jaccard), the team determined that the IAT framework "requires restrictive causal assumptions and makes measurement assumptions that can be questionable."

A piece written for the American Psychological Association's Monitor on Psychology affirms the "noisiness" of the IAT when quoting Ohio State University social psychologist Russell Fazio who said, "There's no way to determine whether it's measuring unconscious attitudes or simply associations picked up from the environment." In the same article, author Beth Azar laments the IAT's unreliability as a singular test of individual bias, observing that "people's scores often change from one test to another" (Azar,

claim that we harbor deep and evolutionarily informed parochial bigotries (or, in less ideological terms, filial and kinship loyalties).[154] "Even the least racist people in the world have unconscious racial biases," Dr. Bloom tells us, which means that the suffering of all those young college-aged Whites is for naught: they still are, and always will be, racists, according to proponents of the IAT like Paul Bloom.

Despite his attempts to exonerate humanity of its essential racism, Paul Bloom nonetheless finds himself condemning us and our antiquated psychology. Of the IAT, Bloom says:

> This research illustrates how we can be at war with ourselves. Part of a person might believe that race should play no role in hiring decisions (or even that racial minorities should get an advantage), while another part guides the person against choosing a black person. This tension can reflect moral struggle; one's explicit views about what's right clashes with one's gut feelings.[155]

Morality is definitionally equalitarian, according to Bloom's halfhearted semi-formalization, and we must be educated into it. Group

---

"IAT"). German Lopez, a writer for Vox observes the same phenomenon when he says, "it turns out the IAT might not tell individuals much about their individual bias. According to a growing body of research and the researchers who created the test and maintain it at the Project Implicit website, the IAT is not good for predicting individual biases based on just one test. It requires a collection—an aggregate—of tests before it can really make any sort of conclusions" (Lopez, "For Years"). This fact runs contrary to the public relations campaign carried out by popular writers like Malcolm Gladwell and institutions such as *The New York Times*, who had presented the IAT as being capable of just that: decoding individual bias.

There is in fact a tremendous body of research which is critical of the IAT, so much so that an entire book could be devoted to just this one subject. Enthusiasm for the implicit association test has waned greatly because of this critical examination; whereas a decade ago, there was much public discussion about the IAT, today that is no longer the case. At least within the court of public opinion, the implicit association test has been soundly defeated (I would argue, as well, that its scientific merits have been similarly nullified).

[154] Bloom, *Just Babies*, 125.
[155] Ibid., 126.

differences do exist,[156] and our tightest bonds are those of kinship,[157] which is why we stubbornly resist affirming equalitarianism in our day-to-day lives (and consequently, why we also require social engineering). But there is another aspect of our psychology which locks us into our essential bigotry: our evolved capacity for disgust. Of disgust, Bloom shares the following:

> Earlier in the book, we explored the role that empathy plays in motivating moral behavior. Empathy makes one more likely to care: it boosts compassion and altruism. Disgust has the opposite effect: it makes us indifferent to the suffering of others and has the power to incite cruelty and dehumanization.[158]

Evolution clearly wants us to be racists! The only problem here is that Bloom greatly misrepresents the role disgust plays in human affairs. Calling upon the research of Paul Rozin, Paul Bloom invokes the concept of core disgust—the idea that humans naturally respond with revulsion to certain things like blood, gore, vomit, feces, urine, and rotten flesh. Once again, Bloom problematizes biology to make room for his preferred (and highly totalitarian) psychology. Consider the following excerpt:

> Unfortunately for us, these substances are also the stuff of life. These vary in how repulsive they are. Feces, urine, and pus are bad, indeed, but people willingly ingest one another's semen and saliva; sweat is not as bad as snot; and, at least in vampire fiction, the drinking of blood can be erotic, not gross. Intriguingly, one body product is hardly disgusting at all—tears. Rosen suggests that tears are immune from disgust because we think of them as uniquely human. I find William Ian Miller's explanation more plausible: tears lack the physical properties of disgusting

---

[156] Ibid.
[157] Ibid., 127.
[158] Ibid., 133.

substances because of their clarity, their liquidity, their non-adhering nature, their lack of odor, and their clean taste.[159]

Here Bloom demonstrates his fundamental misunderstanding of disgust and the role that it plays. We are provoked to disgust by those things which tend to bring about disease, infirmity, and death. Disgust correlates with the "avoidance" side of our approach-avoid neurophysiology, driving us away from harmful, threatening, or otherwise dangerous environmental stimuli (even when said stimulus derives from the body and its functions). Importantly, however, whether some bodily functions or stimuli provoke disgust while others do not is immaterial to the larger question at hand and indicates, at least to me, Bloom's desire to obfuscate basic realities about evolutionary development and human behavior. For instance, fictional non-aversion to blood is meaningless when faced with the factual reality of diseases like HIV and AIDS. Or, that tears don't provoke the same neurophysiological response as, say, urine, means nothing to the larger investigation at hand. Either Paul Bloom gets paid by the word or he cannot make his case in plain and uncomplicated terms, working instead to overtly upset reader comprehension.

Disgust functions, as I have said, to keep us from encountering potentially harmful environmental stimuli. Human social affairs cannot be reduced to disgust alone, however. Using this reductionistic framework, Bloom reduces the complex world of human social affairs to the functioning of a single biological process. Dr. Bloom references the once popular television game show *Fear Factor* to highlight man's capacity to overcome feelings of disgust, thereby elevating him to greater heights of performance and self-satisfaction than ever before. This is evidential of his reductionism, for he regards the success of contestants on *Fear Factor* as explainable by this "will to overcome" which overrides the individual aspirant's near-paralyzing biological disgust response. Bloom's harebrained justification misses the mark in several crucial ways.

---

[159] Ibid., 134.

For starters, the show was called *Fear Factor* and not *Disgust Factor*; while this may seem pedantic, it is difficult to draw exact parallels between discrete phenomena. Fear and disgust are both emotions, and while they may at times yield similar behaviors, they are not identical (nor are the circumstances which trigger or resolve them). Secondly, Joe Rogan's *Fear Factor* offered contestants camaraderie, wealth, and fame as rewards for overcoming their automatic and evolutionarily informed aversions to challenges as diverse as mountain climbing, bug eating, and other feats of physical (or intestinal) endurance. What we commonly observe in the real world, evinced as well by the account of racially anxious White youths shared above, is that all attempts made to secure equalitarianism hinge on the exact opposite: shame, guilt, ostracism, humiliation, financial duress, and more.

If *Fear Factor* demonstrates anything at all, it is that a higher and infinitely more gratifying appeal must be made to compel the individual to overcome strong physiological states (even with this incentive structure in place, many *Fear Factor* contestants would still fail). By lending his support and credibility to the IAT, Bloom reveals that he is not capable of the kind of magnanimity necessary for such a transformation. Even among the most devout equalitarians—that is, people willing to suffer every day so that systemic racism may yet be defeated—Bloom continues to pick at them until, at last, he finds their inner racists.

Categorically, anti-racism and anti-Semitism are all stick and no carrot, which further betrays the true intention behind inquiries like Bloom's: political control of a given population. An Ivy League psychologist like Paul Bloom works not to discover (or even uncover) knowledge, but to lend the academy's credibility to tyrannical power. This is the meaning of our critical inquiry into ethnoscience. Ethnoscience, understood in a naive way, is merely a recapitulation of the myth of the noble savage. In our view, ethnoscience can also be understood as the indirect pursuit of political power and demographic control. Ethnosciences can be expressions of folk curiosity, or they may be organized attempts at information warfare.

Bloom once again resumes his tired and dishonest defense of infant moral psychology in the following passages:

> But we don't start off this way; babies are innocent of disgust. If left unattended, young children will touch and even eat all manner of disgusting things. . . .
>
> Core disgust serves an adaptive purpose. According to [a more plausible] theory, disgust isn't learned, but rather emerges naturally once babies have reached a certain point in development. There is some sense to this timing; if disgust kicked in too early, babies would be disgusted all the time at their wastes and wouldn't be able to do anything about it. Natural selection wouldn't be that needlessly cruel.[160]

Whenever Bloom needs to substantiate his claims, he slips into non sequiturs and paralogical interpretations of Darwinian evolution. His claims are so *prima facie* preposterous that they hardly warrant rebuttal, for any response would unduly legitimate the text's existence as a serious academic investigation. Padding his non-arguments with a shallow review of differing theoretical interpretations verbally adds to the mystique of the text, permitting it a greater and certainly undeserved authorial status. It is precisely this status which makes Bloom's argument noteworthy at all.

But to play devil's advocate, if we take Bloom's proposal seriously then I believe there is no reason, by his own logic, to admit the necessity of his investigation in the first place. If disgust plays a crucial role in moral cognition but it doesn't emerge until later in our development, then it stands to reason that we cannot actually say very much about the moral life of the infant—certainly not in total—for our picture is, owing to the underdeveloped life of the human infant, necessarily incomplete. All that is achieved through Bloom's research, that is, the use of looking-time and reaching-method studies, is the establishment of an arbitrarily "normative" mode for understanding infant moral psychology. Which isn't to say that such investigations tell us nothing, rather that they only speak to an *aspect* of human psychology which must be weighed against alternative methodological inquiries into this phenomenon.

---

[160] Ibid., 135, 137.

The chief consequence of this style of scientific investigation—the teleo-arbitrary establishment of a norm upon which grand sweeping claims about human existence may be made—is that it so neatly lends itself to application in the form of public policy. Bloom tells us himself that he seeks justification for a greater, more far-reaching, and more successful program of moral education than that which currently exists. His program, however, is predicated on the same underlying principles which govern the current dispensation, those being principles illustrative of devout equalitarianism. From the view of a critical ethnoscience, the only functional utility to his new program would be either a 1) fortification of the existing paradigm; and/or 2) an intensification of the existing paradigm.

To my mind his research accomplishes both. And that's giving the devil his due. Once more, Bloom applies an artificial dialectic to drive home his anti-disgust polemic:

> Disgust is the opposite of empathy. Just as empathy leads to compassion in many, but not all circumstances, disgust usually but not always leads to repulsion. Empathy triggers an appreciation of another's personhood; disgust leads you to construe the other as diminished and revolting, lacking humanity.[161]

Using psychological language, Bloom is again addressing the fundamental approach-avoidance apparatus of the brain, which if we were to engage in reductionism ourselves, would ultimately be the home of a great many conflicted human behaviors (i.e., sex-violence, sadism-masochism, narcissism-codependence, et cetera). But within the paradigm of psychology, and trying to cautiously affirm Bloom's hypothesis here, a "truer" dialectic would be between openness and disgust, with disgust representing (in a multitude of empirically observable ways) closedness. Openness would imply curiosity, which would further lend itself to the outcomes which Bloom attributes to empathy. It may be that there is a greater relationship between openness and empathy, as has been suggested in the psychological literature of the last twenty years, though

---

[161] Ibid., 140.

even if it were to ultimately validate Bloom's hypothesis, it would nonetheless require a deeper investigation into this dynamic to establish a proper ordering.

But I must once again protest this tendency to fall into the dialectic, not as a polemic against all dialectics, but to affirm the grander point, which is this: there can be no fundamental antagonism built into the brain, at least, not one that can be justified by appeals to Darwinian evolution. Is disgust the opposite of empathy? What if they were neighbors? Or co-workers? As in, sharing the same space and acting on the same materials, but having different but ultimately collaborative roles within the hierarchy of the nervous system? The two can function differently without functioning oppositionally. This presumption of disharmony is an entirely ideological one, justifiable only from the point of view of an extreme equalitarian (such as Paul Bloom). Its only purpose can be the justification of some disciplinary policy or proposal.

Picking up again on his anti-disgust polemics, Bloom further problematizes disgust by arguing that 1) disgust cannot be entirely hardwired due to the intense variability and subjectivity of the disgust-experience;[162] 2) high disgust-sensitivity leads to harsher attitudes towards immigrants and foreigners;[163] 3) homosexualistic disgust is evolutionarily implausible due to the non-reproductivity of its participants;[164] 4) sex disgusts us because bodies are disgusting;[165] 5) racialistic disgust is disproven by evolutionary logic;[166] and 6) moral intuitions are influenced by concerns about purity.[167]

Summarizing his thoughts on the matter, Bloom shares the following about disgust and morality:

> I think that the intuitions associated with disgust are at best unnecessary and the worst harmful, in that they motivate irrational policies and license savage behavior. For one thing, even if we

---

[162] Ibid., 138.
[163] Ibid., 141.
[164] Ibid., 143.
[165] Ibid., 150.
[166] Ibid.
[167] Ibid.

knew nothing about psychology or evolution, a brief look at the history of disgust illustrates its unreliability as a moral cue. The revulsion that Nazis felt towards the Jews, or that most Americans felt toward interracial marriage, is precisely the same sort of revulsion that many of us currently feel towards certain groups and activities. Since it is clear that disgust got it wrong in the past, why should we trust it now?

Disgust gives the wrong answer for the same reason that it sometimes gives the right answer—by accident.[168]

While the force that drives the evolution of morality toward kin is genetic overlap, and the force that drives morality toward the in-group is the logic of mutual benefits, the force that drives morality towards strangers is . . . nothing. We are capable of judging the actions of strangers as good and bad, but we have no natural altruism toward them, no innate desire to be kind to them.[169]

None of the claims Bloom makes are true in any unqualified sense, but more importantly, the general thrust of his investigation cuts against the very axioms he draws upon as an evolutionist (as we have noted time and time again). It is not plausible to accept that, through countless generations of intense selective pressures, the human brain developed its reasoning and decision-making skills to be about as precise as a random coin flip. As with the revelation about angst-ridden White anti-racism, this too would prove to be a major scientific discovery worth seizing upon. How is it that this accident comes about? How have we been able to have the success we've enjoyed as a species when we apparently have no idea what we're doing?

In truth, the real question is this: how does Bloom's non sequitur make any rational sense? It doesn't, nor does it have to, for Bloom's work is about closing the door to intellectual possibility, not opening it.

Disgust is adaptive because it helps us avoid harmful things, but this is problematized by the fact that it leads us to harm others (more on this in a moment). Kinship is adaptive because it grants us group

---

[168] Ibid., 156.
[169] Ibid., 178.

solidarity, but is also problematized due to its parochial racism. And ultimately, as Bloom never ceases to point out, Jewish people are affected most of all. Dr. Bloom opens his book by discussing the holocaust, and how as a child, he had heard "of gas chambers and sadistic doctors and children being turned into soap and lampshades." It is a matter of historical record that this transmogrification-of-flesh-into-furniture didn't take place, and so the incorporation of such an obvious falsehood so early into the book fatally thrashes the author's credibility as a scientist and public intellectual. Which is why I designate this work, and those like it, as ethnoscience. The pretense towards objectivity, a brotherhood of man, a shared civil liberal society, etc., is only that: a pretense.

But consider this claim with the knowledge Bloom himself presents in the text. Disgust, a component of our physiological avoidance response, works to keep us away from things that could lead to infection, poisoning, contamination, and death. Psychologically, we may come to see social others in these same immunological terms, responding to them as we would a rotting corpse on the side of the road. Which is to say, with revulsion and not organized bloodlust. Bloom never demonstrates that disgust leads to persecution per se, though he says as much repeatedly throughout the book. But persecution is an active pursuit, one which draws upon the body's approach physiology. I don't think anyone believes that some mid-century German equivalent of Joe Rogan served at Dachau, lavishly rewarding the select few who could muster the fortitude to walk Mort and Gertrude into the industrial-strength Nazi soap-inator. I also don't think anyone believes that the purity-obsessed Germans, repulsed by the Jews enough to persecute them, would then feel comfortable bathing themselves through means of this supposed racial-hygienic alchemy. Psychologically, the claim doesn't stand scrutiny. But by having come this far we've already missed the more important point: the premise should not have been granted from the outset. Some claims strain credulity, but this manages to warp the boundaries of the absurd, too. And this is the case, as well, with the idea that young children and infants ought to be subjected to a radical program of "moral" re-education wherein they are fed a daily stream of self-hatred until they internalize the doctrine and regurgitate it silently to themselves until they die.

If the unnecessary suffering endured in the here and now, induced unjustly by the powerful, is of no particular interest to Paul Bloom, then the unnecessary suffering of his dead ancestors is of no particular interest to us. Certainly, it is of no scientific import. It should carry no special moral significance, and its inclusion in any text which purports itself to be a source of meaningful and objective knowledge ought to be met with intense criticism, if not outright derision. Often, we are enjoined to "believe the science," and to accept that "science is real." I don't disagree with such messages, left-coded as they may be. I would simply add that as a pre-requisite, one must acknowledge the existence of ethnoscience and understand it as categorically opposed to proper science. Only then can we be sure what and whom to believe.

As it relates to the question of suspicion culture, the antagonistic practice of ethnoscience undoubtedly contributes to an overall climate of distrust by delegitimizing critically important social roles in the eyes of the average person (e.g., academic scholarship, education, public policy, etc.). In a society as rapaciously capitalistic as our own, this only furthers the cultural divide in terms of employment and representation, for many people are already inclined against taking up unprofitable careers. It is one thing to dismiss a set of labors because they do not help provide our daily bread, but it is another to spurn them (and their practitioners) for appearing inherently, inexorably fallacious and deceptive. Whole sectors of society grow to resent others due to the methodically constructed misperception of their import and function by free-riding and antisocial partisans, themselves bent on sowing chaos to their exclusive benefit.

Those who come to such a position of doubt typically misunderstand their reasons for doing so and are, as a result, rendered unable to cogently articulate their perceptions. Owing to this, they unintentionally become culture war fodder for commentators and public intellectuals who seek to fortify regime positions by highlighting the irrationality of the *hoi polloi*. All sides suffer, for all are forced to labor under conditions of mass delusion and avarice regardless of their partisan affiliations.

One such mass delusion which enables the promulgation of an antagonizing ethnoscience is the belief that we are a homogeneous people, lacking entirely in differentiated motivations, aptitudes, and desires.

Important as this observation is, we must also reckon with the psychic tendencies which allow us a degree of agency in selectively acting upon this delusion. Prejudice, solipsism, despair, and resentment all operate in tandem, permitting us to betray our belief in this delusion at will (even if we do, ultimately, resign ourselves to it).

Some examples of just how we skirt the edges of delusion:

1) We believe in the universal dignity of man, and yet we carve out exemptions and political privileges for some at the expense of others.
2) We bemoan the mistreatment and denigration of certain people-groups even as we heap ever more special considerations upon them.
3) We deny any essential basis for man's most exemplary and laudable qualities, except when we seek to exalt a privileged group.
4) We reserve much of our contempt and criticism for those groups who are the least deserving while exempting others whole stock.
5) We suppress feelings of doubt and skepticism for some, while excessively indulging it towards others.

One way to overturn this delusion of homogenization (while at the same time safeguarding ourselves against the seductive influence of our lower affective tendencies) is by listening to our inner voice and affirming the indelible wisdom we call *intuition*. Earlier in this essay I explained that it is possible to justify ourselves against the powerful, against the credentialed, against the respected and unimpeachable members of our society, by affirming the "irrational" voice within. We would be better suited to term it *the ineffable* rather than the irrational, for it is not the case that our inner voice is irrational; rather, it simply eludes comprehensive articulation. That is, at least at first anyway.

We can come to know it more perfectly and learn to express it more completely by listening more closely to that voice, and by trusting in its logic. When we conceive of our inner voice as "irrational," we are ceding to the regime—and to hostile parties more generally—a great power that we must protect if we seek to grow its potential. Just because we don't always understand some feeling or thought does not mean that it is necessarily irrational, or that it ought to be callously dismissed. Lack of understanding causes fear, and it is often this fear which leads us to a rushed judgment, thereby impairing our discernment. Proper discernment comes from maintaining a state of inner harmony such that we can hear and understand that inner, ineffable voice when it speaks to us. It is by hearing and acting upon this voice that we can develop the ability to resist those who seek to manipulate and deceive us.

ADDENDUM

As I have argued throughout the course of this book (as well as in its predecessor, *Understanding Conspiracy Theories*), our modern lifestyle enjoins us to participate in the great Enlightenment tradition of doubt. There's no escaping it, for every vector of social life is awash with skepticism and paranoid doubting. Secular liberalism has unfolded in such a way that our present circumstance now appears predetermined, unavoidable. While I don't believe that to be the case, nevertheless, Western liberalism's progression into a sort of political theology has profoundly affected the way we think about concepts like sovereignty and authority, cause and effect, as well as responsibility and freedom. A confluence of events produced this condition, though chief among them would certainly be the emergence of the technological society (and along with it, mass democracy).

Owing to the challenges of mass and scale (as Sam Francis termed it), traditional communities and the pastoral power they wielded broke down, only to be replaced by imagined communities and the power of the welfare state. The confessional booth gave way to the psychoanalyst's chair, and with this transformation, the priest to the social worker. Religious and ethnic affiliations overcoded by consumerism and a cynically reconstituted patriotism became impoverished and kitschified simulations. Political initiatives like forced integration and the eruption of the Cold War served as the backdrop for an ever-intensifying American schizoidism, though to be sure, the precursors to this crisis were established long before.

Certainly, the most profound of all technological influences is the internet, the most refined and awe-inspiring expression of what Marshall McLuhan once called "the web of electric light." Thanks to advancements in communication technologies such as the internet, it became possible to manipulate social and ideological developments with a speed never previously witnessed in human history. Combinated technologies such as the smartphone (internet + mobile phone) have allowed for all manner of social contagions and cultural movements to spread across the globe, from extremist Islamism and trans ideology to the Alt-Right and Donald Trump, upending whole societies in just a handful of years. Old tribal filiations are worn away by alienation, while newer ones take their place through screen-mediated engrossment.

Hence my development of the concept of suspicion culture to highlight the social forces which generate distrust and skepticism. I argued in my previous book that this culture of suspicion has had far-ranging psychological consequences—largely negative ones. I view what Dr. Robert Malone has called "mass formation psychosis" as simply a generalized schizoid character within the population, cultivated in part by ideological developments as well as technological ones. But these are not the only methods by which suspicion culture is propagated. The focus of this book has been to highlight how the laborers of academia (predominantly social scientists) accelerated these developments. If this relationship still seems unclear, allow me to further elaborate on this hypothesis.

I began by focusing on the work of historian Richard Hofstadter, whose essay "The Paranoid Style in American Politics" cemented the view, now commonplace today, that those who deign to examine the relations and structure of power operating within American society are merely paranoid and parochial conspiracy theorists. Appropriating the language of psychoanalysis, Hofstadter made a pejorative out of what was otherwise understood as a clinical term for the purpose of stigmatizing and delegitimating anyone critical of governmental policy.

Massively influential upon its publication, acceptance of the arguments presented in Hofstadter's essay would only grow over time, finding similar adherents across other disciplines. Later generations of academics, such as Frank P. Mintz (a political scientist who coined the term "conspiracism") held that, just as with Hofstadter's much maligned "paranoid pseudo-conservatives," to be a conspiracy theorist was to extol "the primacy of conspiracies in the unfolding of history."[170] In other words, to take notice of power relations is to fixate on them. Of course, it is true that relations and structures of power *do* drive historical events, but Mintz, like Hofstadter, coins a pejorative to describe those who observe them. Türkay Salim Nefes, a sociologist, also reinforced Hofstadter's view of the essentially political nature of conspiratorialism by emphasizing their tendency to identify the hidden power relations operating between various social groups.[171] It is not so much the case that such observations are false or illegitimate; rather, it is that they are deployed in service of a tyrannical regime which seeks to dominate its rivals and trample over free and open discourse. Despite their transparent servility, the prominence of Hofstadter's arguments has not diminished with time.

The function of such pejorative and polemical concepts (e.g., conspiracy theorist, paranoid style, etc.) is to fortify the regime against folk accounts of history by creating its own culture of suspicion which can be directed against rival powers, whether indirectly through polemics, or directly through cognitive infiltration (as was Cass Sunstein's preferred method). In the case of the former, individuals are encouraged to doubt their own powers of observation and deduction, or at least to doubt the powers of those around them. With regards to the latter, a new economy of suspicion is produced through the promulgation of deliberate fictions masquerading as authentic folk accounts (i.e., conspiracy theories). Conspiracy theories are merely informal analyses of power relations and most regimes have a vested interest in suspending the production of such inquiries, or misleading them in directions harmless to the regime. Hofstadter's publications were among the first in the United States to wield psychology as a weapon against the mind

---

[170] Mintz, *Liberty Lobby*.
[171] Nefes, "History of the Social Constructions"; "Political parties' perceptions."

of the average American.

Following the discussion of Hofstadter's work, I moved on to two publications by the philosopher Karl Popper: his book *The Open Society and Its Enemies* and the essay "The Conspiracy Theory of Society." Karl Popper seemed a natural choice for a discussion of conspiratorialism and liberal democracy for several reasons. Chief among them: 1) he mentored both advocates of liberal democracy as well as critics of so-called conspiratorialism; 2) the foremost grantmaking network in the world, Open Society Foundations, is named after his book; and 3) he has written extensively on both subjects.

Karl Popper's polemics against the closed society (i.e., non-democratic societies) and the study of power relations (i.e., conspiracism) are direct, sustained, attacks aimed against folk political organization and epistemology. Playing the game of philosophy, Popper bends the universality of logical construction to his needs, fully conscious of the fact that if his arguments ever translated into public policy, that they would completely decimate the populations that implemented them (he admits as much within the text). Effectively, his legacy makes him the arch-architect of the present demographic crisis facing the Western world and the philosopher extraordinaire of the Great Replacement. The most relevant conspiracy theory of our time begins with his social theory, therefore making him a necessary target for an investigation such as my own.

Jonathan Haidt's work on moral intuition, though well-intentioned, also contributed to American suspicion culture by virtue of its implications. According to his social intuitionist model, we possess six basic moral intuitions: care/harm, fairness/cheating, loyalty/betrayal, authority/subversion, sanctity/degradation, and liberty/oppression. Haidt's research found that political conservatives are in touch with all six moral intuitions, while political liberals can only access three, unintentionally leading many to the conclusion that liberals are psychologically defective, and therefore, the moral inferiors of conservative Americans.

In an era of ever-escalating hyperpolarization, Haidt's attempt to balance the scales of political culture in fact created a popular perception which helped to strip American liberals of their humanity. Now to be fair, the utterly disreputable conduct of upper-class liberals did far more to create that perception; however, the stamp of approval from a credentialed expert was all that was needed to seal the fate of liberal America in the eyes of its conservative population.

Conservatives and Republicans being natural losers in the ongoing culture war against progressive liberalism had already primed them to perceive the Democratic Party as manipulative, deceitful, treacherous, and perhaps even evil. Of course, this was not merely a perception, as the American left has long dealt in underhanded and antisocial tactics to help them secure their desired political victories. But where one has a rival, one must also have rationality, or else risk falling into bitter solipsism and forfeiting victory time and time again. It is my view that, rather than lend clarity to the situation, Haidt's research has only deepened the political divide in America.

The heuristics and biases program which arose out of the social sciences' probabilistic revolution changed the way we think about ourselves. Thanks to decades of behavioral economics research premised on the idea that human decision-making operates more-or-less on a set of unreliable irrationalities, we are less certain of our own minds. And now that we stand at the forefront of another revolution, this time in machine learning and artificial intelligence, the groundwork laid down by scientists like Daniel Kahneman and Amos Tversky may finally be exploited, thereby securing the next stage of development for our technological society.

Framing human cognition in this hostile manner and then formalizing this hypothesis through decades of social science has allowed for the prospect of a uniquely tyrannical political resolution to the many social ailments facing our civilization. Owing to our deeply entrenched power structure (and the families and networks which occupy it), a fair and honest solution to the problems of exploitation, injustice, and inequality cannot be implemented. Instead, we appear poised to follow the technological society all the way to its conclusion in the vain hope that we can innovate our way out of the human condition.

From the point of view of conventional conspiratorialism, this seemingly foregone conclusion conjures up all kinds of fantastical expectations seen only in expensive Hollywood films (e.g., precognitive crime units as seen in *Minority Report*, a battle to the death with killer robots like in the *Terminator* series, and so on). The more mundane conspiratorial ideations center on the nature of the technocrats in charge of this posthuman transition (e.g., WEF attendees and the like). Change is often preceded by fear, and rapid change by intense and overwhelming panic. But the real conspiracy is not what will come after the posthuman revolution, or what techno-oligarchs hope to achieve at the end of their machinations. Superficially minded conspiracists get lost in speculating about some four-dimensional chess game rather than recognizing that the hellscape they so intensely fear is already here (and has been for some time).

Speaking strictly from the perspective of suspicion culture however, by popularizing a paradigm of human consciousness which encourages people to doubt their own capacity to process information and make decisions, Kahneman and Tversky have done irreparable harm to the collective mind of the secular West. Their philosophy has set the mind at war with itself, cognitively crippling countless men and women across the globe.

The last chapter of this book most fully represents what I am calling the art of intolerant interpretation. In truth, this hermeneutic has guided me all throughout the process of researching for and writing this book. However, it is most deftly applied in the service of deconstructing Paul Bloom's psychological theorizing; Bloom's logic is so thin and his credibility so lacking that I was left with no choice but to subject his book to scrutiny of the highest order. Anything less would have been intellectually dishonest.

Intolerance has come to be synonymous with irrational hatred, as though the person or group subjected to such invective were a benign or even benevolent entity. But intolerance in fact refers to "an inability to endure or survive exposure to," the implication being the opposite of what conventional wisdom has come to assume. Intolerance is something you practice when you are in proximity to something dangerous; tolerance is something you can only practice in limited amounts for a specific duration of time. In other words, no one can be indefinitely tolerant, and similarly, no one can indefinitely suspend their intolerance. Not if they hope to live a long and fruitful life, anyway.

So, to practice the art of intolerant interpretation is to hermeneutically defend oneself against arguments and ideas which, if not properly guarded against, would in fact prove fatal to the mind and the soul. The arguments proffered by liberal and Jewish social scientists and theoreticians in this book certainly fit that description. Having now concluded this work, you too should be practiced in the art of intolerant interpretation. Let it guide your thinking, wherever it may lead you.

BIBLIOGRAPHY

Azar, Beth. "IAT: Fad or fabulous?" *Monitor on Psychology*, July 1, 2008. https://www.apa.org/monitor/2008/07-08/psychometric.
Blanton, Hart, James Jaccard, and Christopher N. Burrows. "Implications of the Implicit Association Test D-Transformation for Psychological Assessment." *Assessment*, 22, no. 4 (2015): 429-440. https://doi.org/10.1177/1073191114551382.
Bloom, Paul. *Just Babies: The Origins of Good and Evil*. Crown Publishers, 2013.
Bloom, Paul. "The Moral Life of Babies." *The New York Times*, May 5, 2010. https://tinyurl.com/3hhw5v5b.
Boissoneault, Lorraine. "How the 19th-Century Know Nothing Party Reshaped American Politics." *Smithsonian Magazine*, January 26, 2017. https://tinyurl.com/4hxvc3v2.
Bollyn, Christopher. "The Man Who Solved 9/11." Interview by Adam Green, *Know More News*. Posted October 31, 2018, by Brandon Smith. YouTube, 1:20:37. https://www.youtube.com/watch?v=ep6ZwWfsxs4.
Burnham, James. *The Managerial Revolution*. Indiana University Press, 1973.
Cheathem, Mark R. "Conspiracy Theories Abounded in 19th-Century American Politics." *Smithsonian Magazine*, April 11, 2019. https://tinyurl.com/4e6pysnw.

Clifton, Jon. "The Global Rise of Unhappiness." Gallup, September 15 2022, https://tinyurl.com/3732v9us.

Diaz, Jaclyn. "Facebook's New Whistleblower Is Renewing Scrutiny of the Social Media Giant." NPR, October 4, 2021. https://tinyurl.com/369nbaev.

Elia-Shalev, Asaf. "How an ADL Spy Operation Helped Bring down the Far-Right John Birch Society." *The Times of Israel*, May 21, 2023. https://tinyurl.com/3yz6vywz.

Ellul, Jacques. *The Technological Society*. Translated by John Wilkinson. Vintage Books, 1964. Originally published 1954.

Fitzgerald, Margaret E. "The Philadelphia Nativists Riots." Irish Cultural Society of the Garden City Area, 1992. https://tinyurl.com/mrxm5m7e.

Francis, Samuel T. *Leviathan and Its Enemies: Mass Organization and Managerial Power in Twentieth-Century America*. Washington Summit Publishers, 2016.

Frantzman, Seth J. "Was the Russian Revolution Jewish?" *The Jerusalem Post*, February 7, 2018. https://tinyurl.com/muj5h8kn.

Gigerenzer, Gerd. "The bounded rationality of probabilistic mental models." In *Rationality: Psychological and Philosophical Perspectives*, edited by K. I. Manktelow and D. E. Over. Routledge, 1993.

Gigerenzer, Gerd. *Gut Feelings: The Intelligence of the Unconscious*. Penguin Books, 2008.

Gigerenzer, Gerd. "How to Make Cognitive Illusions Disappear: Beyond 'Heuristics and Biases.'" *European Review of Social Psychology* 2, no. 1 (1991): 83–115. https://doi.org/10.1080/14792779143000033.

Gottfried, Paul. *After Liberalism: Mass Democracy in the Managerial State*. Princeton University Press, 2001.

Haag, Chad A. "The Philosophy of Jacques Ellul The Technological Society (La Technique) Summary." Posted May 23, 2019, by Chad A Haag Philosophy Channel. YouTube, 43:51. https://www.youtube.com/watch?v=Et0PUYLV7Ek.

Haidt, Jonathan. *The Righteous Mind: Why Good People Are Divided by Politics and Religion*. Vintage Books, 2012.

Hamlin, J. Kiley, Karen Wynn, and Paul Bloom. "Social evaluation by preverbal infants." *Nature* 450, no. 7169 (2007): 557–559. http://dx.doi.org/10.1038/nature06288.

Hamlin, J. Kiley, Karen Wynn, and Paul Bloom. "Three-month-olds show a negativity bias in their social evaluations." *Developmental Science* 13, no. 6 (2010): 923–929. https://doi.org/10.1111/j.1467-7687.2010.00951.x.

Hasson, Mary Rice. "The Trans-Industrial Complex." *Ethics & Public Policy Center*, October 15, 2018. https://eppc.org/publication/the-trans-industrial-complex/.

Hofstadter, Richard. *The Paranoid Style in American Politics, and Other Essays.* Knopf, 1965.

Huebner, Robin. "North Dakota Link to Notorious Son of Sam Murders Part of New Netflix Documentary." *InForum*, May 20, 2021. https://tinyurl.com/ke5crxfa.

JTA Archive. "Wide Distribution of Anti-Semitic Material Reported in Massachusetts." *Jewish Telegraphic Agency*, March 7, 1962. https://tinyurl.com/4pdek9kk.

Jung, C. G. *The Archetypes and the Collective Unconscious.* Princeton University Press, 1968.

Kahneman, Daniel, and Amos Tversky. "Theoretical Notes: On the Reality of Cognitive Illusions," *Psychological Review* 103, no. 3 (1996): 582–591.

Kahneman, Daniel. *Thinking, Fast & Slow.* Farrar, Straus and Giroux, 2011.

Keller, Morton. *America's Three Regimes: A New Political History.* Oxford University Press, 2007.

Klages, Ludwig. *The Science of Character.* Translated by W. H. Johnston. Rogue Scholar Press, 2021. Originally published 1929.

Kurzban, Robert, John Tooby, and Leda Cosmides. "Can race be erased? Coalitional computation and social categorization." *Proceedings of the National Academy of Sciences* 98, no. 26 (2011): 15387–15392. https://doi.org/10.1073/pnas.251541498.

Lehmann, Chris. "We All Live in the John Birch Society's World Now." *The New Republic*, November 23 2021. https://tinyurl.com/37hx9baj.

Lieberman, Debra, Robert Oum, and Robert Kurzban. "The family of fundamental social categories includes kinship: evidence from the memory confusion paradigm." *European Journal of Social Psychology* 38, no. 6 (2008): 998–1012. https://doi.org/10.1002/ejsp.528.

Little, Becky. "How America's First Third Party Influenced Politics." HISTORY, last modified January 17, 2024. https://tinyurl.com/b5ry8tjm.

Lopez, German. "For Years, This Popular Test Measured Anyone's Racial Bias. But It Might Not Work After All." *Vox*, March 7, 2017. https://tinyurl.com/3je69r9x.

Louie, David. "Suspect in 1974 Stanford Murder Case Contemplated Suicide Before." *ABC7 San Francisco*, June 29, 2018. https://tinyurl.com/55539996.

Mahdawi, Arwa. "Millennials Aren't Getting More Rightwing with Age. I Suspect I Know Why." *The Guardian*, January 3, 2023. https://tinyurl.com/2tvct6hk.

McLuhan, Marshall. *Understanding Media: The Extensions of Man*. McGraw-Hill, 1964.

Mintz, Frank P. *The Liberty Lobby and the American Right: Race, Conspiracy, and Culture*. Greenwood Press, 1985.

Monacelli, Steven. "The John Birch Society Sees a Renaissance in North Texas." *The Texas Observer*, July 21 2022. https://tinyurl.com/33rk6v7n.

Moore, Robert, and Douglas Gillette. *King, Warrior, Magician, Lover: Rediscovering Masculinity Through the Lens of Archetypal Psychology - A Journey into the Male Psyche and Its Four Essential Aspects*. Harper Collins, 1990.

Mulloy, D.J. *The World of the John Birch Society: Conspiracy, Conservatism, and the Cold War*. Vanderbilt University Press, 2014.

N.C. "Conspiracy theories are dangerous—here's how to crush them." *The Economist*, August 12, 2019. https://tinyurl.com/4c4tbctv.

Nefes, Türkay Salim. "The History of the Social Constructions of Dönmes (Converts)*." *Journal of Historical Sociology* 25, no. 3 (2012): 413–439. https://doi.org/10.1111/j.1467-6443.2012.01434.x.

Nefes, Türkay Salim. "Political parties' perceptions and uses of anti-Semitic conspiracy theories in Turkey." *The Sociological Review* 61, no. 2 (2013): 247–264. https://doi.org/10.1111/1467-954X.12016.

Pizarro, David and Paul Bloom. "The intelligence of the moral intuitions: A comment on Haidt (2001)." *Psychological Review* 110, no. 1 (2003): 193–196. https://doi.org/10.1037/0033-295X.110.1.193.

Popper, Karl. "The Conspiracy Theory of Society." In *Conspiracy Theories: The Philosophical Debate*, edited by David Coady. Routledge, 2018.

Popper, Karl. *The Open Society and Its Enemies*. Princeton University Press, 2013.

Postel, Danny. "It Wasn't About Oil, and It Wasn't About the Free Market: Why We Invaded Iraq." *In These Times*, February 11, 2015. https://tinyurl.com/bdfjun2r.

Rabinowitz, Howard N. "Nativism, Bigotry and Anti-Semitism in the South." *American Jewish History* 77, no. 3 (1988): 437–451. http://www.jstor.org/stable/23883316.

Robertson, Robin. *Jungian Archetypes: Jung, Gödel, and the History of Archetypes*. iUniverse, 2009.

Schimmack, Ulrich. "The Implicit Association Test: A method in search of a construct." *Perspectives on Psychological Science* 16, no. 2 (2021): 396–414. https://doi.org/10.1177/1745691619863798.

Schimmack, Ulrich. "Invalid Claims About the Validity of Implicit Association Tests by Prisoners of the Implicit Social-Cognition Paradigm." *Perspectives on Psychological Science* 16, no. 2 (2021): 435–442. https://doi.org/10.1177/1745691621991860.

Tron, Gina. "How The 'Son of Sam' Terrorized NYC and the Evidence That Led to His Capture." *Oxygen*, May 4, 2021. https://tinyurl.com/34u8pud4.

Yad Vashem. "Weimar Republic (1918–1933)." Accessed June 3, 2023. https://tinyurl.com/pvmsmvam.

ENJOYED THIS BOOK?

TO READ MORE, VISIT US AT

ANTELOPEHILLPUBLISHING.COM

www.ingramcontent.com/pod-product-compliance
Lightning Source LLC
Chambersburg PA
CBHW020537030426
42337CB00013B/890